An Introduction to
Cognitive Behaviour Therapy

David Westbrook, Helen Kennerley and Joan Kirk

An Introduction to
Cognitive Behaviour Therapy

Skills and Applications

Los Angeles • London • New Delhi • Singapore • Washington DC

First published 2007

Reprinted 2008

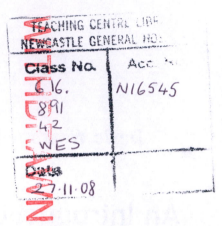

 SAGE Publications Ltd
1 Oliver's Yard
55 City Road
London EC1Y 1SP

SAGE Publications Inc.
2455 Teller Road
Thousand Oaks, California 91320

SAGE Publications India Pvt Ltd
B 1/I 1 Mohan Cooperative Industrial Area
Mathura Road, Post Bag 7
New Delhi 110 044

SAGE Publications Asia-Pacific Pte Ltd
33 Pekin Street #02-01
Far East Square
Singapore 048763

British Library Cataloguing in Publication data

A catalogue record for this book is available from
the British Library

ISBN 978-1-4129-0839-9
ISBN 978-1-4129-0840-5 (pbk)

Library of Congress Control Number available

Typeset by C&M Digitals (P) Ltd., Chennai, India
Printed in Great Britain by
TJ International Ltd, Padstow, Cornwall
Printed on paper from sustainable resources

FSC
Mixed Sources
Product group from well-managed
forests and other controlled sources
Cert no. SGS-COC-2482
www.fsc.org
© 1996 Forest Stewardship Council

Contents

Basic Theory, Development and Current Status of CBT

Introduction

In this chapter we want to introduce you to some of the essential background to cognitive behaviour therapy (CBT), including the basic theory and the development of the approach. We start here because CBT is sometimes criticised for being a rather simple-minded 'cook-book' approach to therapy: if the client has *this* problem then use *that* technique. However, the approach we take in this book is based not on the mechanical application of techniques but on *understanding*: understanding your patient, understanding CBT theory, and bringing the two together in a formulation (see Chapter 4). You should already have some ideas about understanding people, based on your clinical and personal experience. This chapter will start you on the road to understanding CBT theory.

One further clarification. Talking about CBT as if it were a single therapy is misleading. Modern CBT is not a monolithic structure, but a broad movement that is still developing, and full of controversies. The approach we take in this book is based on the 'Beckian' model, first formulated by A.T. Beck in the 1960s and 1970s (Beck, 1963, 1964; Beck et al., 1979). This model has been dominant in the UK for the past 25 years, and we would therefore see ourselves as being in the mainstream of CBT in this country. However, other CBT theorists and clinicians might differ, in major or minor ways, with some of the approaches expounded here. We should also say that although we think that some of the newer ideas in CBT, such as the 'Third Wave' therapies (Hayes, 2004), are exciting developments that have the potential to enrich CBT greatly, our aim here is primarily to provide a foundation for 'basic' CBT. We therefore restrict our consideration of those developments to a separate chapter (Chapter 17).

A brief history of CBT

Just as some knowledge of a client's background can be helpful in understanding his current state, an appreciation of how CBT developed can help us to understand its modern form. Modern CBT has two main influences: first, behaviour therapy as developed by Wolpe and others in the 1950s and 1960s (Wolpe, 1958); and second, the cognitive therapy approach developed by A.T. Beck, beginning in the 1960s but becoming far more influential with the 'cognitive revolution' of the 1970s.

Behaviour therapy (BT) arose as a reaction against the Freudian psychodynamic paradigm that had dominated psychotherapy from the nineteenth century onwards. In the 1950s, Freudian psychoanalysis was questioned by scientific psychology because of the lack of empirical evidence to support either its theory or its effectiveness (Eysenck, 1952). BT was strongly influenced by the behaviourist movement in academic psychology, which took the view that what went on inside a person's mind was not directly observable and therefore not amenable to scientific study. Instead behaviourists looked for reproducible associations between observable events, particularly between *stimuli* (features or events in the environment) and *responses* (observable and measurable reactions from the people or animals being studied). Learning theory, a major model in psychology at that time, looked for general principles to explain how organisms learn new associations between stimuli and responses.

In this spirit, BT avoided speculations about unconscious processes, hidden motivations and unobservable structures of the mind and instead used the principles of learning theory to modify unwanted behaviour and emotional reactions. For instance, instead of trying to probe the unconscious roots of an animal phobia, as Freud famously did with 'Little Hans' (a boy who had a fear of horses: Freud, 1909), behaviour therapists constructed procedures, based on learning theory, which they believed would help people learn new ways of responding. The BT view was that someone like Little Hans had learned an association between the stimulus of a horse and a fear response, and the task of therapy was therefore to establish a new, non-fearful, response to that stimulus. The resulting treatment for anxiety disorders, known as *systematic desensitization*, asked clients to repeatedly imagine the feared stimulus whilst practising relaxation, so that the fearful response would be replaced by a relaxed response. Later developments often replaced *imaginal* exposure (e.g., thinking about a mental picture of the horse) with *in vivo* exposure (approaching a real horse).

BT rapidly became successful, especially with anxiety disorders such as phobias and obsessive-compulsive disorder (OCD), for two main reasons. First, in keeping with its roots in scientific psychology, BT had always taken an empirical approach, which soon allowed it to provide solid evidence that it was effective in relieving anxiety problems. Second, BT was a far more economical treatment than traditional psychotherapy, typically taking six to twelve sessions.

Despite this early success, there was some dissatisfaction with the limitations of a purely behavioural approach. Mental processes such as thoughts, beliefs, interpretations, imagery and so on, are such an obvious part of life that it began to seem absurd for psychology not to deal with them. During the 1970s this dissatisfaction developed into what became known as the 'cognitive revolution', wherein ways were sought to bring cognitive phenomena into psychology and therapy, whilst still trying to maintain an empirical approach that would avoid ungrounded speculation. Beck and others had in fact begun to develop ideas about cognitive therapy (CT) during the 1950s and early 1960s, but their ideas became increasingly influential. The publication of Beck's book on cognitive therapy for depression (Beck et al., 1979), and research trials showing that CT was as effective a treatment for depression as anti-depressant medication (e.g., Rush et al., 1977), fuelled the revolution. Over the succeeding years, BT and

CT grew together and influenced each other to such an extent that the resulting amalgam is now most commonly known as cognitive behaviour therapy – CBT.

Some basic principles

So, what elements of BT and CT have emerged to form the foundation of modern CBT? Here we set out what we see as the most basic principles and beliefs on which our model of CBT is based, so that you can decide for yourself whether you think they make sense – or at least enough sense to be worth giving CBT a try. Below are what we consider to be the fundamental beliefs about people, problems and therapy that are central to CBT. We are not suggesting that these beliefs are necessarily unique to CBT – many of them may be shared by other approaches – but the combination of these principles goes some way towards characterising CBT.

The cognitive principle

The core idea of any therapy calling itself 'cognitive' is that people's emotional reactions and behaviour are strongly influenced by *cognitions* (in other words, their thoughts, beliefs and interpretations about themselves or the situations in which they find themselves – fundamentally the *meaning* they give to the events of their lives). What does this mean?

It may be easiest to start from a 'non-cognitive' perspective. In ordinary life, if we ask people what has made them sad (or happy, or angry, or whatever), they often give us accounts of *events* or *situations*: for example, 'I am fed up because I have just had a row with my girlfriend'. However, it cannot be quite that simple. If an event automatically gave rise to an emotion in such a straightforward way, then it would follow that the same event would have to result in the same emotion for anyone who experienced that event. What we actually see is that to a greater or lesser degree, people react *differently* to similar events. Even events as obviously terrible as suffering a bereavement, or being diagnosed with a terminal illness, do not produce the same emotional state in everyone: some may be completely crushed by such events, whilst others cope reasonably well. So it is not just the event that determines emotion: there must be something else. CBT says that the 'something else' is cognition, i.e., the interpretations people make of the event. When two people react differently to an event it is because they are seeing it differently, and when one person reacts in what seems to be an unusual way, it is because he has unusual thoughts or beliefs about the event: it has an idiosyncratic *meaning* for him. Figure 1.1 illustrates this.

Let us look at a simple example of this process. Suppose you are walking down the street and you see someone you know coming the other way, but she does not seem to notice you. Below are a number of possible thoughts about this event, and some possible emotional responses arising from those interpretations.

- 'I can't think of anything to say to her, she'll think I'm really boring and stupid' (Leading to anxiety)
- 'Nobody would ever want to talk to me anyway, no one seems to like me' (Depression)
- 'She's got a nerve being so snooty, I've not done anything wrong' (Anger)
- 'She's probably still hung over from that party last night!' (Amusement)

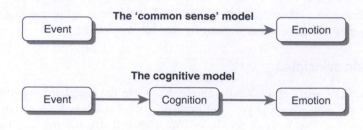

Figure 1.1   The basic cognitive principle

This illustrates the fundamental cognitive principle, that different cognitions give rise to different emotions. It also shows the association between certain kinds of cognition and corresponding emotional states: for instance, that thoughts about others being unfair, or breaking rules that we hold dear, are likely to be associated with anger. We shall have more to say about this idea later.

There is of course nothing new about the idea that meaning is important. The ancient Greek Stoic philosopher Epictetus said over 1,800 years ago that 'Men are disturbed, not by things, but by the principles and notions which they form concerning things.' Yet as we shall see in the rest of this book, the ramifications and elaborations of this simple idea have led to the development of a powerful approach to helping people in distress. By helping people to change their cognitions, we may be able to help them change the way they feel.

The behavioural principle

Part of the inheritance from BT is that CBT considers behaviour (what we *do*) as crucial in maintaining – or in changing – psychological states. Consider the above example again. If you had either the first or second cognition, then your subsequent behaviour might have a significant effect on whether your anxiety or depression persisted. If you approached your acquaintance and chatted, you might discover that she was actually friendly towards you. As a result, you might be less inclined to think negatively in future. On the other hand, if you pretended not to see her, you would not have a chance to find out that your thoughts were inaccurate, and negative thoughts and associated emotions might persist. Thus, CBT believes that behaviour can have a strong impact on thought and emotion, and, in particular, that changing what you do is often a powerful way of changing thoughts and emotions.

The 'continuum' principle

In contrast to some more traditional medical approaches, CBT believes that it is usually more helpful to see mental-health problems as arising from exaggerated or extreme versions of normal processes, rather than as pathological states which are qualitatively different from, and inexplicable by, normal states and processes. In other words, psychological problems are at one end of a continuum, not in a different dimension altogether. Related to this belief are the further ideas that (a) psychological problems can happen to anyone, rather than being some freakish oddity; and (b) that CBT theory applies to therapists as much as to clients.

The 'here and now' principle

Traditional psychodynamic therapy took the view that looking at the symptoms of a problem – for example, the anxiety of a phobic person – was superficial, and that successful treatment must uncover the developmental processes, hidden motivations and unconscious conflicts that were supposed to lie at the root of a problem. BT took the view that the main target of treatment was the symptoms themselves and that one could tackle the anxiety (or whatever) directly, by looking at what processes currently maintained it and then changing those processes. Psychoanalysis argued that treating symptoms rather than the supposed 'root causes' would result in *symptom substitution*, i.e., the unresolved unconscious conflict would result in the client's developing new symptoms. In fact, a wealth of research in BT showed that such an outcome, although possible, was rare: more commonly, tackling symptoms directly actually resulted in more global improvement.

Modern CBT has inherited BT's approach. The main focus of therapy, at least most of the time, is on what is happening in the present, and our main concerns are the processes currently maintaining the problem, rather than the processes that might have led to its development many years ago. Chapter 4 on assessment and formulation discusses this further.

The 'interacting systems' principle

This is the view that problems should be thought of as interactions between various 'systems' within the person and in their environment, and is another legacy from BT (Lang, 1968). Modern CBT commonly identifies four such systems:

- cognition
- affect, or emotion
- behaviour
- physiology.

These systems interact with each other in complex feedback processes and also interact with the environment – where 'environment' is to be understood in the widest possible sense, including not just the obvious physical environment but also the social, family, cultural and economic environment. Figure 1.2, based on the 'hot cross bun' model (Padesky and Greenberger, 1995), illustrates these interactions.

This kind of analysis helps us to describe problems in more detail, to target specific aspects of a problem and also to consider times when one or more systems are not correlated with the others. For example, 'courage' could be said to describe a state where a person's behaviour is not correlated with her emotional state: although she is feeling fearful, her behaviour is not fearful.

The empirical principle

CBT believes we should evaluate theories and treatments as rigorously as possible, using scientific evidence rather than just clinical anecdote. This is important for several reasons:

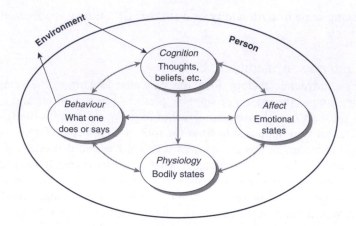

Figure 1.2   Interacting systems

- Scientifically, so that our treatments can be founded on sound, well-established theories. One of the characteristic features of CBT is that, in contrast to some schools of therapy that have remained little changed since they were first devised, it has developed and made steady advances into new areas through the use of scientific research.
- Ethically, so that we can have confidence in telling people who are receiving and/or purchasing our treatments that they are likely to be effective.
- Economically, so that we can make sure that limited mental-health resources are used in the way that will bring most benefit.

Summary

These then are we what we would take as the basic principles at the heart of CBT. To summarise:

- The cognitive principle: it is interpretations of events, not events themselves, which are crucial.
- The behavioural principle: what we do has a powerful influence on our thoughts and emotions.
- The continuum principle: mental-health problems are best conceptualised as exaggerations of normal processes.
- The here-and-now principle: it is usually more fruitful to focus on current processes rather than the past.
- The interacting-systems principle: it is helpful to look at problems as interactions between thoughts, emotions, behaviour and physiology and the environment in which the person operates.
- The empirical principle: it is important to evaluate both our theories and our therapy empirically.

Let us now turn to an elaboration of the fundamental cognitive principles.

'Levels' of cognition

So far we have talked about 'cognition' as if it were a single concept. In fact, CBT usually distinguishes between different kinds or 'levels' of cognition. The following account of levels of cognition is based on what has been found clinically useful; a later section will briefly consider the scientific evidence for some of these ideas. Note that different CBT practitioners might categorise cognitions differently, and although the following classification is commonly used, it is not the only one.

Negative automatic thoughts (NATs)

Negative automatic thoughts,[1] as first described by Beck, are fundamental to CBT. This term is used to describe a stream of thoughts that almost all of us can notice if we try to pay attention to them. They are negatively tinged appraisals or interpretations – *meanings* we take from what happens around us or within us.

Think of a recent time when you became upset: anxious, annoyed, fed up or whatever. Put yourself back in that situation and remember what was going through your mind. Most people can fairly easily pick out NATs. For example, if you were anxious, you might have had thoughts about the threat of something bad happening to you or people you care about; if you were annoyed, you might have had thoughts about others being unfair, or not following rules you consider important; if you were fed up, there might have been thoughts about loss or defeat, or negative views of yourself.

NATs are thought to exert a direct influence over mood from moment to moment, and they are therefore of central importance to any CBT therapy. They have several common characteristics:

- As the name suggests, one does not have to try to think NATs – they just happen, automatically and without effort (although it may take effort to pay attention to them and notice them).
- They are specific thoughts about specific events or situations. Although they may become stereotyped, particularly in chronic problems, they may also vary a great deal from time to time and situation to situation.
- They are, or can easily become, conscious. Most people are either aware of this kind of thought, or can soon learn to be aware of them with some practice in monitoring them.
- They may be so brief and frequent, and so habitual, that they are not 'heard'. They are so much a part of our ordinary mental environment that unless we focus on them we may not notice them, any more than we notice breathing most of the time.
- They are often plausible and taken as obviously true, especially when emotions are strong. Most of the time we do not question them, but simply swallow them whole. If I think 'I am useless' when I am feeling fed up about something's having gone wrong, it seems a simple statement of the truth. One of the crucial steps in therapy is to help clients stop swallowing their NATs in this way, so that they can step back and consider their accuracy. As a common CBT motto has it, 'Thoughts are opinions not facts' – and like all opinions they may or may not be accurate.

---

1. Note that there can also be positive automatic thoughts, or indeed neutral ones; but clients do not tend to want help with those, so we will not consider them further here.

- Although we usually talk about NATs as if they were verbal constructs – e.g., 'I am useless' – it is important to be aware that they may also take the form of images. For example, in social phobia, rather than thinking in words, 'Other people think I'm peculiar', a person may get a mental image of himself looking red-faced, sweaty and incoherent.
- Because of their immediate effect on emotional states, and their accessibility, NATs are usually tackled early on in therapy.

Core beliefs

At the other end of the scale from NATs, core beliefs represent a person's 'bottom line', their fundamental beliefs about themselves, other people, or the world in general. Characteristics of core beliefs are:

- Most of the time they are not immediately accessible to consciousness. They may have to be inferred by observation of one's characteristic thoughts and behaviours in many different situations.
- They manifest as general and absolute statements, e.g., 'I am bad', or 'Others are not to be trusted'. Unlike NATs, they do not typically vary much across times or situations but are seen by the person as fundamental truths that apply in all situations.
- They are usually learned early on in life as a result of childhood experiences, but they may sometimes develop or change later in life, e.g., as a result of severe trauma.
- They are generally not tackled directly in short-term therapy for focal problems such as anxiety disorders or major depression (although they may change anyway). Tackling them directly may be more important in therapy for chronic problems like personality disorders (see Chapter 17).

Dysfunctional assumptions

Dysfunctional assumptions (DAs) can be considered as bridging the gap between core beliefs and NATs. They provide the 'soil' from which NATs sprout. DAs can be thought of as 'rules for living', more specific in their applicability than core beliefs, but more general than NATs. They often take the form of conditional 'If . . . then . . .' propositions, or are framed as 'should' or 'must' statements. They often represent attempts to live with negative core beliefs. For example, if I believe that I am fundamentally unlovable, I may develop the assumption, 'If I always try to please other people then they will tolerate me, but if I stand up for my own needs I will be rejected' or 'I must always put other's needs first, otherwise they will reject me'. Such a DA offers me a guide to how to live my life so as to overcome some of the effects of the core belief, but it is always a fragile truce: if I fail to please someone, then I am in trouble. When one of my DAs is violated, then NATs and strong emotions are likely to be triggered. Characteristics of DAs are:

- Like core beliefs, they are not as obvious as NATs and may not be easily verbalised. They often have to be inferred from actions or from patterns of common NATs.
- They are usually conditional statements, taking the form of 'If . . . then . . .', or 'should/must . . . otherwise . . .' statements.
- Some may be culturally reinforced: for example, beliefs about putting others first, or the importance of success, may be approved of in some cultures.

- What makes them dysfunctional is that they are too rigid and over-generalised, not flexible enough to cope with the inevitable complications and setbacks of life.
- They are usually tackled later on in therapy, after the client has developed some ability to work with challenging NATs. It is thought that modifying DAs may be helpful in making clients more resistant to future relapse (Beck. et al., 1979).

Figure 1.3 illustrates these levels of cognitions for one kind of belief and also shows some of the dimensions along which the levels vary.

It is easy to assume that core beliefs are 'at the root' of the problem, or are the 'underlying' cause, and that therefore they must be tackled directly for therapy to be effective. We would question this assumption. Core beliefs are certainly more *general* than NATs, but that does not necessarily mean they are more important. Most successful CBT research to date targets NATs, but that does not make the therapy ineffective or short-lived. This is probably because people with common mental-health problems such as anxiety or depression have a *range* of core beliefs, not just negative and unhelpful ones. Through the process of therapy they can bring their more positive beliefs back into operation. Although there is not yet much research evidence, working with core beliefs may be more important in lifelong problems such as personality disorders, where clients may never have formed much in the way of positive beliefs.

Characteristic cognitions in different problems

We mentioned earlier that modern CBT theories see characteristic forms of cognition associated with particular kinds of problem. These characteristic patterns involve both the

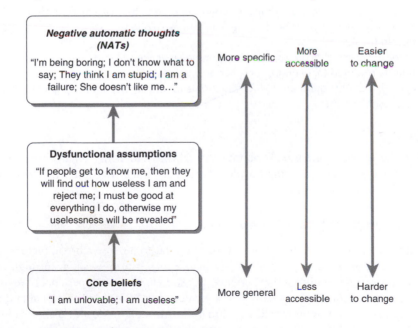

Figure 1.3   Illustration of levels of cognition

content of cognitions and the *process* of cognition. If we take depression as an example, then the thoughts of depressed people are likely to contain characteristic *contents*, e.g., negative thoughts about themselves or others. Depressed people are also likely to show characteristic general biases in the *way* that they think, e.g., towards perceiving and remembering negative events more than positive ones; or tending to see anything that goes wrong as being their fault; or over generalising from one small negative event to a broad negative conclusion. Here we briefly consider some examples. (See also later chapters on specific problems.)

Depression

As first described by Beck, the characteristic cognitions in depression are the *negative cognitive triad*, namely negatively biased views of *oneself*, of the *world in general* and of the *future*. In other words, the typical depressed view is that I am bad (useless, unlovable, incompetent, worthless, a failure, etc.); the world is bad (nothing good happens, life is just a series of trials); and the future is also bad (not only are myself and the world bad, but it will always be like this and nothing I can do will make any difference).

Anxiety

The general process here is a bias towards the over estimation of threat, i.e., perceiving a high risk of some unwanted outcome. The exact nature of the threat, and therefore the content of cognitions, is different in different disorders. For example:

- In *panic*, there is catastrophic misinterpretation of harmless anxiety symptoms as indicating some imminent disaster, e.g., dying or 'going mad'.
- In *health anxiety*, there is a similar misinterpretation of harmless symptoms as indicating illness, but on a longer time scale: e.g., I might have a disease that will make me die sometime in the future.
- In *social anxiety*, thoughts are about being negatively evaluated by others, e.g., 'They will think I am stupid (or boring, or peculiar, or ...).'
- In *OCD*, thoughts are about being responsible for, and/or needing to prevent, some harm to oneself or others.

Anger

In anger, the thoughts are usually about others' behaviour being *unfair*, breaking some implicit or explicit *rule*, or having hostile intent: 'They ought not to do that, it's not fair, they're trying to put me down.'

Generic CBT model of problem development

We shall finally put together the ideas introduced so far to develop a broad picture of how CBT sees the development of problems (see Figure 1.4). It proposes that through experience (most commonly childhood experience, but sometimes later experience), we develop core beliefs and assumptions which are to a greater or lesser extent functional and which allow us to make sense of our world and find a way through it. Most of us have a mixture of functional and dysfunctional beliefs, with the functional ones allowing us to cope

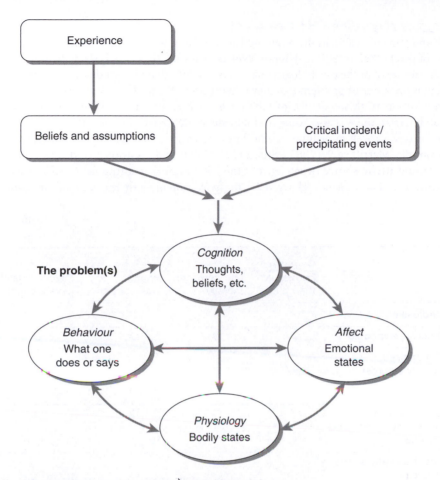

Figure 1.4   Generic problem development model

reasonably well most of the time. Even quite dysfunctional beliefs may not cause any particular problems for many years. However, if we encounter an event or series of events that violates a core belief or assumption and cannot be handled by our more positive beliefs (sometimes called a *critical incident*), then dysfunctional assumptions become more active, negative thoughts are evoked, and unpleasant emotional states such as anxiety or depression result. Interactions between negative thoughts, emotions, behaviour and physiological changes may then result in persisting dysfunctional patterns, and we get locked into vicious cycles or feedback loops that serve to maintain the problem.

The current status of CBT

Finally, since we have talked about CBT's commitment to empiricism, we should consider the empirical status of CBT. What is the evidence that CBT is effective? And what is the evidence that CBT theory is an accurate model of human functioning?

Evidence regarding CBT treatment

Roth and Fonagy (2005), in the recent update of *What works for whom?* (their landmark summary of psychotherapy efficacy), report evidence showing that CBT is strongly supported as a therapy for most of the psychological disorders in adults that they studied, and has more support in more kinds of problem than any other therapy. Figure 1.5 summarises this.

In addition to this evidence of CBT's *efficacy* (i.e., that it works in tightly controlled research trials), there is also some useful evidence demonstrating its *effectiveness* (i.e., that it can also work well in ordinary clinical practice, outside specialist research centres). See, for example, Merrill et al. (2003); Stuart et al. (2000) and Westbrook and Kirk (2005).

A second useful source of evidence is the UK National Institute for Clinical Excellence (NICE). This is an agency charged by the government with the task of surveying the

	Cognitive/ behaviour therapies	Interpersonal therapy	Family interventions	Psychodynamic psychotherapy
Depression	✓	✓	O	?
Panic/agoraphobia	✓	O	O	O
Generalised anxiety disorder	✓	O	O	O
Specific phobias	✓	O	O	O
Social phobia	✓	O	O	O
Obsessive-compulsive disorder	✓	O	O	O
Post-traumatic stress disorder	✓	O	O	?
Anorexia	?	O	?	?
Bulimia	✓	✓	O	O
(Some) personality disorders	✓	O	O	✓
Schizophrenia	?	O	✓	O
Bipolar disorder	?	O	O	O

Key to summary:
✓ = Clear evidence of efficacy
? = Some limited support for efficacy
O = Not currently well validated (NB this indicates a lack of sufficient evidence to support efficacy; it does not necessarily imply that there is good evidence of *in*effectiveness)

Figure 1.5   Summary by the current authors, adapted from Roth & Fonagy (2005), Chapter 17

evidence for the effectiveness of different treatments and making recommendations about which treatments ought therefore to be made available in the National Health Service (NHS). In the past three years, NICE has produced guidelines on several major mental-health problems, which include the following recommendations:

- Schizophrenia (NICE, 2002):'Cognitive behavioural therapy (CBT) should be available as a treatment option for people with schizophrenia ...' (p. 13);
- Depression (NICE, 2004a):'For patients with mild depression, healthcare professionals should consider recommending a guided self-help programme based on cognitive behavioural therapy (CBT) ...'(p. 5);'When considering individual psychological treatments for moderate, severe and treatment-resistant depression, the treatment of choice is CBT ...' (p. 27);
- Eating disorders (NICE, 2004b):'Cognitive behaviour therapy for bulimia nervosa ... should be offered to adults with bulimia nervosa ...' (p. 4);'Cognitive behaviour therapy for binge eating disorder ... should be offered to adults with binge eating disorder ...' (p. 5);
- Generalised anxiety and panic (NICE, 2004c): 'The interventions that have evidence for the longest duration of effect, in descending order, are: [first] cognitive behavioural therapy; ...' (p. 6);
- Post-traumatic stress disorder (PTSD) (NICE, 2005):'All people with PTSD should be offered a course of trauma-focused psychological treatment (trauma-focused cognitive behavioural therapy [CBT] or eye movement desensitisation and reprocessing [EMDR]) ...' (p. 4).

In summary then, at the time of writing, CBT is the psychological therapy with the most solid and wide evidence base for efficacy and effectiveness.

Evidence regarding CBT theory

It is a fallacy to think that demonstrating the efficacy of a treatment proves the truth of the theory on which that treatment is based. The treatment's efficacy could be due to some combination of factors not imagined in the theory. Thus, for most of us, even a randomised controlled trial (RCT) showing that a treatment based on traditional witchcraft was effective for depression would not necessarily convince us that depression was in fact caused by evil spirits; instead we might investigate whether there was a powerful placebo effect, or perhaps whether the herbal potions used in the treatment contained a psychoactive substance. In the same way, the efficacy of CBT as a treatment does not show that CBT theory is true. In fact, the evidence for some of the fundamental theoretical ideas of CBT is more patchy than the evidence for the treatment's efficacy. Clark et al. (1999) present a detailed consideration of the balance of scientific evidence in the case of the cognitive theory of depression. In summary, they conclude that regarding the supposed patterns of negative thinking in depression, there is evidence that:

- there is an increase in negative thinking about oneself, the future and (less clearly) the world;
- there is a reduction in positive thinking about the self, but this change is less marked and may be less specific to depression (in other words, the same thing also happens in other problems);
- there is a specific increase in thoughts and beliefs about loss and failure (more so than people who suffer from anxiety problems).

Regarding the proposed *causal* role of negative thoughts, i.e., the suggestion that negative thinking can provoke low mood, they conclude that there is some experimental evidence that negative self-referent thinking can indeed induce subjective, behavioural, motivational and physiological features similar to mild to moderate depression. If we experimentally provoke negative thoughts about themselves in non-depressed people, we can produce temporary states quite similar to depression.

There is also some evidence that the proposed cognitive processing biases can be identified in experiments, with evidence that in depressed people there is:

- a bias towards processing negative information relevant to themselves (but no such bias for neutral or impersonal information);
- enhanced recall of negative events, and increased negative beliefs.

Furthermore, there is evidence that these changes in processing can occur at an automatic, pre-conscious level.

The least well-supported part of the theory is the suggestion that people are vulnerable to depression because of negative beliefs that are still present in 'latent' form even when they are not depressed. Clark et al. suggest that there is a little supportive evidence for this idea, but that it has proved difficult to get clear evidence (perhaps not surprisingly, when one considers the difficulties of identifying such 'latent' beliefs experimentally).

A similar picture is found for specific CBT models for other disorders: in some areas there is good solid research support and in others the evidence is equivocal. Overall, then, the evidence is

(a) that CBT is undoubtedly an effective treatment for many problems; and
(b) that there is support for CBT theory but that there is still room for exploring and developing this approach further in some areas.

Distinctive Characteristics of CBT

CBT has many features in common with other therapies, but it is also different in important respects. In this chapter we describe the fundamental characteristics of the CBT approach, and we also explore some of the myths about CBT. We hope this is helpful for you, but also for your clients: giving them accurate information about therapy allows them to make an informed choice about whether they want to proceed (Garfield, 1986) and may also improve outcome (Duckro et al., 1979).

CBT is distinguished by a combination of characteristics which are described in this chapter. It is collaborative, structured and active, time limited and brief, empirical and problem oriented; it also frequently employs the techniques of guided discovery, behavioural methods, 'in vivo work', summaries and feedback.

Collaboration

CBT is fundamentally a *collaborative* project between therapist and client. Both are active participants, with their own areas of expertise: the therapist has knowledge about effective ways to solve problems, and the client has expertise in his own experience of his problems. This collaborative emphasis may be different from what the client expected, so clarify what the client anticipated in order to establish a shared view from the outset. Part of the initial induction into therapy would include a statement about the client's crucial role. For example, you might say:

> We both have an important role in the treatment. I know quite a lot about CBT, and about how particular sorts of problems can present difficulties for people. However, you know very much more than I can about the details of how your problem affects you, and it is this knowledge that will allow us to understand and gradually change the situation for you. This really is a joint enterprise.

This also implies you cannot be expected to know all of the answers all of the time. If you are unsure, you can always ask the client for clarification, more information, or their view of the situation.

When a client described a vivid dream to a therapist and asked, 'What am I supposed to make of that?' the therapist asked, 'What do you think was important about your having that dream?' and 'What did it leave you feeling?'

Remember that CBT encourages openness and honesty between therapist and client: be overt about what you are doing and why, and ask the client to give honest feedback about what he finds helpful and what he does not.

Collaboration should develop as treatment proceeds. Encourage your client gradually to take a more active role in setting agendas, devising homework and giving feedback. Enhance this by being genuinely respectful of the client and by fostering the sense that he is becoming his own therapist. The hope is that clients will leave therapy as skilled CBT practitioners, so they are encouraged to use the approach independently and to be prepared for relapse (see Chapter 6).

Structure and active engagement

CBT is problem focused and structured, and the therapist works with the client to maintain structure in the sessions. For example, at the beginning of each session, we set an explicit agenda with the client, and then (by and large) stick to it (see Chapter 11, which elaborates on the process of agenda-setting).

CBT therapists are *actively* engaged with the client and may talk more than in some other therapies – perhaps as much as 50 per cent of the time in the early stages. This can feel onerous to new therapists. However, much of your input is in the form of questions, and the way the session develops is the result of a joint effort. In the early stages of therapy, the content of sessions will be directed to a greater extent by the therapist, but responsibility is increasingly picked up by the client as sessions progress. For example, homework tasks are likely to be devised by you at first, but as treatment proceeds, your clients will have a greater role in setting up tasks for subsequent meetings. The extent to which the client determines the content of sessions is partly a function of his personality, beliefs and attitudes. An autonomous person might assume control from early in treatment, whereas a more dependent person will benefit from a slower handover of responsibility.

Time-limited and brief

CBT is attractive to clients and commissioners of services partly because it is often relatively brief. In this context, 'brief' means somewhere between six and 20 sessions. The number of sessions is guided by treatment trials involving the target problem but is also influenced by the problem and the client, as well as available resources. As resources are often scarce, it is important to help people efficiently, and the structure and focus of CBT contribute to achieving that. Table 2.1 gives some suggestions about possible lengths of treatment for different types of problem.

Evidence does not suggest that a long history necessarily demands lengthy treatment (Fairburn et al., 1987), and neither do clients who have been on long waiting lists necessarily require an equally lengthy treatment. For therapists used to other treatment

Table 2.1 Guidelines on length of treatment

Type of problem	Number of sessions
Mild	Up to 6
Mild to moderate	6–12
Moderate to severe *or*	
moderate problems with co-existing personality disorder	12–20
Severe problems with co-existing personality disorders	> 20

approaches, the rapid move from one or two sessions of assessment and formulation into a six- or eight-session therapy may feel uncomfortably rushed, but this is likely to become less difficult as you become more familiar with the approach.

It is helpful to give your clients an indication of how long treatment is likely to last and to build in regular progress reviews. If it appears that the therapy is not helpful, or if progress has reached a plateau, it is easier to bring treatment to a close if reviews have been pre-established. If the client is making progress but residual problems are still present, then it is probably worth continuing with treatment. However, it is worth considering the benefits of allowing your client to manage such difficulties independently. This is best done by gradually increasing the length of time between sessions, so that the client takes increasing responsibility for dealing with residual problems and setbacks, whilst there continue to be opportunities for review with the therapist.

There is no commitment within CBT to a standard '50-minute hour', or any other standard session length. A session involving in-vivo, experiments, for example, with a client with agoraphobia, may last 2 or 3 hours. On the other hand, a review session towards the end of treatment may last only 20 minutes. Bear in mind that if relevant and productive homework assignments have been set up, then the majority of treatment can be considered to be taking place outside the 'therapy hour'.

Empirical in approach

There is a strong emphasis within CBT on using empirical psychological knowledge. For example, that early loss of a parent predisposes one to depression in adult life (Brown et al., 1986); acting out anger increases rather than diminishes angry feelings (Tavris, 1989); and current mood affects memory for past events (Williams, 1992). Therapy rests on this kind of knowledge base. CBT has also borrowed from behaviour therapy a commitment to establishing the efficacy of treatment in individual clinical cases (see Chapters 5 and 18).

As a therapist, you need to keep informed about the evidence from research trials and use this to guide interventions in individual cases. It is sometimes claimed that the samples studied by research teams are atypical of those found in clinical settings and therefore trial data are not relevant. However, unless you have good evidence to demonstrate why another approach would be likely to be more successful, then it is fairer to the client if the available empirical evidence is given appropriate weight. This is not to discount therapist intuition about what is likely to be helpful, merely to suggest that such insights should be built into a formulation that is consistent with evidence about psychological processes. None of us should be cavalier about discounting well-described and apparently relevant data, and we need to be aware that there is some indication that clients may do better if a treatment protocol is followed than if treatment is individually tailored (Schulte et al., 1992), although the evidence is not conclusive (Ghaderi, 2006).

Within individual therapy, the client is also encouraged to tackle his problems in an empirical way:

- *Thoughts and beliefs are considered as hypotheses to be investigated* – for example, a woman who thought, 'I am a useless mother' was encouraged to see this as one possible view among other possibilities and to look at the evidence supporting each view.
- *Data can be collected to test out ideas* – for example, a man who feared spiders because he believed that they would run towards him was encouraged to collect data about how frequently a spider on a tray ran towards a (therapist's!) hand, rather than away from it.
- *New beliefs can be formulated in the light of evidence and subsequently tested out* – there is an emphasis on 'discovering how it is' by trying out new behaviours, new ways of thinking, new ways of interacting, and not simply relying on verbal discussion or new insights for changes in feelings and beliefs. It is as important as ever to be guided by the client about what would be helpful:

    Following discussions with her therapist, a woman was developing a new belief: 'Things can be done for their own sake, and still feel satisfying and enjoyable. You do not need to be making the most of your potential.' To test this out, she joined a non-auditioned choir for the fun of it, and she began to learn French so that she could 'get by', with no intention of becoming fluent.

Problem-oriented in approach

Your client's problem may be a dysphoric mood, a relationship difficulty, an unhelpful behaviour (for example, a repetitive habit), or an occupational problem (for example, frequent loss of jobs). CBT identifies the pertinent *problems* for the client and then focuses on resolving or reducing them, and problems are described in specific terms, not at the general level of diagnosis. For example, if a client was suffering from depression, you would want to know how this was actually affecting him and what specific aspects of the problem he wanted help with: e.g., self-critical thoughts, low mood, social withdrawal, reduced interests, etc.

Once you have agreed what problems will be tackled, goals are set for each problem and these goals provide the focus for treatment. The process of goal-setting explicitly focuses the client on where he hopes to be at the end of treatment, and in what ways he wants to be different from how he is now (see Chapter 11).

In choosing strategies to address your clients' difficulties you might well find that you draw on other strategies in addition to those laid out in this text. Interventions such as skills training (assertiveness, time management, etc.), or grief work, or couple therapy, may also be relevant. As ever in CBT, interventions should be evaluated and you should review the efficacy of the strategies you use.

Guided discovery

The therapist uses a form of questioning often described as 'Socratic' in a process of guided discovery, helping the client to clarify his thoughts and beliefs (see Chapter 7). CBT therefore involves carefully constructed questioning, to help clients understand the idiosyncratic meanings of situations, to work out alternative ways of looking at things and to test out the usefulness of new perspectives, *for themselves.*

Behavioural methods

Behavioural interventions are a necessary element of CBT, so many assignments include behavioural tasks and experiments. These are used to test out new perspectives derived in treatment sessions, to enhance learning and also to encourage generalisation from treatment sessions to everyday life – where the changes really need to be made. There is a wide variety of possible behavioural interventions (see Chapter 9 for a thorough review of behavioural strategies), and some of the principles of behaviour therapy have been directly adopted by CBT: for example, taking a graded approach to new tasks and breaking them down into manageable chunks.

In-vivo work

CBT therapists often take therapy out of the office and into the real world, in order to help with assessment or to carry out a behavioural experiment. Such real-life '*in vivo*' work can be invaluable. For example, a client with long-standing OCD may have become unaware of the detail of his obsessional rituals, and you may underestimate his problems unless you directly observe them. Similarly, it is important to check out that changes in belief in a clinic setting are translated into real-life settings, so it may be helpful to do experiments *in vivo*, possibly with the therapist accompanying the client.

> *A man with health anxiety believed that if he became short of breath, he could pass out and die; he therefore made sure that he always stayed within reach of a doctor's surgery. During therapy he challenged this belief. The therapist then drove him into the countryside where neither of them knew the whereabouts of doctors' surgeries, and they ran up and down the road to make him breathless (an activity he had been avoiding), so that he could test out his new belief that he would not pass out.*

If the client is trying out a difficult new behaviour, it may be helpful for you to be there to offer encouragement and support. In some instances, therapist modelling of behaviours may be useful, although you should withdraw as soon as possible, and allow the client to continue alone in such experiments.

> *A woman with agoraphobia had catastrophic concerns about the consequences of becoming anxious, particularly that she would be publicly ridiculed if she were to soil herself. The client accompanied the therapist to a local shopping centre and observed from a distance the responses of members of the public to an obvious brown stain on the back of the therapist's skirt – responses best described as studied indifference.*

It is often possible to draw on the assistance of relatives or friends for in-vivo work, but this must be planned carefully, with an eye to detail, and it may be necessary to help the aide identify and challenge unhelpful thoughts of their own. For example, a spouse may believe that exposing their loved one to panic may be harmful, and such a belief would be counterproductive in a behavioural experiment about the consequences of panic.

Summaries and feedback

CBT makes frequent use of summaries and feedback during sessions, which is one way of keeping the session to the agenda. You might pause to summarise the main points under discussion approximately every 5 minutes, and more frequently than that in the early stages of therapy. Summaries should include the emotions that the client has described, and the meaning of the event or situation for him. This is not supposed to be an *interpretation* of what the client has said. It is better to use the client's own words as far as possible, rather than substitute your own, as this may significantly change the meaning for the client, especially if he has used a metaphor or some idiosyncratic phrasing. It is equally helpful to ask your client to summarise the discussion, by saying, for example: 'Can you feed back to me what you think the main points of our discussion are so far? I would just like to check out that I am on the same track as you.'

This provision of summaries helps ensure a shared understanding of key points. It is sometimes startling to learn how misunderstood the client or the therapist has been.

> After discussing why it is helpful to write down NATs, a therapist had mentioned that it was an asset that the client was readily able to identify them. When asked for feedback, the client said that she now understood that, as she was aware of her NATs but still felt bad, it was unlikely that she would benefit from CBT.

Summaries can also be enlightening for the client:

> Therapist: 'It sounds as if the qualities that attracted you to your partner are now the things that you find most upsetting. Is that right?'
> Client: 'Yes, but I had not thought about it like that before.'

It is particularly useful to summarise the key points at the end of the session and to ask the client what is the 'take-home' message for him – again, this will reduce misunderstandings. It is also important to gather feedback on the session, for example: what has been helpful, unhelpful or upsetting? Clients are more likely to give genuine feedback if you take time early in treatment to explain why feedback is valuable and give honest encouragement when you receive it.

Each session can also begin with a request for feedback on the previous one – what had been helpful or whether the client had any new ideas about the previous discussion. Again, it is more likely that your client will review the session and give feedback, if you have discussed the advantages of thinking about the therapy between sessions and taken seriously the client's feedback on this. For example, a client said that he did not like to think about sessions when he was not with the therapist. Exploration revealed that he struggled with negative thoughts about being overwhelmed, thoughts which could then be dealt with.

Myths about CBT

In this section, we will identify and explore some of the common myths surrounding CBT.

The therapeutic relationship is not important in CBT

Therapist qualities recognised in other therapies are equally important within CBT, and warmth, empathy and unconditional regard have been found to be typical of CBT therapists (for example, Wright and Davis, 1994). This contrasts with the mistaken view that CBT is impersonal and not concerned about the therapeutic relationship. At the most basic level, if a client is to be willing to reveal personally significant material, to carry out frightening and difficult new behaviours and to feel safe, then he has to be able to trust the therapist. Therefore, although CBT does not see the relationship as sufficiently therapeutic in itself, it is seen as an essential foundation for effective therapy. It is recognised that the therapist must pay attention to ruptures in the therapeutic relationship and must attempt to understand what client beliefs may have been triggered to produce the difficulty (see Chapter 3).

It is also sometimes believed that CBT therapists have no interest in the client's feelings about the therapist. However, there has been an increasing recognition over the past 20 years of the importance of relationship factors – but construed in cognitive rather than psychodynamic terms (see Orlinsky et al., 1994).

CBT is mechanistic – just apply technique X to problem Y

CBT is based on an explicit model that links emotion, behaviour and cognition, and this model underpins the therapeutic strategies that have been shown to work effectively. At a clinical level, there is often a specific model for many problems presented by clients. There may also be a fairly detailed protocol for treating clients with a specific kind of problem. However, while the formulation for an individual client may be based on the model for his problem, the treatment would not be technique-driven (e.g., 'I think he needs some anxiety management training'), but would instead be based on an understanding of how the model applies to him – what psychological processes are maintaining *his* problem and what relationships between emotions, thoughts, behaviours and physiological features are important in *his* case. This is discussed further in Chapter 4.

CBT is about positive thinking

It is sometimes suggested that CBT is not concerned with the client's circumstances or interpersonal situation but is only interested in getting the client to see things positively. This is not true: CBT aims to help clients *realistically* evaluate their thoughts, not to show that they are always wrong or that things are always positive. Often when people have problems, their thinking is excessively negative, but sometimes it is accurate – your client may think his partner is not interested in him because his partner is not interested in him! The formulation should take account of interpersonal and socio-economic circumstances and not assume that the client's thoughts are distorted.

> *A woman presented with low mood following redundancy from her job in a hotel. This was the third job that she had lost, the first two through redundancy, and the last after interpersonal difficulties with her boss. She was feeling low because however hard she tried, luck was against her, and things went wrong. She felt hopeless about being able to improve things. Rather than assuming that her view was distorted, the therapist helped the client review the evidence, to see what had contributed to each of the job losses and what responsibility she seemed to have for the outcomes. Therapy might have needed to focus on her interpersonal skills, or her occupational standards, or possibly a tendency to attribute blame to others. In the event, it appeared to be much as she had initially thought: luck had been against her, and treatment therefore focused on helping her to tolerate the intrinsic unfairness of events.*

CBT also acknowledges that some unhelpful thoughts may have been accurate in the past but are no longer accurate. For example, a child growing up in an emotionally deprived home may accurately have believed that 'No one is there for me', but this may no longer be true in her adult world. The aim of treatment is to understand and resolve problems, not to fix thinking!

CBT does not deal with the past

Most CBT sessions do focus on the 'here and now', because most therapy is concerned with tackling current problems and hence what is currently maintaining them. But that is not to say that CBT cannot work with past history when necessary, nor that it discounts the importance of past experiences in accounting for problem development (see Chapter 4). The main reason for a 'here-and-now' focus is that the factors that account for the development of a problem are often different from the ones that are maintaining it, and so relatively greater attention is paid to the present situation than to the past.

> *A girl with anxiety about wetting herself had had an experience as a young child when she felt humiliated after wetting herself in front of her friends on a school trip. She had not been able to 'hold on' when instructed to do so by her teacher and had been teased by her friends. As an adult, she knew she was capable of holding on for many hours and no longer had friends who would tease her. The problem now was largely maintained by avoidance of situations where she would not have easy access to a lavatory, by not drinking before going out, and by a range of 'safety behaviours' like wearing long thick socks under her trousers so that urine would be absorbed if she did have an accident.*

CBT deals with superficial symptoms, not the roots of problems, so alternative symptoms are likely to occur

As noted in Chapter 1, there used to be concern that simply 'removing symptoms' would result in the emergence of other manifestations of an underlying problem. However, a number of studies show that CBT clients are, if anything, protected against relapse, rather than developing further problems (e.g., Williams, 1997; Durham & Turvey, 1987).

The strategies taught in CBT are often readily generalised to other problems. In addition, the CBT formulation of a client's problems aims to throw light on the psychological *processes* maintaining them, and to intervene in ways that impact on these processes. In doing so it addresses fundamental maintaining patterns.

CBT is adversarial

It is sometimes suggested that the CBT therapist tells the client what is wrong with his thinking and how he ought to think. As one mental-health information centre leaflet put it, 'Cognitive therapy takes the form of an argument between client and therapist. As such, it is only suitable for the robust.' In reality, only *bad* CBT looks like an argument! You should aim to approach your client open-mindedly so that you can get a sense of what it is to be him, to experience the problem as he does and to help him learn to question his beliefs for *himself*: there are good psychological reasons for encouraging him, via questioning, to work out new perspectives for himself (see Chapter 7).

CBT is for simple problems: you need something else for complex problems

CBT is a wide-ranging and flexible approach to therapy, which skilful practitioners can apply to many psychological problems, provided the client is at least minimally engaged in the process. Within Axis I disorders (defined by DSM; see APA, 2000), clients with very severe and chronic difficulties have been helped by this approach (Tarrier et al., 1998), and there is now increasing evidence of its efficacy for those with personality disorders (see Chapter 17).

CBT is interested in thoughts and not emotions

Obviously, CBT is interested in helping people modify thoughts, but usually as a means to an end, not an end in itself. Most clients want help with mood, feelings or behaviour rather than with dysfunctional thinking. Cognitive change is a means of helping people change those other systems, and therapy is rarely fruitful if it is a purely intellectual discussion of abstract thoughts. If the client is experiencing no emotion during the process, it is very unlikely that he will achieve a shift in emotion or behaviour.

CBT is only for clients who are psychologically minded

Typically, CBT needs clients to be able to recognise and talk about thoughts and emotions and to distinguish them. It is also advantageous if a client can relate to psychological models – a vicious cycle or a preliminary formulation, for example. However, if a client has difficulty in reflecting in this way, the therapist can try to increase his capacity to do that (see Butler and Surawy, 2004), and it is worth offering a trial of a few sessions to see if the client can take to the approach.

CBT is quick to learn and easy to practice

CBT has some powerful strategies that are *relatively* easy to learn and apply, and this book introduces you to the basic skills. However, using the approach in a creative and flexible way is as difficult as any other therapy, and you are reminded that you will need to receive regular supervision (see Chapter 19) and keep yourself updated on developments in CBT.

CBT is not interested in the unconscious

CBT does not use the concept of the unconscious in the Freudian sense but certainly recognises that cognitive processes may not be conscious. In many instances, you and your client are attempting to clarify the meanings of situations that may initially be beyond awareness. This is not generally interpreted as repressed material but is taken to be at a pre-conscious level, out of awareness, but available on reflection to consciousness. Many clients need training to increase their awareness of, for example, NATs or assumptions. Socratic enquiry is used to help the client identify such cognitions and, subsequently, to establish the meaning of them. However, the therapist does not offer an interpretation of her own; the client is by and large considered to be the expert.

There are instances when thoughts or images may be actively blocked by the client. For example, someone who has been sexually abused as a child might use the process of dissociation to detach from an experience or memory which is too distressing to deal with; in OCD, many clients never confront the disturbing thoughts that motivate their ritualistic behaviour, by avoiding situations that would trigger the thoughts. Generally, the CBT techniques described in Chapters 8 and 9 are used to identify the nature of these unconscious thoughts or beliefs.

CBT demands high intelligence

CBT makes no greater demands on intelligence than any other therapy and, indeed, has been adapted for use with people with learning difficulty and for children and young people.

Summary

The basic characteristics of CBT make this a fascinating and satisfying way of working with clients, as you help them develop strategies for managing problems and guide them as they work out new, more adaptive perspectives on their world. We hope some of the myths about CBT have been debunked by this chapter and that the reader is reassured about the nature of the approach.

The Therapeutic Relationship

This chapter reviews the importance of the therapeutic relationship in CBT. We will look at:

- the extent to which the therapeutic relationship is an essential foundation for therapy;
- the role of the therapist in CBT and the importance of non-specific therapist factors;
- ways of building collaborative client-therapist relationships – and of repairing ruptures in the therapeutic alliance;
- boundary issues.

The therapeutic relationship as an essential foundation of therapy

An effective therapist–client relationship is important for treatment, with good evidence relating quality of relationship to therapeutic outcome (Orlinsky et al., 1994). However, within CBT the therapeutic relationship is seen as necessary but not sufficient, and in treatment trials there is typically a beneficial effect from CBT over and above that of being in a therapeutic relationship (Roth and Fonagy, 2005).

Moreover, the evidence indicates that it may be the nature of the *client's* participation in treatment that is the strongest predictor of outcome. For example, a client is more likely to do well if he is engaged with the therapeutic task, offers suggestions about treatment, warmly interacts with the therapist and is trusting of the therapist; and a client who consistently completes homework will do better than one who does not (Burns and Nolen-Hoeksema, 1991). Furthermore, in so far as therapist characteristics are related to outcome, it is the client's *perception* of those characteristics, and not the behaviours themselves, that predicts outcome (Wright and Davis, 1994). For example, if a therapist's empathic skills are assessed by her client and by an independent observer, the client's perception of empathy is a better predictor of outcome. All this means that the client is an active contributor to the therapy process.

The therapeutic relationship can be viewed as a useful laboratory for working on problems, providing an opportunity to acquire new skills that can then be transferred to situations in real life. An example would be learning to evaluate a 'hot' thought in a therapy session, with coaching from the therapist, before applying the same techniques in 'real life'. The client may also use sessions to review and modify unhelpful beliefs as they are played out with the therapist in the clinical setting. Safran and Muran (1995) suggest that the therapist can act in ways that provide new, constructive interpersonal experiences for the client, with the client and therapist stepping back together from the interaction and examining what is currently going on between them.

> *A client's formulation included beliefs about others failing to be there for him when he was in trouble. In a session where there seemed to be difficulties emerging in the relationship, the therapist used her own feelings as the cue for a discussion, saying 'I am feeling quite defensive just now, and I wonder why. Could we explore this together?' The discussion revealed that the client was uncertain whether or not the therapist could help him. They then went on to look at whether the therapist would be likely to withdraw if things became difficult, or whether she would want to find ways of hanging in there even in the face of difficulty, a discussion that was highly relevant to the client's fears, and which led to the therapeutic relationship becoming a 'laboratory' for testing out those fears.*

Within this model, the ways in which the client responds to the therapist may be influenced by beliefs developed early in life (possibly modified by subsequent experience), and the characteristics and behaviour of the therapist herself will also influence the client's reactions to her. The therapeutic relationship is not construed in terms of 'transference', in the psychoanalytic sense that it is a representation of another relationship from early life, but instead is considered as *a relationship in its own right*, with the potential for providing the client with new evidence about the range of possibilities for relationships – for example, 'People may stay with you even if difficulties emerge in the relationship.' The extent to which any corrective interpersonal experience in therapy will generalise to other relationships should be considered empirically. If the issues are being openly discussed, it is easier to check out whether there is any generalisation to everyday life.

Bordin's (1979) analysis of the therapeutic relationships as a *working alliance* is useful. He suggested that three components are necessary for a successful working alliance:

- Agreement on the task – what needs to be done in therapy, what the process of change will be, what activities and techniques will be used.
- Agreement on therapy goals – what is being sought from therapy in the short and long term, with client and therapist each contributing personal commitment to the goals.
- A positive therapist–client bond, typified by mutual liking, respect, trust and commitment.

It is clear that a good working alliance is necessary for a good outcome. At its most basic, you cannot carry out effective therapy with a client who drops out because he finds you cold and unempathic. The alliance needs to be established within the first three or four sessions (Horvarth, 1995), but this is not to say that the quality of the relationship remains fixed. It varies as treatment progresses, and it may be necessary to attend to breakdowns in the alliance in order for therapy to succeed. Thus, the quality of your therapeutic relationship should continue to be a focus of concern throughout the course of treatment.

Although it is not clear whether effective CBT is typified by a particular kind of alliance, it appears from a number of studies (e.g., Raue and Goldfried, 1994) that whatever the therapeutic modality, clients consider similar qualities of the working alliance to be important. These include:

- being helped to understand their problems;
- being encouraged to face whatever situations cause them distress;
- being able to talk to an understanding person;
- being at ease with the personality of the therapist.

Some of these features map onto central features of CBT – for example, presenting a formulation of the client's problems for him to comment on and designing behavioural experiments to test out unhelpful beliefs. As some of the factors relate to the qualities of the therapist, these will now be considered.

The role of the therapist

One of the guiding principles of CBT is that, as therapist, you work empathically and collaboratively to engage the client in therapy (Beck, 1967). Chapter 7 below, on Socratic method, develops this idea further, but the general approach is that you function as a guide and mentor rather than an instructor. You are 'walking alongside' your client as he explores new options for feeling and behaving, and your role is to open up new opportunities for exploration, by asking questions, or giving information, that may lead him into previously unexplored areas. You need to have a good understanding of his current bearings in order to do this, so you need to adopt an open-minded curiosity and respect about your client's beliefs, emotions and behaviours and not assume that you know how he feels or thinks.

As this demands a lot of active questioning on your part, the tone of the interaction is crucial: it should not be accusatory ('You can't really mean you think that!'), nor persuasive or haranguing ('Do you think it is possible that most people respond in this way and that you are not picking up the cues?'). You should reflect a genuine, concerned interest in the client's current perspectives or feelings. This is a fine balance because, while you are trying to get a detailed sense of what it is like to be your client in the current situation, you also need to maintain a measure of scepticism about what he is saying since it is possible that he is making cognitive errors that will significantly distort the picture he presents.

Although the therapist's role as guide is paramount, it may be appropriate to adopt an educative, information-giving role from time to time:

A young person was troubled by a recurrent image of himself in an embarrassing situation from a few years previously. He was given the information that this is relatively common for people with social anxiety, and this was supplemented by appropriate reading.

Another important role for the therapist is *practical scientist*, providing a model for the client to adopt in relation to both current and future problems. Adopting an open-minded approach to problems and experiences, in which hypotheses are set up and tested and new conclusions drawn if appropriate, is relevant throughout therapy. The importance of look-ing for evidence that contradicts your initial hypothesis is particularly important – and this is as true for the therapist's initial formulation as it is for the client's initial beliefs. Evidence inconsistent with your ideas is the royal road to new perspectives!

The collaborative nature of the therapeutic relationship means that you relate to your client in an adult-to-adult way as far as possible. Thus you are open about your ideas con-cerning his problems and share your formulation in a way that allows the client to give feedback on its relevance or accuracy; you may disclose information about yourself if this is in the client's interest; and you are free to say 'I don't know' or 'Can I just think that over for a minute', without needing to appear all-knowing. It is acceptable for you and your client to problem-solve together. The only occasional exceptions to this openness are when it is clearly in the client's interest – for example, you might choose not to disclose too early your ideas about a possible final weight for an eating-disordered client, in case this demotivated the client.

Within the complex web of interactions between therapist, client and techniques, it is clear that a good cognitive therapist also needs the characteristics identified by Rogers as necessary for all therapies, namely warmth, empathy, genuineness and unconditional regard for the client (Beck et al., 1979). Therapists who act in this way have been shown in many studies to achieve better outcomes (Lambert and Bergin, 1994; Orlinsky et al., 1994).

In a survey, Wright and Davis (1994) found that clients wanted their therapist to:

- offer a physically safe, private, confidential setting, comfortable and free from distraction;
- be respectful;
- treat client concerns seriously;
- prioritize client interests over their own;
- be competent;
- share practical information about how to make life improvements;
- permit the client to make personal choices when using information and therapist suggestions;
- be flexible in evaluating the client – not assume that the client fits a theory or is now totally understood;
- review how the client gets on if therapist recommendations are followed;
- pace herself well, not rush, or keep changing appointments.

Although none of these qualities are specific to CBT, they nevertheless give a useful check-list of general rules to follow. Many of them are consistent with the general approach of CBT, and many would fall under the general rubric of treating one's clients in a respectful and empathic way.

Ways of building a positive and collaborative client–therapist relationship

The general principles of the cognitive-behavioural approach provide a sound foundation for building a good client–therapist relationship. For example:

- careful listening to get a real sense of how it is to be the client;
- taking time to set a shared agenda;
- making it clear that feedback is welcome;
- carefully establishing the client's goals for treatment.

Clients differ in what they bring to therapy, and consideration of these factors can ease the development of a good relationship. For example, some clients may be at a relatively early stage in their 'preparedness to change' (Prochaska and DiClemente, 1986), and the therapist needs to be aware of this. A client with an eating disorder may be willing to think about extending the range of food she is eating only if she can be assured of no weight gain; or a client with substance misuse may not be willing to consider abstinence. In such cases, collaboration might be better achieved through initial motivational work (Miller and Rollnick, 1991) rather than active CBT.

It seems that inexperienced therapists are able to create a good working relationship with their clients, but that more experienced clinicians are better able to spot potential ruptures in an alliance. We will now consider how to deal with ruptures when they occur, but an experienced supervisor is invaluable in this area (see Chapter 19).

Ruptures in the therapeutic alliance

Do not be surprised that ruptures in the working alliance occur: your client's problems have often become so well entrenched that he is unable to deal with them independently, and this means that change is likely to be difficult. As a result, he may experience a range of unhelpful emotions and thoughts while struggling to deal with his problems.

Signs of a rupture in the therapeutic alliance

These may be reflected in non-verbal cues related to emotional states such as discomfort, anger or mistrust. There may also be behavioural signs, such as not carrying out homework tasks, expressing scepticism about the approach, or high levels of expressed emotion. The important issue is to be mindful of the quality of the interaction between you and your client, so that you can take early steps to intervene when difficulties arise. Do not ignore it and hope that it will go away.

How to deal with ruptures in the alliance

Watson and Greenberg (1995) point out that ruptures can be related to:

- the goals or tasks of therapy (for example, the client does not understand or agree with the goals or strategies used in treatment);
- the client–therapist bond (for example, the client is not collaborative, or does not trust or respect the therapist).

They argue for dealing with the former problems by approaching them directly, e.g., by clarifying the rationale for treatment, or possibly changing the approach. For example, if the client believes that reducing avoidance is important but does not believe that reducing safety behaviours (see Chapters 4 and 13) would be helpful, it may be best to switch in the short term to reducing avoidance, unless he is willing to do a behavioural experiment to investigate the role of safety behaviours.

If the rupture in the alliance seems to be related to your bond with the client, first deal with this within your current therapeutic relationship, without assuming that the problem is a reflection of your client's characteristic interpersonal relationships. If such work is unsuccessful, or if the formulation indicates that the client may, for example, find it difficult to trust *anyone*, then it may be necessary to consider the rupture as a characteristic pattern and to use the therapeutic relationship to provide the client with a corrective emotional experience (Safran and Muran, 1995).

Newman (1994) makes the point that you should consider what contribution you are making to any therapeutic impasse, rather than assume that all the problem resides within the client:

> *A woman with health anxiety was making little consistent progress, despite a formulation that apparently accounted well for her problem, and her being committed to homework tasks. The therapist was aware that the client frequently had moist eyes, but she always denied that she was upset when the therapist questioned her about it. In supervision, the therapist became aware that she was reluctant to discover that the client had the potential for becoming very upset, because the client was slightly histrionic in style, and the therapist had automatic thoughts about being 'washed away' by the woman's distress. She therefore asked the client about her feelings in a neutral voice, and never reflected her own perception of the woman's sadness. The client did not feel able to share her feelings with the therapist, and denied that she was upset.*

If it seems that the impasse is related to your client's issues, then, rather than viewing this as an indication of poor motivation or ambivalence, it is more useful to formulate the issue in the same way as any other problem. For example, you could consider:

- What function the behaviour may have.
  (e.g., if the client is hostile, he may be protecting himself against feared rejection)
- What idiosyncratic beliefs may be fuelling it.
  (e.g., the client may believe that a competent therapist would be able to read his mind)
- What fears the client may have about complying.
  (e.g., if he were to change, he may be faced with challenges he could not tackle)
- What skills he may lack.
  (e.g., in reflecting on his emotional experience)
- What environmental features may be contributing.
  (e.g., he may be exhausted through caring for an elderly mother)

The problem can then be tackled in CBT in the same way as other problems. This could include:

- revisiting the formulation and rationale;
- using Socratic method to clarify the issues;

- collaborating and providing choices, while providing structure, limits and guidance;
- reviewing the pros and cons of change versus no change;
- communicating with the client's language, metaphors or images;
- gently persisting when the client subtly avoids – don't take 'I don't know' for an answer;
- maintaining an empathic attitude, and avoiding blaming or making negative interpretations of your client's behaviour.

Again, we remind budding CBT therapists that effective clinical supervision (see Chapter 19) will be invaluable in tackling this kind of problem.

We will now turn to considering issues about boundaries in CBT.

Boundary issues

'[*Keep*] far from all intentional ill-doings and all seduction, and especially from the pleasures of love with women and men.'

The Hippocratic Oath

The relationship between therapist and client is different from other social relationships, and boundary issues need careful and serious consideration in CBT, just as they do in other approaches. Treatment boundaries provide a framework for appropriate roles for the therapist and client, and include structural components – such as where, when and at what cost – as well as what happens in the therapy between the therapist and client. The main governing principles are common to all therapeutic encounters:

- The client's needs must have primacy.
- Gratification of the therapist's needs (beyond professional satisfaction) is excluded from consideration in the therapeutic setting.

Therapeutic boundaries are set in such a way that the client can:

- feel safes;
- trust the therapist to act in his interest;
- feel free to disclose material of deep personal significance;
- be confident that he understands the therapist.

(In addition, the therapist must also feel safe). The following guidelines for appropriate boundaries within CBT may be useful:

- Refrain from self-seeking or personal gratification.
- Maintain confidentiality unless it involves a significant risk to the safety of the client or others.
- Evaluate the effect of a boundary violation on the client. Rather than adopting an absolute rule like 'never accept a gift', consider the impact of such behaviour on the client and the

therapeutic relationship. For example, a gift of a jar of home-made chutney from one client could mean that a further attempt was being made to identify the therapist as a family friend; while for another it may mean that the client was at last beginning to see himself as an independent adult, equal in the relationship.

- Make choices about boundaries that minimise the risk of harm to the client. This means only departing from ordinary clinical practice when it will clearly benefit the client.
- Do not express opinions about, or otherwise interfere in, aspects of the client's life other than those relevant to the formulation and goals of therapy. If your client sought help for his panic attacks, bear that in mind when he begins to tell you about the way his children's school is dealing with the child's frequent absences – unless it relates to his panic attacks, do not give your advice, opinion or similar experiences.
- Seek to increase the client's independence and autonomy, hence increasing his freedom to explore and the choices available to him.

Maintaining treatment boundaries

The therapeutic relationship is non-reciprocal in a number of ways, putting the therapist in a powerful role, even in the relatively collaborative mode of CBT. This non-reciprocity includes:

- extensive self-disclosure by the client, with almost total non-disclosure of significant material by the therapist;
- the emotional neediness of the client, compared with the exclusion of any of the therapist's emotional needs;
- the power attributed to healers in many societies in order for them to reduce suffering and restore health.

Crucially, maintaining appropriate boundaries is the responsibility of the therapist: it is never reasonable to blame the client for infringements. The maintenance of boundaries is unequivocally your responsibility, whatever the behaviour of the client, so it is incumbent on you to seek sufficient supervision and support. In rare cases (such as clients with sociopathy) it may be necessary to terminate therapy if the client cannot maintain reasonable boundaries even with coaching and encouragement.

Although the power differential between therapist and client is generally acknowledged, some therapists have felt exploited by their clients. For example, Smith and Fitzpatrick (1995) described reports of clients with severe or borderline personality disorders forming 'special' relationships with their therapists, where contact outside the therapy became established. Some therapists have blamed clients for 'leading' them into flagrant boundary violations. You might find yourself potentially over-involved with, and feeling manipulated by, your client; but you must be alert to this and be prepared to discuss the situation with both client and other professionals.

It is sometimes argued that the nature of the transference relationship means that the client may seek the fulfilment of needs arising from unresolved conflicts, and that boundaries must therefore be very strictly enforced and contained by the therapist. Transference in this psychoanalytic sense is not part of CBT theory, so although some boundaries are important (as discussed in this section and below), such strict adherence to inflexible boundaries is not necessary in all aspects of therapy. Hence in CBT, treatment sessions do not have to take place at the same time every week, nor happen in the same place, nor last the same length of time. If a client has to postpone a session for some reason, this would usually be accepted by the therapist and would only be considered to be resistance if it happened repeatedly, with no other explanation.

Effective CBT may mean that you need to visit your client at home, possibly at unusual times of the day. For example, a client with obsessional rituals that are preventing him from starting the day may need visiting first thing in the morning. Do not undertake this lightly. Consider whether you should put safeguards in place to reduce the possibility of misinterpretations of your behaviour by the client: for example, an assistant could be taken along for a home visit or a relative included in the setting-up of the session.

You might also need to accompany clients into a range of everyday situations, for example in order to do behavioural experiments. It is helpful to make the aims of such sessions very explicit, by spending time agreeing what predictions are being tested out, how the experiment will be carried out, and so on (see Chapter 9). This makes good technical sense and it also sets boundaries for the session, making it clear that this is a treatment session with a specific purpose, and not a social event. This can be difficult for some needy clients to understand, especially if the therapist contact is the only social event of the week.

A woman with obsessional problems was finding it difficult to test out the effects of exposure and response prevention on her fears of pushing people off the pavement into the path of cars. The therapist and client therefore spent two lengthy sessions walking in crowded streets, busy with cars. Although they planned what specific 'tasks' she should do as they walked along, and discussed changes in her distress level as she walked past people near the edge of the pavement, they nevertheless had quite long periods of time when they were not specifically addressing the problem. The therapist then discussed general topics of a non-emotional and relatively non-personal nature, like annual holidays, but continued to be mindful of the nature of any disclosure and its possible impact on the client.

Finally, the open, collaborative style of CBT can sometimes be compromised if the therapist is involved in a compulsory admission to an institution. The repercussions can be minimised if you discuss it openly with the client, including what it meant to him, and any associated misperceptions, either beforehand or after the crisis has resolved.

Kinds of boundary violation

Although there is a continuum of boundary violations, *any* straying over boundaries should be done in awareness of the principles sketched out earlier in this chapter. There are particular kinds of violation which are worth specific consideration:

Dual relationships, where the therapist and client are in a second relationship in addition to the therapeutic one: for example, being school governors together. Although therapists are usually advised against such dual relationships, it is sometimes difficult to avoid them.

If a therapist lives in a small community, for example a rural setting or an academic group, then barring her from treating all those with whom she had an existing relationship might mean that they have no access to treatment at all. Similarly, if you are involved in groups related to your political, religious, ethnic or sexual identity, then dual relationships may be inevitable as people tend to seek out a therapist with similar values to themselves. In addition, despite ethical guidelines prohibiting dual relationships for therapists, it is not uncommon for therapists to accept invitations to, for example, a client's special event.

It may be possible to differentiate those dual relationships that are harmful to the client or therapy from those that are innocuous. Gottleib (1993) suggested that the therapist should consider the other (non-therapeutic) relationship along three dimensions – power, duration and whether the other relationship had a planned finite end – with risk to the client increasing with increasing values on any of the three dimensions. You should be mindful of such factors before entering into a dual relationship.

Self-disclosure would almost always by seen as inappropriate in psychodynamic therapy or counselling, but there is a less rigidly drawn line within CBT. Self-disclosure can be useful if it is done with the client's interests in mind. For example, a therapist could disclose information about a past problem of her own that she had overcome, in order to increase the client's hope for improvement and confidence in the proposed method. Beck et al. (1979) suggested that it is more appropriate to use self-disclosure with more severely depressed clients, as this may facilitate their engagement in treatment. It would never be helpful to describe current problems, whether psychological or financial, social or sexual, to a client: he can reasonably expect that the focus should be on his own problems.

It may sometimes be necessary to disclose personal details to a client – for example, illness in the therapist or her family, or pregnancy – if the circumstances are likely to have an impact on the delivery of treatment. But judgements of this kind may be less clear-cut than they seem, and you should make use of supervision if you have concerns about sharing information of this kind.

> *A young client in her twenties was discussing whether to try and forgive her emotionally abusive mother. Her therapist had been recently bereaved, and was grieving for the close supportive relationship that she had with her own mother. In the course of the session, the client said to the therapist, 'I feel that you really want me to make moves towards my mother', and the therapist became aware that she had too much emotional involvement in the client achieving that closeness for herself.*

Non-sexual physical contact may feel comfortable to some therapists, who would give a distressed or frightened client a reassuring pat, but they may still confine this to clients of the same gender as themselves. However, never underestimate the potential for clients to misinterpret such actions. Departures from normal practice should not be made casually – always be aware and mindful of your client's formulation. For example, a touch on the arm could be alarming to someone with a history of abuse, who has rules about maintaining her distance from people; while a pat on the leg could be misinterpreted as sexual by a client longing for physical closeness to another person, especially someone showing unconditional warmth and empathy. A useful way to deal with this is to find a time when your client is calm and to ask him how he would like you to react when he is highly distressed. For example, you could say:

You were obviously very distressed when we were talking earlier. I wonder how I could be most help at times like that. Some people like to simply express the feelings, and to deal with it themselves; others may find a little pat on the arm comforting. Is there any particular way you would like me to react?

Obviously such discussion must be constrained by what you feel is right for your own therapeutic boundaries.

Pope et al. (1987) reviewed three kinds of physical contact between therapists and clients and found that a sizeable minority of therapists had experience of each kind of touching. According to a survey of therapists, the least unacceptable was shaking hands with the client; that was practised often by 76% of therapists and was generally seen as ethically acceptable. Hugging was considered acceptable in some circumstances by 44%, but was only practised regularly by 12%. Kissing was seen as unacceptable or rarely acceptable by 85% of therapists, and was practised only infrequently by 24% and never at all by 71%.

The distinction between erotic and non-erotic physical contact falls along a continuum: it is not 'all or nothing'. As ever, cultural influences are relevant here. In many European and South American cultures, kissing on both cheeks is a customary form of greeting and may be only rarely interpreted as erotic, even in a therapy situation. Holding back from kissing could be seen by some clients as distant and aloof. In other words, the therapist has to draw boundaries flexibly and sensitively and cannot simply use rules about proscribed behaviour.

Sexual relationships between therapist and client are the most harmful kind of boundary violation, with possible negative impacts on vulnerable individuals, as well as damage to the therapeutic relationship. It is difficult to get data on the frequency of such behaviour, and estimates of the number of therapists who have had sexual intercourse with at least one client range from 1% to 12%, but these are likely to be under-estimates because of the compelling reasons for therapists to conceal the behaviour. There is an extensive literature on the harmful effects on clients of such boundary transgressions (Pope and Bouhoutsos, 1986), and some authors have suggested that in such cases the therapist should be charged with rape, since the client could not be capable of informed consent within that relationship.

Therapists who engage in sexual behaviour with clients tend to gradually blur boundaries rather than suddenly descend into inappropriate behaviour, and inappropriate self-disclosure, rather than other boundary violations, tends to precede sexual transgressions (Simon, 1991). Sexual violation of boundaries appears to be more common among middle-aged male therapists who are professionally isolated and currently experiencing personal problems, often including marital problems. They typically begin to cross appropriate boundaries by discussing their own problems with younger, female clients (Gabbard, 1991).

It is therefore incumbent on you as therapist to be aware of any gradual change in boundaries with any particular client and to raise this with your supervisor if it seems that your relationship may be subtly changing. It may seem that your client's needs may be met via a relationship different from a typical clinical one, but in that case, discuss it openly with your supervisor, to protect both yourself, from allegations by a client who may possibly misinterpret your motivation, and your client from possible abuse. Another sensible rule of thumb is that in situations where there is a grey area, it is probably in the interests of both client and therapist to err on the side of caution.

Summary

In summary, a good working alliance between you and your client is a necessary condition for successful CBT, without which the sophisticated models of CBT would be irrelevant.

Assessment and Formulation

Central to the successful use of CBT is developing a *formulation* (sometimes known as a *case conceptualisation*): an individualised picture that helps us to understand and explain a client's problems. This chapter describes the role of formulations, the assessment process that is used to develop a formulation, how to construct formulations and some of the common pitfalls in this phase of treatment.

Formulation in CBT

Definitions and approaches differ, and there is no one 'correct' way of doing formulations (see for example Persons, 1989; Bruch and Bond, 1998; Butler, 1998). However, most approaches share core features (Bieling and Kuyken, 2003). Our working definition of a CBT formulation is therefore that a CBT formulation uses the CBT model to develop:

- a description of the current problem(s);
- an account of why and how these problems might have developed;
- an analysis of the key maintaining processes hypothesised to keep the problems going.

Some of the benefits of making a formulation like this are:

- The formulation helps both client and therapist understand the problems, so that what may present as a baffling collection of random symptoms moves from chaotic confusion to something which *makes sense*. This process can begin to combat the demoralisation which is common in clients at initial presentation (and sometimes in therapists, when faced with difficult and complex problems).
- The formulation acts as a bridge between CBT theories about problem development and maintenance and the individual client's experience. It is 'the lynch pin that holds theory and practice together' (Butler, 1998). CBT theories are necessarily pitched at a general level: they describe typical clients who have panic attacks, or depression, or whatever; and they describe

the processes involved in each disorder in general terms and at a somewhat abstract level – as is appropriate for scientific theories. But to apply those theories to an individual in a clinical setting, we need to move from these generalisations to the specific experience of *this* person in front of us. One important function of the formulation is to bridge this gap.

- The formulation provides a shared rationale and guide for the therapy which may follow. If we have a reasonable understanding of the processes causing and maintaining a client's problems, then we can more easily see what interventions might be useful to overcome those problems. A good formulation therefore makes it easy to establish what therapy needs to do, at least in broad terms, and helps clients understand why particular strategies may be useful.

- The formulation begins the process of opening up new ways of thinking – a key part of CBT – by giving clients a different way of understanding their symptoms. Many clients come to the initial assessment with a view of their problems which is either threatening, or self-critical, or both. For example, in OCD, clients often see the fact that they have unpleasant thoughts as meaning that they must be evil or immoral; or in health anxiety, they may see bodily symptoms as indicating that they are seriously ill. The process of constructing a formulation can be a first step in considering alternative views of the symptoms and can free clients to see different ways of tackling them.

- Finally, the formulation can help the therapist to understand, or even predict, difficulties in therapy or in the therapeutic relationship. For example, if low self-esteem and self-critical thoughts are important elements in the formulation, we can predict that this client may have difficulties in doing homework, because he will be worrying about not doing it 'well enough' or worrying that the therapist will disapprove of his thoughts. By taking account of such predictions from the formulation, we may be able to avoid difficulties or manage them better.

Formulation: art or science?

Although the benefits described above might seem obvious, the scientific status of formulation in CBT is actually far from clear. For example, there is a relative lack of research evidence indicating whether formulations are *reliable*, i.e., whether different therapists agree on a formulation for the same client (Bieling & Kuyken, 2003); and there is also little evidence about whether treatment based on formulation is more effective than purely protocol-driven therapy (i.e. therapy given in a standardised way so that all clients with a particular problem get essentially the same treatment). In fact, there is one fascinating study which suggests that behaviour therapy based on an individual formulation may sometimes result in *worse* outcomes than completely standardised therapy (Schulte et al., 1992), although another more recent study found some evidence of superiority for CBT based on an individual formulation in bulimia nervosa (Ghaderi, 2006). It is not our intention to explore these controversies in detail, but we think it is worth describing our position on some of them.

First, as noted above, one of the roles of formulation is to act as a bridge between CBT theories and the experience of an individual client. In fulfilling this role, it seems to us inevitable that the process of formulation lies somewhere in the no-man's land between science and art (or at least craft). On the one hand, we are attempting to use empirically validated and evidence-based CBT models, derived using scientific principles, to help our clients. On the other hand, we have to apply these theories to the unique individuals with whom we are working, and we therefore need to work with their idiosyncratic thoughts and feelings. Such a process cannot be completely described in objective and generalisable terms: the ideal formulation is not just 'true' in a scientific sense, it must also 'make sense' to the client at the level of subjective meaning – and that is a task which involves as much craft as science.

Second, even the most rigid treatment protocol needs some individualising: no treatment manual can or should prescribe the therapist's every word. There is, therefore, a need to translate general guidelines into what is appropriate for *this* client at *this* time, which is one of the roles of the formulation.

Finally, clinical practice inevitably brings us clients who do not 'fit' the protocols, clients for whom an intervention according to the protocol does not work, or clients for whom there simply is no clearly recommended protocol (either from CBT or any other form of treatment). In such cases, the only thing we can do – other than giving up – is to build an individual formulation and develop a course of therapy based on that formulation.

Our view is, therefore, that CBT practitioners should start by assessing whether there is some well-established treatment protocol which has been shown to be effective and, if there is, then they should use that to inform the formulation and as a basis for treatment. But they always need to apply the protocol within the framework of a formulation that can guide its application to the individual client, and they also need to know when to leave the protocols behind and develop an idiosyncratic treatment plan. An individual formulation is the best tool we have for achieving both those ends.

Focus on maintenance processes

The main focus for CBT formulations and treatment plans is usually on current maintenance processes. Several linked beliefs contribute to this focus:

- The processes that start a problem are not necessarily the same as the processes that keep it going. Once a problem has begun, maintenance processes can take on a life of their own and keep a problem going, even if the original cause has long since disappeared.
- It is generally easier to get clear evidence about current processes than it is about original causes, which may have happened many years ago.
- It is easier to change maintenance processes that are happening here and now than to change developmental processes, which by definition are in the past. In any case, if past events are indeed still having important effects, then they must be doing so through some current psychological process.

Thus, the main focus of CBT, most of the time, tends to be on 'the here and now', and the main focus of assessment and formulation tends to be the same. A client described the key role of maintenance processes versus original causes to one of the authors thus:

Imagine you're walking along a crumbly and unstable cliff-top. Whilst you're walking near the edge, a seagull flies down and lands near to your feet, and the weight of the seagull is enough to make the edge of the cliff crumble. You fall over the edge, but you just manage to grab on to a branch 20 feet down, so you're left hanging there, clinging to the branch. Now if you're dangling there, and you want to get out of this situation and get safely back up to the top of the cliff ... then it's no use looking for the seagull!

A more prosaic analogy which makes the same point is that if you want to put out a fire then you had better tackle what keeps it going – heat, fuel, oxygen, etc. – rather than look for the match that started the fire.

This is not to say that history or development are irrelevant. We are talking about what is *usually* the *main* focus of CBT, not about what is *always* the *only* focus. There are several reasons why developmental history can be important.

- Information about the past is essential if one is to answer the question 'How did I get here?', which is often important to clients. They want some understanding of what led to their problems, and it is important to try to help them in that goal (although not always possible in practice – sometimes the developmental causes of a problem remain mysterious despite our best efforts).
- It may be useful to identify original causes in order to prevent their operating again in the future. Following the analogy above, once the fire is out then it may well be a good idea to find out where the match came from, so that we can avoid future fires from the same cause.
- There are some difficulties where an important part of the problem is inherently about the past. PTSD, or the consequences of childhood trauma, are obvious examples where it is clear that past events might need to be a focus of therapy. Another area is 'schema-focused' therapy for people with personality disorders or participatory complex problems. But even in these areas, the main focus is often on how the past is operating in the present.

Thus, CBT assessment and therapy neither can nor should *exclude* the exploration of past events and their implications, but the main focus of CBT is typically more biased towards the present than the past and towards specific examples rather than general rules.

The process of assessment

The aim of CBT assessment is primarily to arrive at a formulation which is agreed as satisfactory by both client and therapist, and which will serve the purposes outlined above.[1] Assessment within this framework is not a simple matter of ticking off a checklist of symptoms or completing a standard life history. Rather, it is an active and flexible process of repeatedly building and testing hypotheses. Figure 4.1 illustrates this cycle.

The therapist is constantly trying to make sense of the information coming from the client and building up tentative ideas about what processes might be important in the formulation. Further assessment is then aimed at testing those hypotheses. If further evidence seems to support the hypothesis, it may become part of the formulation; if not, then the hypothesis will need to be modified and further evidence will be sought. This process continues until the therapist feels that there is enough of a formulation to begin discussing it with the client. Eventually a working draft formulation is agreed. But even after that point, further

---

1. Of course, in many service contexts, an assessment may have other, more generic, purposes as well, such as risk assessment, establishing urgency, or screening for particular treatments. However, we shall not consider such assessments further here.

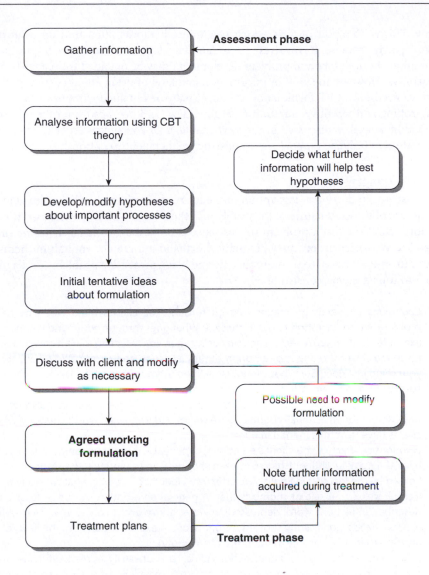

Figure 4.1   The process of assessment

information which emerges during treatment may lead to modifications or additions to the formulation. Most of the time such modifications will be minor 'tweaks', but sometimes new information will emerge which demands a significant reformulation of the problem.

Assessing current problems

In keeping with the centrality of maintenance processes in CBT, relatively more time tends to be spent on exploring details of current experience than in some other approaches to therapy. This is an aspect of CBT which beginning therapists often find uncomfortable, perhaps partly because it involves an unfamiliar degree of structured questioning. Information about history and problem development may be obtained from a fairly ordinary narrative. However, the kind of information and level of detail about current problems which we need for a CBT formulation cannot usually be obtained without careful, sometimes probing and repetitive, questioning at interview (and perhaps from other sources of information as well, as discussed in the next chapter). Of course it is crucial that you also pay attention to building rapport and a constructive therapeutic relationship (see below).

Problem description

The first step is to develop a description in the form of a problem list. Your aim is to get a clear picture of the exact nature of the problem, at the level of specific patterns of thoughts, behaviour, etc. Note that a problem in this sense is not a diagnostic label. Terms such as 'depression' or 'social anxiety' may be useful shorthand but are not enough in themselves for our purposes. We need to be more specific and break presenting problems or diagnostic labels into four 'systems', consisting of:

- *Cognitions*, i.e. words or images that go through the client's mind when he has the problem. A good question to get at these is: 'What goes through your mind when …?' (for example '…when you're feeling anxious' or '…when you're feeling low'). It can also be useful to look out for changes of emotion during a session and to ask: 'What went through your mind just now?' Such 'hot thoughts', i.e. thoughts accessed whilst they are generating strong emotions, are often much more informative than thoughts reported in calm moments days or weeks later. Thought records as part of homework can also be useful here. Remember that not all cognitions are verbal, and it is always worth checking whether clients have upsetting mental images.
- *Emotions or affect*, i.e. the client's emotional experience. It is not uncommon for clients to have difficulty in distinguishing between thoughts and emotions. The distinction is not helped by the fact that in English we often say 'I feel that …' when what we really mean is 'I think that … ' A rule of thumb is that in general an emotion can be at least crudely described in just one word: 'depressed', 'anxious', 'angry' and so on. If what he is trying to express needs significantly more than one word – e.g. 'I felt that I might have a heart attack' – then it is probably a thought, not an emotion.
- *Behaviour*, i.e. what the client does, actions which are outwardly visible. Useful questions to ask are: 'What do you now *do* because of the problem which you did not used to do?' (e.g. safety behaviours – see later); and, 'What have you *stopped doing* as a result of the problem?' (e.g. avoidance of fear-provoking situations).
- *Physiological changes or bodily symptoms*, e.g. symptoms of autonomic arousal in anxiety, such as increased heart rate, sweating, aches and pains, nausea, etc.; or loss of sexual interest and appetite for food in depression.

A good strategy is to ask the client to go through the most recent occasion he can recall when he experienced the problem symptoms. Having identified the time in question, you then take the client through what happened, from moment to moment, starting with whatever change he first noticed: perhaps a dip in mood, perhaps a worrying physiological symptom, or perhaps a frightening thought. Elicit what happened in each of the four systems: 'What went through your mind when that happened? How did it make you feel? Did you notice any changes in bodily sensations? What did you do? And what was the next thing that happened . . .' and so on.

Triggers and modifying factors

Another area of questioning is to establish the factors currently affecting the problem, in two areas:

- *Triggers*, i.e. what factors make the problem more or less likely to occur.
- *Modifiers*, i.e. what contextual factors make a difference to how *severe* the problem is when it does occur.

As a simple example, a spider phobia by definition will be *triggered* by seeing a spider but may also be triggered by seeing pictures of spiders, by seeing anything in the environment that looks even vaguely like a spider, or even by the word 'spider' (some clients make up different terms for spiders because the word itself is so distressing to them). When the phobia is triggered by such situations, the severity of the fear is likely to be *modified* by other factors: e.g. the spider's size, its speed, how close it is to the person, whether he thinks he can easily escape, and so on.

Be aware that many factors can operate as triggers or modifiers. Amongst those to consider are:

- Situational variables. Are there specific situations, objects or places that make a difference?
- Social/interpersonal variables. Are there particular people who make a difference? The number of people around? Particular kinds of people?
- Cognitive variables. Are there particular kinds or topics of thought which tend to trigger problems?
- Behavioural variables. Does the problem occur when the client or other people are doing specific activities?
- Physiological variables. Is the problem affected by taking alcohol or drugs? Are the problems more likely when the person is tense, tired or hungry? Does a woman's menstrual cycle affect the problem?
- Affective variables. Is a problem worse when the person is depressed, bored or upset? Some clients may react badly to any kind of strong emotion, even positive emotion, because it makes them feel out of control.

Some clients will respond to this line of questioning by saying that they are *always* anxious or depressed and nothing makes any difference. This is almost never true. Such a response often arises because the client has become so distressed and overwhelmed by the problem that he has lost the ability to 'step outside' and think about it objectively. Careful, gentle questioning will usually bring out some factors which do make a difference. One question which may begin to offer some clues is to ask the client what situation would be his worst nightmare. By noting what dimensions the client uses to describe this worst situation, you may get clues as to what variables are important. Another useful approach is to use self-monitoring homework to spot differences that the client may not recall at interview.

Information about triggers and modifiers is useful in two ways. First, it starts to give the therapist useful clues about possible beliefs and maintaining processes, by considering what themes might lie behind the variables discovered. If someone is especially anxious in situations where his behaviour might be observed by others, perhaps there is some element of fear of negative evaluation; if he is particularly depressed when he perceives others as rejecting him, perhaps there are some beliefs about being unlovable or unworthy. These clues can then prompt further questions which can help to confirm or refute the initial guesses. Later chapters will give you ideas about the kind of beliefs which are frequently found in different disorders.

The second benefit of this information is that it can be useful in treatment. It may be helpful in identifying targets for treatment (e.g. if the client feels anxious in restaurants or supermarkets, those might be areas he wants to work on); or in planning interventions (e.g. when planning a behavioural experiment on what happens if the client panics, it is helpful to know that he is more likely to panic in crowded shops and less likely to panic if accompanied by a trusted person).

Consequences

The last major area of the current problems is to look at what happens as a result of the problems. This may be explored in four main aspects:

- What impact has the problem had on the client's life? How has his life changed because of the problem?
- How have important others (friends, family, doctors, work colleagues, etc.) responded to the problem?
- What coping strategies has he tried, and how successful has he been?
- Is he using either prescribed medication or other substances to help him cope?

The first question here is important to get a picture of what the client has lost (or, occasionally, gained) as a result of having the problem. The next questions may give you important clues about maintaining processes. Many maintaining processes arise from perfectly reasonable 'common-sense' attempts by the client or others to cope with the problem. Unfortunately such responses may sometimes serve to maintain the problem. For instance, it is almost a universal of human nature to avoid or escape from a situation perceived as threatening – indeed, it is an entirely functional response in many situations (for example, if threatened with physical attack). It just happens that escape and avoidance may also serve to maintain unnecessary fears. Similarly, if your partner is worried about something and asks for reassurance about it, then it is a perfectly natural reaction to give them the reassurance they want; again it is just an unfortunate fact that this can be at best ineffective and at worst can exacerbate the problem. There are many other examples where such natural responses to a problem turn out to be unhelpful in the long run. Note that this is *not* necessarily to suggest that either clients or other people are in any sense motivated (even unconsciously) to keep the problem (see notes on possible problems, p. 60 below.

Another reason for exploring coping is that sometimes clients have developed quite good coping strategies. With a bit of shaping up – perhaps being more consistent or taking things further – these coping attempts can provide effective treatment strategies. It is always worth asking clients about what they think helps: often they have good ideas!

Maintaining processes

A crucial focus of assessment and formulation is trying to identify maintenance patterns, i.e. the psychological processes which keep a problem going. These are often in the form of vicious circles, or feedback loops: cycles in which the original thought, behaviour, affective or physiological response gives rise to effects which ultimately feed back to the original symptom so as to maintain or even worsen it. In later chapters we will look at some of the specific processes which CBT theories suggest may be important in different disorders. In this section we summarise some of the most common vicious circles which you will meet repeatedly in many different disorders. This should serve as a guide to some of the things to look for during an assessment.

Safety behaviours

The concept of safety behaviour has assumed a central place in many current theories of anxiety disorders since it was outlined by Salkovskis (1991). Anxious clients frequently take steps to do something which they believe protects them from whatever threat it is that they fear. For example, someone who fears collapsing in a supermarket may cling tightly on to the shopping trolley so as not to fall over; someone who fears being seen as boring and dislikeable may take care not to reveal anything about himself. People are endlessly inventive, and no matter how many clients you see, they will still come up with safety behaviours that you have never met before. Although this kind of behaviour is easily understandable, it can have an unnoticed and unintended side effect. It blocks the threat beliefs from being disconfirmed, because when nothing happens, the 'lucky escape' is attributed to the success of the safety behaviour instead of resulting in a decreased perception of threat (see Figure 4.2).

There are several popular stories which illustrate this concept to clients. One concerns a man who comes across a friend standing in the street waving his arms up and down. When he asks the friend what he is doing, the answer is 'Keeping the dragons away'. 'But there are no dragons around here,' he replies. To which his friend says, 'See, that's how well it works!'

Stories like this can naturally lead on to therapeutic strategies by helping clients to think about how the dragon-fearing man might learn that actually there are no dragons. Most clients will easily come up with the answer that he needs to stop waving his arms so that he can see that there are still no dragons. They can then be asked to consider whether that might have any lessons for their own problems and thus build on the formulation (see also Chapters 13 and 14 on anxiety disorders).

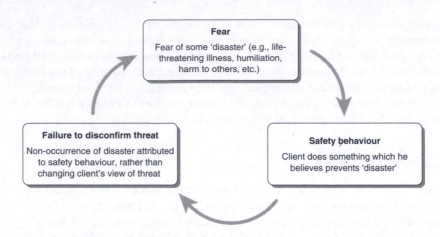

Figure 4.2   Safety behaviours

Escape/avoidance

Avoidance (or escape) can be considered as a particularly common form of safety behaviour. However, it is worth identifying avoidance separately, partly because of its near-universal prevalence in anxiety problems and, partly, because its unhelpfulness is immediately clear to clients in a way that those of other safety behaviours may not be. This is perhaps because the notion is part of 'folk psychology', as shown in the advice that if you fall off a horse, the best thing to do is to get straight back on it. (See Figure 4.3.)

Note that avoidance is not necessarily as obvious as running away when one meets an anxiety-provoking situation. For example, someone who gets anxious in social situations might accurately report that he does not avoid such situations. However, careful exploration might reveal that although he talks to people, he never looks them in the eyes, or he never talks about himself. In other words, there is more subtle avoidance despite the lack of obvious avoidance.

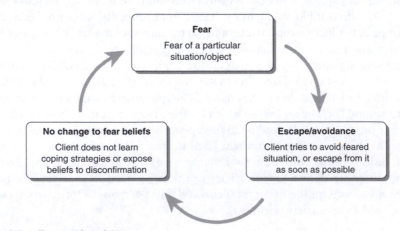

Figure 4.3   Escape/avoidance

Reduction of activity

This maintaining process, illustrated in Figure 4.4, is as common in depression as avoidance is in anxiety. Low mood leads to reduced activity, which then leads to the loss of most of what used to give positive feelings of pleasure, achievement or social acceptance. Lack of positive rewards in turn maintains low mood.

Catastrophic misinterpretation

Originally conceived by Clark (1986) as the central cognitive process in panic disorder, this cycle (Figure 4.5) can also be important in clients with other problems such as health anxiety or OCD. The central idea is that bodily or cognitive changes – most often symptoms caused by anxiety, such as increased heart rate, breathing difficulties or other signs of autonomic arousal – are interpreted as indicating some immediate and serious threat: that I am about to have a heart attack, or a stroke, or that I am 'going mad'. Naturally enough, such a thought causes yet more anxiety, and hence more symptoms, which seems to confirm the imminent threat ... and so it goes round.

Scanning or hypervigilance

This process is common in health anxiety and is also seen in other problems such as PTSD. Figure 4.6 shows how the worry that one might have a serious illness leads to scanning or checking for the symptoms that one believes indicate the illness. This scanning, and the increased salience of the symptoms due to their significance for health, leads one to notice what may actually be perfectly normal bodily symptoms. Those symptoms are then interpreted as confirmation of one's fears. In some cases, the checking behaviour may even *produce* worrying symptoms. For example, a client who feared that her throat would close up and she would choke would frequently and strenuously try to clear her throat with a loud 'Ahem'. As a result, she produced unpleasant feelings in her throat, which she then took as confirmation that there was indeed something wrong.

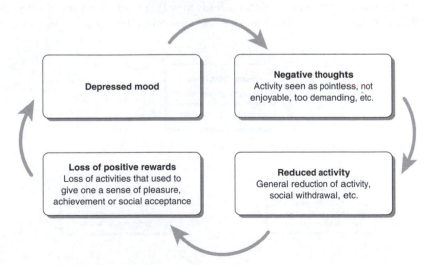

Figure 4.4   Reduction of activity

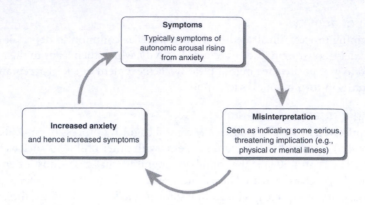

Figure 4.5   Catastrophic misinterpretation

A useful metaphor to illustrate this kind of process is to ask clients to remember a time when they have been thinking about buying a particular model of car. They may have noticed that at such times it seemed as if suddenly the roads were absolutely full of that kind of car. What can we make of this? Most clients will readily concede that it is unlikely that the owners' club for that particular car has decided to follow them around. Those cars were actually always there, it's just that they were not noticed until they became important. Now that they have become important, they see them everywhere.

Self-fulfilling prophesies

This refers to a process through which people with negative beliefs about others' attitudes towards them may elicit reactions which appear to confirm those beliefs. Figure 4.7 illustrates this process for two examples: socially anxious and hostile behaviour. In the first case, the expectation of rejection by others leads to withdrawing from social interactions: e.g. declining invitations to social events, or not joining in attempts at conversation. Over

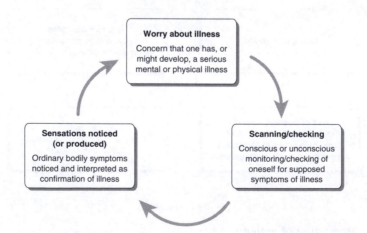

Figure 4.6   Scanning or hypervigilance

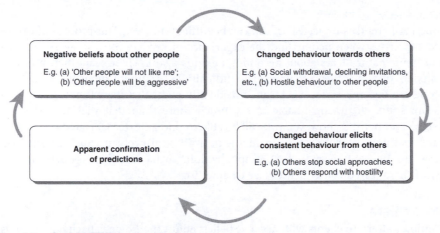

Figure 4.7   Self-fulfilling prophesies

time this behaviour may lead to others ceasing to make such social approaches – which of course proves that other people do not like me.

A similar pattern can be seen in some forms of hostile or aggressive behaviour. The expectation of hostility from others can lead to aggressive behaviour, for example in order to show that one is not to be intimidated. The aggression may then elicit hostile behaviour from others, thus confirming one's prediction of hostility.

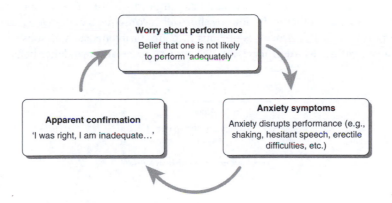

Figure 4.8   Performance anxiety

Performance anxiety

This pattern (Figure 4.8) is common in social anxiety, in male erectile dysfunction and in some less common problems such as people who are unable to urinate in public toilets (*paruresis* or 'shy bladder syndrome'). Worry that one is not going to be able to perform 'adequately' (talk coherently, or maintain an erection, or urinate) leads to anxiety, which in turn may indeed disrupt performance, resulting in hesitant speech, erectile difficulties, inhibition of bladder release, etc. This, of course, strengthens the negative beliefs about performance.

Fear of fear

Although apparently simple, fear of fear can be difficult to treat. This process, illustrated in Figure 4.9, arises when people find the experience of anxiety itself so aversive that they develop anticipatory fears about becoming anxious again. These fears then produce the very anxiety of which they are afraid. The difficulty in treatment stems from the fact that this cycle can become so detached from outside influences that there is nothing tangible to focus on: some clients are unable to say much more than that they find the anxiety intolerable. Sometimes, however, you will be able to find an external feared consequence – perhaps that anxiety will result in madness or a physical problem. Such external consequences can give you a way in, for example by doing behavioural experiments to test the reality of these feared consequences (see Chapter 9).

Perfectionism

A common pattern in clients with negative beliefs about their own capacity or worth is the cycle involving perfectionism shown in Figure 4.10. The desire to prove oneself not completely worthless or incapable results in such high standards that one can never meet them consistently, and, therefore, the sense of worthlessness is maintained rather than reduced.

Short-term rewards

We end with one of the most basic maintaining processes, going right back to the days of learning theory and operant conditioning. Figure 4.11 shows the process of behaviour being maintained by rewarding short-term consequences, despite negative longer-term consequences. This process occurs because humans – indeed, all animals – have evolved to be more strongly shaped in their behaviour by short-term consequences than long-term ones.

The importance of this process is obvious in many problems such as substance abuse, some forms of eating disorder, aggressive behaviour, escape and avoidance behaviour, and so on.

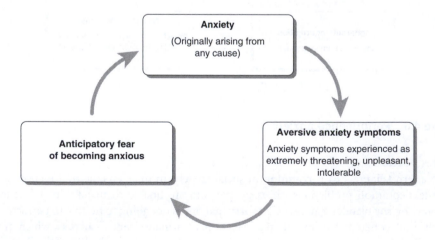

Figure 4.9　Fear of fear

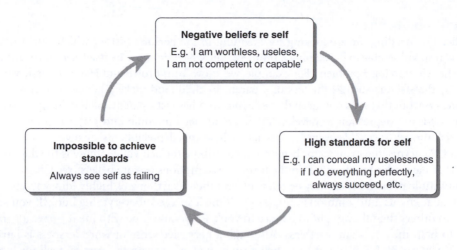

Figure 4.10   Perfectionism

Note that all the above cycles are intended as general outlines of possible processes, not universal laws: use them as ways to start your thinking and adapt them as necessary for an individual client.

Assessing past history and problem development

Having considered common current maintenance patterns, we move on to looking at the past: the client's history and the development of the problem. This part of the assessment aims to identify vulnerability factors, precipitating factors and modifying factors.

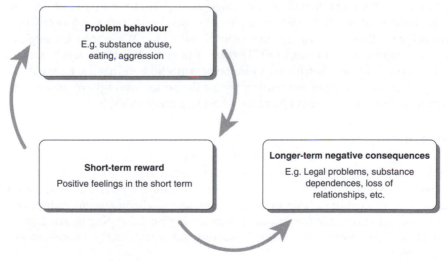

Figure 4.11   Short-term reward

Vulnerability factors

Under this heading, we are looking for anything in the person's history which might have made him vulnerable to developing a problem, but which does not by itself *necessarily* mean that he will develop a problem. For example, we know from Brown and Harris's classic work (1978) that factors such as the loss of a parent in childhood make a person vulnerable to depression, but that does not mean that *everyone* who has lost a parent will inevitably become depressed. For depression to develop, other events need to come into play (in Brown and Harris's model, 'severe life events' – or what we have called 'precipitants' below).

In CBT terms, the main factor believed to contribute to such vulnerability is the development of particular beliefs, either in the form of assumptions or core beliefs (see Chapter 1). A multitude of such beliefs may be relevant, and their exact form is highly idiosyncratic to particular clients, but common examples are: 'I must succeed at everything I do'; 'If you are nice to others then they ought to be nice to you'; 'I can only cope with life if I have a partner to help me'; or 'I am worthless'. Although a pervasive sense of worthlessness is fairly obviously unhelpful, many of these beliefs may enable a person to function well for long periods of time. It is only when they come up against some situation that resonates with the belief in an unhelpful way that problems may result: in the above examples, when they do not succeed, or do not get the respect they crave, or do not have a partner. Later chapters will look at some beliefs commonly thought to be linked to particular problems.

Precipitants

The events or situations which actually provoke the onset of a problem are known as the precipitants. In the standard cognitive-therapy model they are also known as 'critical incidents'. Precipitants are factors which seem to be closely associated with the actual onset of a problem or with a significant worsening of a long-standing problem. Although there may be a single significant event which precipitates a problem (perhaps most obviously in PTSD), it is often the case that there is no single event, but rather a series of more minor stresses, any one of which the person might have coped with, but which overwhelm the individual when they occur together in a relatively brief time. When there *is* a single event, other than major trauma leading to PTSD, then we often find that the event in some sense 'matches' a pre-existing belief: for example, the person who feels that it is essential to be in a relationship loses an important relationship, or the person who believes he must always be coping and in control comes up against something uncontrollable.

Modifiers

Just as we look for modifying factors in the current problems, so it may also be useful to look at modifying factors across time. Clients often report that the problems have just slowly grown worse, but sometimes careful exploration reveals that there have been times of improvement or of rapid worsening. Common modifying factors include changes in relationships; major role transitions such as leaving home, getting married or having one's children leave home; and changes in responsibilities such as a promotion at work or having a child.

The order of assessment components

In what order should you explore these different aspects of the client's problems? We do not believe there is any one 'right' way of doing this, for the simple reason that both clients and therapists vary. Some clients have little idea of what to expect from a psychological assessment and no strong preferences about how to proceed and are happy to follow a structure largely set by the therapist. Other clients may be set on telling their story in chronological order, from birth to the present day. Yet others may at first want nothing more than a space to express their distress. Therapists need to be responsive to these differences.

That said, all other things being equal, our preference is to begin an assessment by exploring the current problems. Starting here is relatively easy for most clients, and it helps to orient the therapist in later stages of the assessment. You know quite a bit about the problem and, therefore, have some hypotheses about what kind of area may be important to explore when looking at problem development and personal history.

At first, you may prefer to take a structured approach to assessment, keeping the focus fairly tightly on one area at a time. Later on, as you gain experience and the structure becomes second nature, you may find that you can 'loosen up' and allow the conversation to wander around more, whilst still retaining in your mind the structure and how different aspects of the problem fit together.

'Non-specific' factors and the therapeutic relationship

We noted in Chapter 3 that one of the common myths about CBT is that it has little interest in the therapeutic relationship, and we hope it is clear that this is not true. Whilst CBT does not generally give the therapeutic relationship a central curative role, it still regards the relationship as an essential vehicle for change. This is particularly important during the assessment, when that relationship is being established. Although we have talked about some of the technical aspects of assessment, we want to make it clear that paying attention to the human relationship between client and therapist is just as important – indeed, probably even more important. If you forget to ask a particular question you can always come back to it later, whereas if you fail to respond with warmth and humanity to your clients, they may not come back at all! It is therefore crucial not to get so absorbed in the pursuit of information that you stop genuinely listening to what the client is saying or fail to notice and respond to distress.

Newcomers to CBT sometimes worry that asking the number of questions that a CBT assessment demands must automatically mean that the client feels harassed and intruded upon. Our experience is that this is not usually so. If questions are asked with warmth and empathy, in a genuine spirit of curiosity and desire to understand, most clients will see the assessment as a positive experience with someone who is interested in, and wants to understand, their way of looking at the world.

A good technique, throughout therapy but perhaps especially during assessment, is to pause frequently to summarise your understanding of what the client has told you and to ask for their feedback on whether you have got it right. This has several benefits. It gives you time to reflect and to think about where to go next. It helps reduce the risk of misunderstanding, by giving the client a chance to correct differences between your summary and what they meant to convey. And the request for feedback conveys the message that the client is an active partner and that the therapist is not necessarily all-wise and all-knowing.

Making formulations

Not too fast; not too slow

The process of assessment and formulation is worth spending time on, because developing a good formulation will pay dividends in more efficient and focused therapy. But how much time? You may feel two opposing pressures. Sometimes, there is an urge to 'get stuck in' and get into treatment as quickly as possible. On the other hand, therapists sometimes feel that they cannot come up with a satisfactory formulation until they know absolutely everything about their client's history, from the moment of birth to the present day. The best answer is probably somewhere in the middle.

In general we would recommend a two-session assessment, at least until you are familiar with the CBT approach. In the first session, aim to get as much as you can of the necessary information. You then have the time between sessions to try to make sense of the information and develop a formulation. Trying to construct a formulation will very quickly highlight any important gaps in the assessment. You can then go into the second session with a clear idea of what else you need to know and, in most cases, develop the formulation in discussion with the client by the end of the second session. This is not a hard and fast rule. In some cases, perhaps with very complex problems or with clients with whom you find it difficult to form a relationship, the process of assessment may take longer. On the other hand, as you become more experienced in CBT you will probably find that with clients with straightforward problems you can develop at least a rough formulation within one session. But the two-session approach works well for most beginners most of the time.

Diagrams

The best way of communicating formulations is through diagrams rather than words. There are two common approaches to drawing formulations. Many CBT therapists have a whiteboard in their office and use this to draw up formulations. Others just draw them onto paper. The whiteboard has the advantage of being larger and therefore easier to see and also easier to rub out as changes are made. On the other hand, doing the formulation on paper means that it is easier to make a photocopy for the client to take away.

In either case, it is helpful to make the process of drawing up a formulation as collaborative as possible. Don't just produce a beautiful formulation like a rabbit out of a hat. Involve your client in the process, asking him or her what should go where: 'From what we have discussed so far, what do you think might have led to the problem starting?', 'What do you think the effect is when you do that?', and so on.

Figure 4.12 shows a possible template for formulations. This is not meant to be prescriptive. There are many different ways of showing formulations, and you will probably develop your own style. This is just one possible approach, which does at least give a clear picture of the most important elements in any formulation.

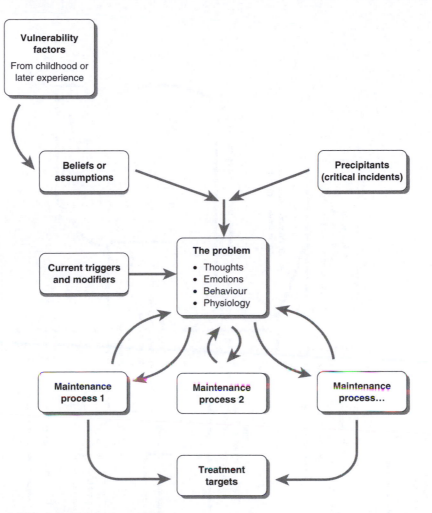

Figure 4.12   A template formulation

Sample formulation

Figure 4.13 shows an example of a formulation for a client who presented with a fear of becoming incontinent of faeces whilst driving. This had led to his being unable to drive more than a mile or two from home. That was just far enough for him to continue to get to work but was only achieved by plotting an intricate route that kept him in easy reach of a public toilet. The relevant information summarised in the formulation is as follows.

Vulnerability

Two factors seemed important. First, that he had been brought up in a family where bowel functioning was of more than average concern: in his words, they were 'obsessed by

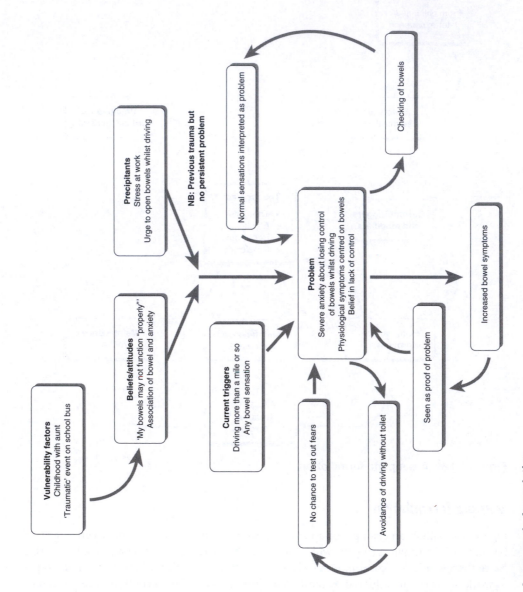

Figure 4.13   An example formulation

bowels'. He recalled that as a child he would be asked every day whether he had opened his bowels and, if he had not, he would be given laxative medication.

Second, and probably more important, he recalled with some distress an incident when he was eleven or twelve when, whilst he had a stomach bug, he had in fact been incontinent on the school bus on the way home. Not surprisingly, he remembered this as an extremely shameful and humiliating experience.

Beliefs

It was hypothesised that these earlier experiences had led to beliefs that his bowels were liable to malfunction, and that if they did the results could be catastrophic. Perhaps related to this, he reported that he had always felt a slight association between bowels and anxiety: when he felt anxious, he would tend to want to go to the toilet, and when he felt an urge to open his bowels, there was some degree of anxiety.

Precipitants

This client's history is an interesting illustration of the earlier point about the 'fit' between precipitants and pre-existing beliefs. Some years before the incident which started the presenting problem, he had suffered what would seem a far more 'traumatic' experience, when he had hit someone in his car who had died as a result. The accident was not his fault – the other person had run out into the road in front of him and he had no chance to avoid them – but nevertheless it was obviously upsetting. However, despite significant temporary distress, it did not lead to persisting problems.

What did lead to the presenting problem seems a much more trivial incident, but because it linked with his beliefs, it proved more powerful as a precipitant. The incident occurred at a time when he was under a great deal of stress at work, due to conflict within the company. During this time, whilst driving to work and feeling a bit under the weather, he had a sudden urge to open his bowels and he became very anxious that he would lose control. Nothing disastrous actually happened. He found a place to pull over, went behind a hedge and carried on to work. However, this immediately led to further anxiety, which increased steadily over the next few months.

The problems

He became anxious at the thought of driving more than a short distance from home (*emotion*). He had typical anxiety symptoms, including increased heart rate, muscle tension, feeling hot and so on, but particularly an unsettled stomach (*physiology*). He believed that if he did not reach a toilet within a few minutes of getting an urge to open his bowels, he would lose control (*cognition*). He avoided driving almost entirely except for getting to work and coped with that only by his safety behaviour of staying within range of public toilets. He also focused a great deal of attention on his bowel, checking both before and during any journey whether he needed to go to the toilet and always trying to open his bowels before he set off (*behaviour*).

Maintenance

Three main maintenance processes were identified. First, his avoidance of driving outside 'safe' areas was a safety behaviour that blocked any testing of his beliefs about his lack of control of his bowels. Second, his anxiety created bowel symptoms which were interpreted as proof of lack of control. And, finally, his constant checking of his bowels constituted 'scanning', which led to his noting bowel sensations which were actually perfectly normal.

Suitability for CBT

A common question from beginning therapists is: 'Who is "suitable for CBT?" ' The truth is that there is not much solid evidence about how we should match clients to therapies – whether CBT or any other therapy. One study that has been widely quoted (but not replicated) is Safran et al. (1993), which suggested better outcome in short-term CBT if the client:

- can access NATs in session;
- is aware of, and can differentiate, different emotions;
- relates well to the cognitive model;
- accepts responsibility for change;
- can form a good collaborative therapeutic alliance (using evidence from previous relationships);
- has problems of relatively acute onset and history;
- does not show unhelpful 'security operations', i.e. attempts to control anxiety to such a degree that therapy is difficult;
- shows ability to work on one issue at a time in a relatively focused way;
- is reasonably optimistic about therapy.

These factors are not well established, so use them as a guide rather than a rigid set of criteria. Furthermore, they were devised to assess suitability for short-term CBT – one may be able to overcome less positive factors in longer-term work.

Faced with the lack of evidence about suitability, many therapists offer clients a trial period – perhaps five or six sessions – during which both client and therapist can evaluate how well CBT fits for this individual. Although five or six sessions may not be long enough to resolve the client's problems, it usually is long enough to get an idea of whether CBT seems to be useful. If it is, then the therapy can continue. If not, you can consider other treatment plans. Of course, the decision to discontinue treatment needs thoughtful discussion so as to avoid upset to the client as far as possible.

Possible problems during assessment

As previously noted, a common difficulty for beginners in CBT is getting sufficient detailed information about the problems. This may be due to therapist or client difficulties.

Problems for the therapist

For therapists, the difficulty may lie partly in not yet knowing what information is important. With more experience with a range of psychological problems, you will develop a sense of what areas are likely to be important in particular problems. You should also read about CBT models, so that you know what theorists see as important (we hope that the rest of this book will help!). One of the skills that experienced therapists demonstrate is not so much always asking the right questions but recognising quickly when they are asking the *wrong* question and rapidly moving on to try a different angle.

It is important to try to feel your way between giving up too easily and persisting too long. In most cases, if your client is not managing to tell you much about an area of questioning, it is worth persisting for at least a while and trying different approaches. Clients often find one question easier to answer than another, and what initially seems a totally fruitless line of enquiry may suddenly open up in a more productive way. However, do not be *so* persistent that the client feels as if it is an interrogation rather than an assessment! In general, our experience is that when you are first learning it is worth persisting slightly beyond the point that feels completely comfortable to you; it will usually be acceptable to the client.

Problems for the client

For clients, there may be several difficulties that make it hard for them to answer your questions. In any particular case, it is important to understand what is causing the difficulty, but there are two common classes: those where the client genuinely does not know the answer to your question; and those where he does know, but is reluctant to answer.

Common reasons for clients not knowing the answers include:

- The client has become so used to the problem (or so demoralised by it) that he no longer notices the factors you are trying to assess. Often, further gentle questioning can begin to elicit variations and thus reveal more information. Another useful technique is self-monitoring (see Chapter 5), either done close to the time of emotional upsets so as to increase the accessibility of thoughts or done hourly to pick up variations in mood.
- Avoidance or other safety behaviours have become so widespread or so effective that client no longer experiences negative thoughts and thus cannot report them. A useful metaphor for understanding this is the reaction of an experienced driver seeing a red traffic light. He would not consciously think 'I had better stop, because if I don't a car coming the other way might crash into me, and that would be very unpleasant.' He would just automatically brake on seeing the red light. On the other hand, if he put his foot on the brake and nothing happened, then his negative thoughts and emotions would be easily accessible! A useful strategy, therefore, can be to try a small *behavioural experiment* (see Chapter 9), used as an assessment strategy. If the client is willing to see what happens if he does not avoid or does not perform his usual safety behaviour, then the thoughts and emotions are likely to become much more apparent.
- The client is amongst that small proportion of people who simply find it very difficult to access or report thoughts and emotions. Some people get better with practice, so it is worth persisting for a while, for example via homework, as above. A few people never do get comfortable with thoughts and feelings. In such cases, a more traditional behavioural approach may prove more fruitful.

Examples of knowing the answers but being reluctant to report them, include:

- Fear of the therapist's reactions. For instance, the client may think that you will disapprove of his thoughts or behaviour, or find his symptoms 'silly', or laugh at him. Always try to discover the reason for the client's reluctance before trying to do anything about it. Most clients will be able gradually to talk about the obstructing thoughts, even if they do not yet feel able to talk about the original thoughts themselves. It may also be helpful to offer the client suggestions about the kind of worries other clients have reported, so that he realises that the therapist has heard this kind of thing before (but without putting words into the client's mouth).

- Other feared consequences of reporting the symptoms openly. A client may fear she will be diagnosed as 'mad' and locked away or think that the therapist will contact the police or social services and have her arrested or have her children taken away. With some problems there may be quite idiosyncratic fears. Some people with obsessive-compulsive problems report fearing that their protective rituals, particularly those involving 'magical thinking', will no longer work if they reveal the full details, thus putting the client or others at serious risk. Again, it can be helpful to offer clients examples of common fears and also perhaps to clarify the differences between different kinds of mental-health problem (for example that OCD is different to schizophrenia).

Possible problems in making formulations

Effect is not purpose

It is important to avoid the assumption that clients or their relatives necessarily *intend* (even unconsciously) the consequences of their behaviour. The fact that one of the effects of an agoraphobic client's behaviour is that her husband always has to accompany her does not by itself prove that she is behaving like that *in order* to have her husband always with her. Similarly, an obsessional client's husband reassuring her in a way that seems to maintain the problem does not show that he is doing that *in order* to keep her obsessional. This is not to say that such motivation (sometimes called *secondary gain*) does not exist; just that it is not universal. Some independent evidence is needed, beyond the mere effect, to show that it is important in any particular case. Freud himself is supposed to have said in relation to Freudian symbolism, 'Sometimes a cigar is just a cigar.' We might perhaps extend this to '*Most of the time* a cigar is just a cigar.' Most clients and their families want to get rid of their problems: they just get trapped in patterns of thought and behaviour that do not help them to achieve that goal.

Censoring the formulation

Therapists sometimes ask whether there is any element of a formulation that should *not* be shared with the client. As a general rule, the answer is 'No'. As part of the collaborative approach of CBT, the formulation should be open. A possible, but rare, exception to this is if the full formulation would contain some element that might threaten the therapeutic relationship. Discussions about the formulation will typically happen fairly early on in the relationship, when there may not yet be sufficient trust and confidence to contain conflicts. An obvious example would be if you thought you had sufficient evidence to assume secondary gain as part of the formulation (see above). Even with strong evidence for that kind of process, the client might be offended by such a suggestion early on in therapy. It might be wise not to make it part of the formulation until the relationship has strengthened and such issues can be openly discussed.

Spaghetti junction

It is not necessary for a working formulation to contain *every* piece of information you have about a client. Including too much in a formulation can result in a nightmare of criss-crossing lines and boxes that is confusing rather than clarifying. Remember, the aim of the formulation is to make sense of the information gathered from the client and to explain the key processes involved. A degree of filtering and simplification is necessary and desirable to make the formulation reasonably easy for both client and therapist to grasp. A good motto is the saying attributed to Einstein: 'Everything should be made as simple as possible – but no simpler.'

Tunnel vision

Sometimes we may fix too early on a hypothesis and then get 'stuck', only paying attention to information that confirms the hypothesis and not looking for other information (Kuyken, 2006). It is important to remember that in order to test a hypothesis adequately, we have to look for evidence that would *refute* that hypothesis, not just evidence that supports it.

We can also sometimes try to force clients into fitting the formulation, rather than making the formulation fit the client. It is crucial that you are responsive to what clients tell you and that the formulation is idiosyncratic to your client.

Formulations need to make sense

A common problem is the formulation that has boxes and interlinking arrows which look fine but which, and on closer examination, make no logical sense. This can happen as a result of careless use of the 'hot cross bun' (Padesky and Greenberger, 1995: see Figure 4.14).

Although this model is popular and can be very useful as a simple reminder of the multiple interconnections between the four systems, it needs to be made more specific if it is to form the basis of a useful formulation. Used without enough consideration, it can lead to lumping together miscellaneous thoughts in one box; putting equally disparate piles of behaviours, emotions and bodily changes in other boxes; drawing arrows between the boxes; and then sitting back, satisfied that the problems have been explained. But they have

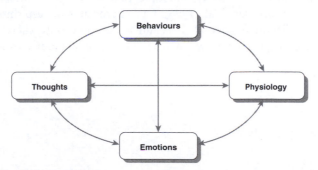

Figure 4.14   The hot cross bun

not, because the arrows do not represent any comprehensible process. Instead of being specific about what behaviour is linked to what thought or what emotion, we just have one big arrow linking all thoughts to all behaviours, all emotions, and so on. Although each one of these links might make sense when taken individually, they make no sense at all when they are all lumped together. As a result, the therapist (not to mention the client) is likely to struggle to explain *how* these supposed links operate.

Always think critically about your formulations and ask yourself what psychological process the arrows and boxes represent. Make sure you can explain *how* a thought in one box leads to a behaviour in another box, or *how* that behaviour has an effect on a specific belief. In short, make sure your formulations make sense.

Formulations need to be used

It may seem obvious that a formulation cannot help if it is not used, but it can be forgotten. Having constructed the formulation, therapists sometimes file it away as a task completed and never think about it again. Remember that the point of the formulation is to guide both therapist and client throughout treatment. Try to get into the habit of referring back to the formulation frequently: 'How does this experience fit with the formulation?'; 'What would our formulation suggest might be a good way forward here?'; 'Is this work [in session or as homework] going to make a difference to an important maintaining process?'

Core beliefs and schemata

Finally, a note of caution about the transition from the formulation to treatment plans. There is sometimes a belief that if your formulation contains core beliefs or schemata, then (a) those must be the primary targets for treatment, because they are more 'fundamental' or 'deeper' than NATs or behaviour; and (b) you should therefore begin by modifying them. This is rarely true. Core beliefs and schemata are certainly broader in their applicability than a typical NAT, but that does not necessarily render them more important or more fundamental and certainly does not imply that working with negative thoughts and behaviours is 'superficial'. On the contrary, almost all the evidence currently available for the effectiveness of CBT is based on working primarily at the level of specific automatic thoughts and their associated behaviours. There is also evidence that working at that level actually results in changes at the wider belief level as well (see, for example, the fascinating 'dismantling' study of Jacobson et al., 1996). Our approach is to keep things as simple as possible and work with more general beliefs and assumptions only when it is clearly necessary because we have got as far as we can with more specific thoughts and behaviours.

Measurement in CBT

Introduction

We have already discussed the commitment within CBT to an empirical approach to establishing the effects of treatment, both for groups of clients and for individual cases, and this issue will be considered in more detail in Chapter 18. This chapter will describe how to translate this empirical approach into action with individual clients. We will look at how measurement can be used to increase understanding of problems at the assessment stage ures and during subsequent treatment. We will also consider why it is worthwhile using measures in this way, how to devise them and give examples of the kinds of measures that might be useful.

The empirical nature of CBT

From the start, we want to encourage the client to view treatment as an experiment, in which thoughts, feelings and behaviour, and the relationships between them, can be investigated, during both assessment and treatment.

Assessment and formulation

At assessment, it is helpful to ask the client to collect data about the nature of the problem, to supplement and fine-tune what he reported in the assessment interview. Such data may contribute to two main goals.

1. To help elaborate the formulation: e.g. it may be helpful to look at triggers for particular thoughts, feelings or behaviours, and how these relate to each other, so that tentative ideas about a formulation can be explored.
2. To provide a baseline against which the problem can be compared in the future: for example, measuring the frequency or severity of the problem.

A client believed that she was ruining her children's lives by continually 'going on' at them, shouting inappropriately and being unable to regain control once she had 'lost it'. She agreed that it would be useful to keep a diary to find out how frequently this occurred, and when it happened (see Figure 5.1). The main thing that she learned at this stage was that in fact she did it rarely, only twice in a week.

Date	Triggers
2nd May	—
3rd May	—
4th	Dan said it was my fault he had forgotten his football boots, and we had to drive back for them
5th	—
6th	Emma doing her hair for so long she missed the bus.
7th	—
8th	—

Figure 5.1   Rating scale for how often a woman 'lost it' with her children, and what triggered it ('losing it' meant shouting for more than a minute)

During and at the end of treatment

Once the client has a good description of the problem, what triggers and maintains it, he can begin to try out new ways of behaving, thinking and interacting and then assess the impact on the problem. Regular measures allow both client and therapist to evaluate the impact of interventions. It is particularly important to gather data at the end of treatment so that overall progress can be assessed.

A client with an OCD recorded how long it took her to leave her house if she planned to go out, and how long it took her to get away from work at the end of the day. As she introduced response prevention into a number of tasks (see Chapter 14), she could clearly see the effect of this intervention on the length of time it took her to leave home and work (see Figure 5.2).

Another example of evaluating treatment changes:

A man who was very anxious away from home realised that arriving for trains early was a safety behaviour that kept in place his belief that 'only by staying 100% in control will I be safe, and not be rejected. 'He experimented with arriving at places either just on time, or even late, in order to find out whether there were catastrophic results and found that no one commented or appeared to notice. To his surprise, he found that he was slightly less anxious on the days that he eliminated the punctuality, not more anxious as he had predicted (see Figure 5.3).

Date	Place	Time taken (mins)
Before response prevention		
5th Jan	home	23 mins
5th Jan	work	37 mins
7th Jan	home	25 mins
7th Jan	home	18 mins
After response prevention		
6th Feb	home	8 mins
7th Feb	home	7 mins
7th Feb	work	11 mins
9th Feb	home	9 mins

Figure 5.2   Length of time spent leaving places when disrupting OCD rituals

Event	How early or late	Comments made by others	Anxiety beforehand, 0–10*
London train	45 mins early	Nil	7
Board meeting	On time	Nil	2
Guilford train	10 mins early	Nil	3

*0 = not at all anxious; 10 = as anxious as I could possibly be

Figure 5.3   Chart of arriving on time (or late) at events and the effect on others and anxiety levels

Why bother with measurement?

You may need to be creative and ingenious in devising useful monitoring to assess problems and evaluate the effects of different interventions. However, this begs the question of why you should use measures at all. There are a number of reasons why it is helpful to gather data to supplement information derived from interviews:

- Regular measures allow you to obtain a baseline of important aspects of the problem and then to use that to assess the effects of future intervention.

- Observations of behaviours, thoughts or feelings made at the time they occur are more reliable than retrospective estimates (Barlow et al., 1984).
- Direct observations by the client in real life can have therapeutic effects in themselves, for example by providing accurate information about the scale of the problem or about its progress.

A client assiduously produced thought records each week and carefully picked the most distressing examples for consideration in the session. This significantly coloured her assessment of how the previous week had been, as her attention was focused on the difficult times. To counteract this, she began to rate her mood three times daily (eventually reducing this to once daily when her mood was more stable) and was very surprised to find that on many days her mood was considerably lighter than she was reporting. This was very encouraging for her, as she had been doubtful that she would be able to use cognitive therapy.

- Once they have begun to improve, many clients lose awareness of how disabling the problem was initially. Baseline measures of the problem can help the client to assess his progress more accurately.

As a client's agoraphobic symptoms improved, he focused on his difficulty driving to nearby market towns, claiming that going into his local town had never really been a problem. This was dispiriting for him, as it seemed that he was making little progress. However, a review of his early diaries was sufficient to reassure him that indeed he had made enormous progress and that tasks that he now took for granted had initially presented real problems for him.

- If an intervention does not have the impact that the formulation would predict, measurement can help you and the client to work out why. For example, it may be that the treatment is not being delivered appropriately.

A client was feeling out of control and overwhelmed by everyday domestic tasks. As a first step, she decided to spend 20 minutes on three days each week tidying up papers that covered the surfaces in her kitchen and to rate how overwhelmed she felt. This intervention appeared to have little impact, but a diary in her therapy notebook indicated that she was only managing to do it once a week and was taking this as further evidence that she was overwhelmed. These data allowed the therapist and client to trouble-shoot and work out how to increase the probability that she would carry out the task – in this case, by doing it at her most productive time, when she was alone in the morning.

There are therefore sound reasons for using measures as part of routine clinical practice. We shall now consider how to do this in ways that will provide you and your client with information which will be genuinely helpful for therapy, beginning with a note on the psychometric qualities of measures.

Psychometric aspects of monitoring

Reactivity of measurement

Whatever is being measured is often affected, positively or negatively, by the process of monitoring. In habits such as smoking, a beneficial reduction may occur if the client becomes aware of triggers and responds to the beginning of a potential cycle by inhibiting a response. On the other hand, change can be in the opposite direction. For example, some clients' response to the initial monitoring of NATs is an increased preoccupation and/or frequency of negative thoughts, which may increase anxiety or depression in the short term. It is helpful to tell your client that a temporary exacerbation of the problem is possible and to encourage him to persist with monitoring long enough to see its longer-term advantages.

Validity and reliability

When standardised measuring instruments such as questionnaires are developed, an enormous amount of attention is paid to psychometric qualities, particularly *validity* and *reliability*.

A *valid* measure is one which measures what it purports to measure and not some ir relevant feature: for example, a questionnaire of social anxiety should not be couched in language so complex that responses to it are affected by a person's verbal ability.

A *reliable* measure achieves the same result or score when repeated under the same conditions at another time, or with another assessor. A measure low in reliability is affected by extraneous features and produces inconsistent findings.

Standardised measures, such as a well-developed mood questionnaire, will usually have been tested for validity and reliability. However, in many cases you need ingenuity to devise more idiosyncratic measures, and it is then important to try to make them as reliable and valid as possible in the circumstances. The following section suggests how this can be achieved.

Obtaining useful and accurate measures

Most of the principles that will be described here are easy to apply but can make an enormous difference to the value of the measures used.

Simplicity

Do not overburden your client. Begin with a limited task that does not ask too much. As your client becomes more persuaded of the value of information obtained through monitoring, and becomes more skilled, you may increase the demands on him, but still keep in mind the difficulty of observing and recording.

It can be instructive to carry out some monitoring for yourself, to get an idea of how onerous it can be. You could, for example, do a thought record (see Chapter 8) for a day; or you could keep records about the frequency of a behaviour that worries you – snapping at people, scratching your head – and what triggers it on each occasion. It will probably become clear that monitoring is not without its challenges!

Consider measures in more than one system

Although it is important to limit demands on the client, you should bear in mind that different aspects of the problem may change in different ways, and that this detail may need to be tracked.

> *A woman with anxieties about her health focused on reducing the amount of time that she discussed her worries with her husband and mother, or asked for reassurance (i.e. a behavioural aspect). She kept records (see Figure 5.4) which included information about behavioural, cognitive and emotional aspects of the problem. In the first two weeks, her success in effecting behavioural change had little impact on her anxiety or on the strength of her beliefs that she may have something seriously wrong with her health.*

Relevance

Only ask for information that you will use and that will make a difference to treatment. It is unlikely that the client will go to the trouble of monitoring unless he sees its relevance, and it may also jeopardise the therapeutic relationship if you ask for information merely 'out of interest'.

Specific, clearly defined targets

In order to improve the reliability of your measures, try and ensure that two observers engaged in the same task would agree on their observations. This means spelling out in detail what you want to be recorded. For example, if you are asking someone to record the frequency with which they 'lose their temper', you could ask, 'Let's try and be specific about what we mean. For the purposes of this exercise, what would you want to include in "losing your temper"? What would you be doing that would mean that you had lost it?' This might include shouting loudly, saying unkind and inappropriate things, banging doors; but would not include talking across someone, feeling angry but not shouting. The advantage of *operationalising* in this way is that, should any incident occur, the client would not have to make a judgement at the time about whether what had happened was included in the definition.

It is not uncommon that an internal state is the focus of measurement, in which case it is not possible to use the criterion of agreement by two observers. Nevertheless, you should take care to minimise the ambiguities in what is being recorded.

> *One client became dissociated in a number of situations and was recording where this happened. It was agreed in advance that she would look for instances where she had been unaware of her surroundings but that she would not include occasions when she felt unpleasantly vague and light-headed but was still aware of where she was.*

Provide clear and simple instructions

Do not expect the client to remember what the task entails, because he may either forget it altogether, or his memory may distort the task: write it down (or, even better, get the client to do so).

Behavioural: Each time you ask for reassurance, or discuss your symptoms with your husband or mother, please put a tally:

Date	Tally	Total
14th	/////////	11
15th	/////	5
16th	//	2
17th	///	3
18th	////////	7
19th	//	2

Cognitive: Rate (daily) how strongly you believe the following statement, from 0–100: 'My eyes are normal, and work as well as most people's.'

Date	Rating
14th	55
15th	45
16th	43
17th	50
18th	43
19th	45

0 = not at all; – 100 = totally believe

Emotional: Rate (daily) from 1–10, the most anxious you have felt, and how anxious you have felt on average, where 0 = not at all anxious, and 10 = as anxious as I could possibly feel.

Date	Peak Anxiety	Average anxiety
14th	8	4
15th	7	5
16th	8	4
17th	9	6
18th	7	5
19th	8	5

Figure 5.4   Records of different aspects of health anxiety

Use sensitive and meaningful measures

In some cases, measures which are most sensitive to change, and therefore helpful in plotting progress, may not capture the characteristics of the problem which are most important for the client. Both sensitive *and* meaningful measures are important but for different reasons: the first because they allow you to look at the effects of interventions relatively quickly, and the second because they focus on what the client believes to be the central, meaningful aspects of the problem.

A depressed woman was most interested in whether her mood was improving in response to treatment. As part of therapy, she was trying to increase the number of pleasurable and satisfying activities she engaged in, and she kept a daily record of how many hours she managed to work, and how many social contacts she had, and these were totalled each week. She also kept a daily mood rating. Although these measures were directly related to an aspect of the formulation (reduced activity), she was more interested in her scores on the Beck Depression Inventory that she completed every fortnight, as she felt that this best captured how she was getting on in general.

Provide aids to recording

Minimise demands on the client by providing as much support as possible for the practical task of monitoring, at least in the early stages of therapy. Rating forms or diaries should be drawn up for the client, with as many copies as will be required. The record sheets should be as simple and discreet as possible, bearing in mind that many clients would be embarrassed to be seen recording personal information. For example, the client could carry a small index card for recording information on a day-to-day basis; he could use differently coloured dedicated pages in his diary; he could use a memo pad in his mobile phone or hand-held computer.

Train the client to use the measure

Even if the task appears to be straightforward, always ask your client to go through a recent example and carry out the recording process with you. This will ensure that the task is clear to him and will allow you to discuss difficulties that crop up. For example, you could say, 'Can we think about the last time that you felt panicky, and fill in the record about that? What would you put in this column here, where it says "Situation"?'

Also spend some time clarifying rating procedures, as they may be unfamiliar to your client. For example, you might say, 'That's interesting; people often experience several emotions, which is why the column is labelled "Emotions". It is also useful to have ratings of the *strength* of the emotions, so let's go over that. Zero on this scale means that you are not feeling anxious at all, and 10 means "as bad as you could possibly imagine feeling". Can you think of a time when you have felt like that? . . . and what about a 5; can you think of a time when you felt moderately anxious, halfway between these two? . . . and what about a 7? Can you think of a time when you have felt quite a bit more than "moderate", but not as extreme as a 10?'

Remember that you are anticipating that your client will learn the *skill* of self-monitoring and be able to use this to manage problems in the future.

Collect data as soon as possible after the event

If records are not completed until some time after the event, it is likely that recall will be less vivid and/or will be biased by the client's mood at the time he completes the record. It may not be possible for him to record an experience immediately as it happens, particularly if he is with other people, but he should be encouraged to go over in his mind what he will record and to complete the task as soon as it is practically possible. Alternatively, it may be possible for him to make a brief note at the time and to complete the full monitoring at a more convenient time.

Pay attention to the monitoring

The therapist should never fail to take notice of information that has been collected. If the information is truly valuable, then the next session should, to some extent, rely on it; but in any case, it is important that the client's efforts are rewarded by genuine interest, so that he will be willing to continue monitoring in future. Ensure that feedback on any such homework is part of your shared agenda for the session.

What sorts of information to collect

There are many different ways of recording useful information, and the following examples give a flavour of this variety. There will be other examples in later chapters, and many academic papers and books will also give measures for specific problems that can be adopted for clinical use.

Frequency counts

A useful rule of thumb is that if there is something relevant to count, then count it. Counting is potentially the most reliable measurement method, even though it may appear to be overly simplistic. The variety of features that can be counted is almost boundless, and it is worth trying to think of aspects of the problem that could be measured in this way. Examples include:

- number of self-critical thoughts;
- number of times of checking (that the house is locked, that there are no spider's webs, etc.);
- number of eye-lashes pulled out (in trichotillomania);
- number of toilet rolls used in a week (to assess OCD problems or bladder/bowel worries);
- number of phone calls received;
- number of times of swearing;
- number of times clothes changed;
- number of urges to binge.

Therapist and client creativity is the only limit to the variety of possible frequency counts.

It is important to have an idea of what the frequency might be before monitoring; it is not helpful to ask someone to record the number of intrusive thoughts in a day if the total is likely to be a few hundred! Should the frequency be very high, then the client can be asked to take a sample at a relevant time of day (for example, a half-hour period when the thoughts are at their most troubling) or, if there is no reason to focus on a particular time, an arbitrary time (for example, between 5 and 6 o'clock).

Duration of event/experience

The duration of an event or experience may also be relevant, and is also likely to be a reliable measure. Examples include:

- Time spent washing for an obsessional client.
- Time spent checking his body for someone with health anxiety.
- Time spent travelling alone for a client with agoraphobia.
- Time able to concentrate on reading for a depressed client.

Again, use your imagination.

Self-ratings

These are amongst the most commonly used measures, as they can capture the quality of internal events such as emotions and cognitions. They are less reliable than frequency counts or measures of duration, but their reliability can be improved if the simple guidelines outlined above are followed. Although they are more reliable than a simple description of the experience, they remain subject to shifts in 'anchor points', in the sense that a rating of 'moderate', or 5- on a 10-point scale, may mean something different at the beginning of treatment compared with the end, as the individual gradually comes to have fewer highly distressing experiences.

If a discrete event is being monitored, then the client can be asked to rate it each time it occurs. For example, a man with anxiety about micturition rated how anxious he felt before going to the lavatory and also rated how much urine he passed (see Figure 5.5).

However, if the phenomenon being measured is continuous (as anxiety may sometimes be) or occurs very frequently, then it may be necessary for the person to choose a time to rate (as described above under 'Frequency Counts'), or to do an average rating for a period of time: for example, to rate average anxiety during the morning, afternoon and evening (see Figure 5.6).

Diaries

Diaries can combine the kinds of measure described above and let you look at the links between different aspects of problems, such as the relationship between the problem and particular triggers, safety behaviours and modulating variables. As they are more multi-faceted, it is even more important to pay attention to setting up the recording and training the client in its use. Unless care is taken, the client may return with information which is inconsistently collected and difficult to analyse. Get feedback from the client about what is relevant, whether the recording sheet seems sensible and whether there are ambiguities which would make it difficult to use.

Whenever you are away from home, rate:

- *How anxious you feel before you go to the lavatory:*
  0 = not at all anxious; 10 = as anxious as you could possibly feel
- *How strong was your urge to go:*
  0 = no urge at all; 10 = very strong urge
- *How much urine you pass:*
  0 = none 1 = a little, 2 = a moderate amount, 3 = a lot, 4 = a great deal

Date and time	Anxiety 0–10	Urge 0–10	Amount 0–4
23th July, 9.15	6	5	2
23th July, 11.00	7	4	1
23th July, 12.15	6	6	1
23th July, 15.20	5	5	2

Figure 5.5   **Diary for a man anxious about micturition**

Rate how anxious you have felt *on average* each morning, afternoon, and evening. If you have a rating greater than 5, note what you were doing at the time.

	Anxiety 0–10	Situation if anxiety > 5
Monday a.m.	4	
p.m.	7	In meeting with seniors
evening	2	
Tuesday a.m.	6	Planning presentation
p.m.	7	Presentation
evening	2	
Wed. a.m.	4	
p.m.	4	

Figure 5.6   Diary of anxiety about work

Figure 5.7 shows a diary from a woman with a phobia about vomiting that prevented her from carrying out a range of social and domestic activities. The diary included aspects that she felt were important, particularly her sense of achievement, which compensated for the anxiety she experienced in the short term.

Two diaries in common use are described later: the Dysfunctional Thought Record (DTR) in Chapter 8, and the Activity Schedule in Chapter 12.

Questionnaires

There is an enormous range of questionnaires available for clinical use, many of them originally developed for use in research trials (see Chapter 18 for some questionnaires commonly used in clinical practice). A major advantage of many questionnaires is that they will provide you with the scores of relevant groups – for example, the normal population, or a group of depressed out-patients – so that you can compare your patient's score to others. However, a questionnaire may not give as sensitive results as a simpler record focused on the client's own problem. In other words, questionnaires are different from rating scales or frequency counts, but not necessarily better: it depends on what information you need. In any event, it is important to use questionnaires that are well standardised and validated, otherwise, the results of the questionnaire may be unreliable.

Date	Situation	Safety behaviours dropped	Anxiety 0–10	Sense of achievement 0–10
23rd June	Made ill friend a cup of tea and drank with her	Did not disinfect tea-cup; held the cup afterwards and drank from it; drank on 'her' side; did not wipe the work surface; took dog for walk so did not sit and think it all through.	8	10
26th June	Walked down passage where someone had been sick	Did not go to the far side; went back the same way, though knew it was there; did not hold my breath; wore clothes in the evening.	9	10
27th June	Ate yoghurt on day date expired	Kept busy in evening and did not sit and ruminate to check whether I felt sick; did not stay up late in case I felt sick in bed	6	9

Figure 5.7   Diary recording success in dropping safety behaviours

Other sources of information

Although the majority of the information used in therapy is provided by the client, different data sources can be relevant: other informants, live observations of behaviour, and physiological data.

Other informants
It may be helpful to interview other people because:

- they have information unavailable to the client – for example, a client may believe he behaves oddly in social situations, and someone else's view can provide useful information;
- the problem has an impact on the other person – for example, if a client with obsessional problems involves relatives or other significant people in his rituals;
- the way someone else responds to the client's problems may be relevant to its maintenance;
- the other person's beliefs about the problem may be important – for example, that medication is likely to be the only effective solution.

It is important to remember that the problem may have major implications for other people, so they should be approached in a similar way to the client, recognising that they will need to be engaged, to be given hope and, possibly, to be educated about CBT. The reasons for using Socratic enquiry will also apply to them just as much as to the client (see Chapter 7).

Although an interview is the most common way of obtaining information from other informants, they can be asked to provide more directly observed material in the same way as the client. Frequency counts, ratings, diaries and questionnaires may all be useful in some circumstances.

The issue of confidentiality should be discussed with both the client and the other informants, to establish whether there are things that either party does not wish to be disclosed. It is worth checking out whether the reasons for this are well founded or, perhaps, based on an erroneous belief. For example, a relative may be concerned that mentioning worries about suicidal ideas might put them into the client's head, when in fact this is not a risk.

Role play and live observation
Observing your client at the time the problem occurs can provide significant information which the client had forgotten or of which he was unaware. For example, a client with a complex hand-washing ritual took for granted some of the details involved, including that she washed the soap and put it back on the sink after completing each stage in the ritual; a man with social phobia was unaware of the extent to which he averted his gaze in casual social interations.

Sometimes, you can observe behaviour in naturalistic settings: for example, a therapist accompanied a client with social anxiety into shops and observed his interactions when he asked for goods or presented items for purchase. At other times, you might contrive a situation: for example, the therapist asked a client with OCD to briefly 'contaminate' herself by touching a doorknob with her bare hands (which she usually avoided) and then to carry out her usual ritual to make things safe.

You can, of course, use the full range of measures while observing the client, including frequency count and rating scales.

Physiological measures

Many research reports, particularly those involving anxiety, include measures of physiological state, and, indeed, it may be the physiological symptoms that are the most upsetting for the client, as, for example, in panic disorder. Although there are simple, portable instruments for measuring, for example, heart rate or galvanic skin response, these are rarely used in routine clinical practice. Often, the client's perception of the physical changes, and their meaning to him, are sufficient index of changes within that response system.

> *A client feared fainting when anxious, and in order to give him information about the state of his blood pressure (BP), he was asked to focus on his heart rate (HR). This was raised, and the therapist questioned him about the relationship between HR and BP, and then explained to him that fainting results from a decrease in BP.*

Thus, the focus was on an indirect measure of a physiological variable and did not demand direct physical recording.

Making the most of the data

Time and energy goes into collecting information, so you should ensure that you make good use of it. First, examine it carefully to see what it says about the hypothesis it was designed to test. This may involve *collating* the data in some way. For example, if the client has produced a series of questionnaires over a number of weeks, graph the results and look for variations. This is shown in Figure 5.8 for a series of Beck Depression Inventory scores from a client being treated for depression.

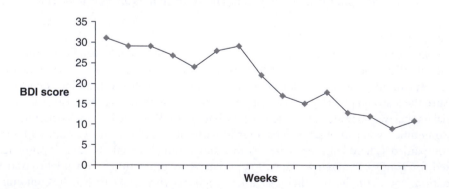

Figure 5.8   Graph of the BDI scores over treatment

However, a series of diaries may be more difficult to summarise, particularly as the client's anxiety scores may not be declining if he is attempting more and more difficult tasks. Figure 5.9 shows data from a client who was severely claustrophobic. It may be helpful to ask him, in the session, to group tasks by their difficulty level. He could then look at improvements in anxiety for activities at each difficulty level.

As the treatment progresses, the responsibility for collating and interpreting information can increasingly be handed over to your client. You can ask your client to review his own diaries and identify themes or the most important incident to discuss. This helps clients develop the ability to review and prioritise, which is necessary for effective problem-solving.

Problems when using measurements

The client does not appreciate its potential value
It is important to discuss your client's doubts and, if necessary, to get agreement to do some measurement as an experiment.

Date	Situation	Anxiety 0–10*	Difficulty 1–5 **
12th November	Small room, door open	5	1
14th November	In lift, up one floor	7	2
15th November	End of row, back of hall	4	2
16th November	Small room, door closed	7	3
17th November	Small room, door closed, smoky air	8	4
19th November	Small room, door open	3	1
21st November	Middle of row, back of hall	4	3
23rd November	Small room, door closed	5	3

*0 = not at all; 10 = as anxious as I could possibly be
**1 = imagined being able to do this; 5 = thought I would never manage this

Figure 5.9   Diary of anxiety scores rising with increasingly difficult tasks

The client cannot read or write
You will then need ingenuity to find other modalities for recording – e.g. using a dictaphone.

Poor reliability or validity of a questionnaire
Always check that it has data on reliability and validity and that its normative data is relevant for your client.

Summary

Measuring the qualities of the problems presented by the client, and then assessing changes as treatment progresses, are crucial aspects of CBT. It can be an interesting, creative and collaborative part of therapy, as you use your ingenuity to design measures, and it can be a useful antidote against either wishful thinking or therapeutic pessimism!

Helping Clients Become Their Own Therapists

Introduction

'One of the most powerful components of the learning model of psychotherapy is that the patient begins to incorporate many of the therapeutic techniques of the therapist.'

(Beck et al., 1979, p. 4)

In CBT we teach the client to become his own therapist, with the skills to manage relapse. Essentially, the cognitive therapist aims to make herself redundant, and this means thoroughly educating the client in the model and methods of CBT. There is more to this than simply sharing the cognitive model and strategies with clients. There are ways in which we can make therapeutic techniques more accessible and more memorable and ways in which we can prepare the client for independent long-term coping. In Chapter 3 we described how the therapeutic relationship is crucial in helping a client to explore and learn, and how collaboration is fundamental to learning the skills of CBT. This chapter will focus on ways in which client learning can be further enhanced and relapse management established.

Helping the client learn and remember

Clients cannot take on the role of therapist unless they can recall the model and methods of CBT. There are many models to explain learning, but perhaps one of the most relevant for us as therapists is the adult learning theory of Lewin (1946) and Kolb (1984).

Adult learning theory

This model emphasises the importance of experiential learning and the value of reflection. It comprises four necessary stages in effective learning:

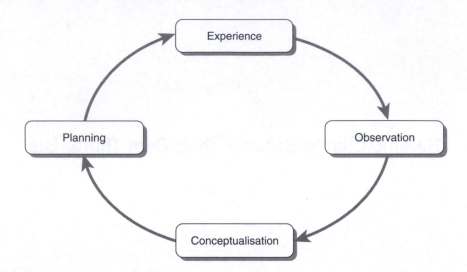

Figure 6.1   The adult learning cycle (adapted from Lewin, 1946 and Kolb, 1984)

- Experience
- Observation
- Conceptualisation
- Planning.

These form a cycle as illustrated in Figure 6.1. For learning to be effective, it needs to move through all the stages of the cycle.

This understanding of the elements of effective learning can help therapists in many ways: for example, in deciding when to provide information and when to use Socratic method and in creating assignments to make learning more memorable. The next chapter focuses on the Socratic method, but it is worth noting here that the Socratic method contains elements of the learning cycle. When using it, we cue clients to reflect on their experiences (observation); use this to develop new understandings of their problems (conceptualisation); then synthesise new possibilities and ways forward (planning new experiences). Similarly, Chapters 8 and 9 focus on cognitive and behavioural techniques respectively, and you will again see how these crucial elements of CBT are linked by the learning cycle: cognitive techniques help the client develop new insights and possibilities (observation–conceptualisation–planning) which are tested 'in the field' (experience).

As an example of the learning cycle, you could present the model of cognitive therapy or illustrate the interactions of feelings, thoughts and actions in a way that takes the client around all four elements:

Experience; Observation:
Therapist: 'How did you feel?'
Client: *'Pretty anxious: I was scared.'*
   'And what was running through your mind?'
   'I thought that I would embarrass myself – look like a fool.'

'So what did you do?'

*'I told my boss that I couldn't do the presentation because I would be on annual leave –
I then booked in annual leave.'*

'So you got out of doing the presentation: how did that leave you feeling and what
was going through your mind then?'

*'After the initial relief, I felt even worse. I still hadn't faced my anxiety of public speak-
ing and now I had the fear that my boss would realise that I'd lied to her.'*

'It seems that you felt scared and you thought that you would embarrass yourself;
so you avoided what frightened you but soon regretted it.'

'Well, yes.'

Conceptualization:

'So, what might you learn from this?'

*'I suppose it's obvious really: if I get scared, I should face up to my fears. Running away
is only making me feel worse about myself and I think that it makes me more anxious.'*

Planning

'Facing up to your fears … do you have any thoughts on how you might go about
doing that?

This could then lead to planning a behavioural experiment which would provide an
experience which could be reviewed, and so on. This incorporation of experience and
cognition has been shown to promote greater cognitive, affective and behavioural change
than purely verbal interventions (Bennett-Levy, 2003) and to help to bridge the 'thinking–
believing gap' that clients often experience ('I know it with my head but I just don't *feel* that
it is so') (Rachman and Hodgson, 1974).

It has been suggested that we each have preferences in the way that we use information
and learn from it. Honey and Munford (1992) mapped these preferences on to the learning cycle and identified four preference types: activist, reflector, theorist and pragmatist. As
you read through the descriptions of each stage in the cycle consider your own preferences.

Experience:	The time of action, engagement, 'doing'. This is the preferred quad-rant of the *activist*, who enjoys being engaged in something tangible. Within therapy this might include role play or setting a behavioural assignment.
Observation:	The part of the cycle where there is reflection upon what has hap-pened: the preferred position of the *reflector*, who takes time to digest events and mull them over. In sessions this could include the process of reviewing a client's thought diary or collecting feedback at the end of a meeting.
Conceptualisation:	Making sense of what happened by relating it to previous experiences and knowledge. This analytical phase is preferred by the *theorist*, who enjoys searching for understanding. In therapy, this might be the process

of reflecting back on the formulation of a problem, generalising from an experience or abstracting principles.

Planning: The phase when practical implications of a new understanding are considered, preferred by the *pragmatist*. This marks the time when plans are made, thus creating the basis for further experience. In therapy this is the time of preparing the next step, setting goals and tasks based on a new understanding.

Personal preferences can result in the under- or over-emphasising of elements of the cycle. For example:

- The *Activist* might dwell disproportionately on the 'doing' part of the task, for instance engaging a client in a behavioural assignment but then failing to review it thoroughly. This means that it is difficult to appreciate the implications of the experience and to take it forward. At worst, the experience is wasted.
- The *Reflector* might review the assignment but fail to make links with previous experiences or to generalise to develop principles. In this case, planning would be impaired as it could lack a theoretical basis and would be unlikely to make links with the client's problem formulation.
- The *Theorist* will make links, but if observation is weak she will have little to work with. If the phase of planning is also weak, then meaningful future opportunities for learning can be lost.
- Finally, the *Pragmatist* will focus on creating concrete plans, but these will be less effective unless she is properly engaged in the active phase and the stages of observation and theorising. Unless all four phases are involved, even the best planning is unlikely to result in new skills being learnt or remembered.

Your own preferences might interact unhelpfully with the preferences of your client. For example, two reflector-theorists might have an agreeable and stimulating time philosophising but not be sufficiently active in therapy, so that experiential learning does not occur. Problems can also arise from an antagonistic combination, such as the Activist–Theorist therapist frustrated by the Reflector or the Pragmatist client, who might seem frustratingly slow or obsessive. Thus, in some instances, difference in preferences can underpin problems in the therapeutic alliance (see Chapter 3).

From the above, it is clear that learning style is relevant to training clients in cognitive therapy, and to the development of the therapeutic alliance. Therefore, it is worth taking time to reflect on it.

Remembering

Learning is not just about *acquiring* knowledge; information also has to be *retained* and it has to be *retrievable*. Since clients need to be able to remember salient points from therapy, an understanding of memory and how we might help clients can be a valuable adjunct to our work. There are several useful resources for understanding more about memory and information-processing, but one of the most informative and readable is Alan Baddeley's *Your memory: a user's guide* (1996). This section owes much to this text.

The main systems involved in remembering are:

- **Short-term memory** (STM): This is the '*temporary holding point*' for information (20–30 seconds): the information will be forgotten if it is not relevant or rehearsed enough to be transferred to long-term memory.
- **Long-term memory** (LTM): This is the '*depot*', where information may be held indefinitely. Contrary to some beliefs, memory is not held like a recording that gets replayed when we recall something. It is more like a jigsaw puzzle, with the pieces being stored in different parts of the brain waiting to be reconstructed when we remember. This is an important point because it makes memory susceptible to distortion.

Is this important in clinical practice? The following example illustrates how understanding something about learning and memory can be relevant to helping a client get the most out of a technique.

Whilst teaching a relaxation technique, a man reclines in a chair in his therapist's office. His sensory memory processes verbal instruction, the tone of his therapist's voice and the physical sensation of relaxing a body part or breathing slowly. This will be held in STM while the client carries out instructions and reflects on the effects of relaxation. If the exercises are considered relevant, they are then more likely to be stored in LTM.

If the exercises are not considered relevant, or are poorly attended to they will be lost.

Let us assume that the rationale for introducing relaxation exercises was initially persuasive and he attended to the instructions, practised at home and returned to the session giving feedback on the experience. However, it emerged that his practise was not as the therapist expected. Although some elements of the regime had been remembered, parts had been forgotten and parts had been mixed up with other exercise instructions. Overall, the exercises had not been helpful. Discussion revealed what might have contributed to this.

1. *He did not remember the rationale for the exercises and so struggled to appreciate their relevance.*
2. *The exercise had only been practised once in session, there had been little debriefing, and nothing written down: thus he had formed a poor memory of the exercise.*
3. *In trying to recall the relaxation exercise the client had unwittingly drawn on memories of yoga techniques learned years earlier, which disrupted his recollection.*
4. *Both therapist and client tended towards the 'activist' quadrant of the learning cycle and were light on planning.*

How might the client's recall have been improved?

- *Relevance:* material which is perceived as important or meaningful is likely to be remembered. This is why sharing a rationale – and checking that the client understands and agrees with the rationale – is so important in therapy.
- *Focus:* distractions impair memory, so clients benefit from being focused. The therapist should minimise distraction and keep the client directed towards the task.
- *Repetition:* repeating information and experiences will render them more memorable. In this case, the therapist might usefully run through the relaxation exercise more than once.

- *Active engagement:* getting feedback from the client would also have helped.
- *Memory aids:* we all forget things, so we all benefit from notes, lists and so on. It might have been helpful to have given this client a handout restating the rationale and the techniques of relaxation, or to have tape-recorded the exercise.
- *Familiarity:* we tend to 'reorganise' our memories in the light of previous experiences and beliefs (Bartlett, 1932). Therefore, it is useful if the therapist checks out the client's responses to, and associations with, a particular technique. Often, previous experiences can helpfully be incorporated – in this example, familiar yoga techniques could have been structured into the exercises, making them more memorable.
- *Working through the learning cycle:* the client would have benefited from being cued to reflect on the exercise, consider what he had learnt and how he might take that forward. The conceptualisation and planning stages of the learning cycle offer an opportunity for trouble-shooting and for making concrete plans to practise.

Principles of effective learning apply to each of the cognitive and behavioural techniques which we introduce to our clients, from simple diary-keeping through to complicated behavioural experiments. By using them you can help clients learn the skills of symptom management; but you also want your clients to be able to manage their difficulties in the longer term, and so they must also become skilled in relapse management. We turn to this now.

Relapse management

As stated earlier, clients must become independent of the therapist, and that means that they need to remember the techniques of CBT *and* to be able to use them in difficult situations and to draw on them after a set-back. It is crucial that clients are able to tackle set-backs productively. You might wonder why this section is called relapse *management* rather than *prevention*. Although some treatment approaches might aim to have no relapses, it can be almost impossible to prevent some degree of relapse in some disorders and with some clients. Clients who anticipate that they can completely prevent relapse are therefore likely to be disappointed. However, it is possible to learn how to *manage* such events and to regain progress that has been lost.

Our recommendation is that relapse management is introduced early on in therapy so that it is developed as a skill which can be refined over the course of treatment. The most basic form of relapse management comprises three questions that the client asks himself following a set-back:

- How can I make sense of this?
- What have I learnt from it?
- With hindsight, what would I do differently?

In this way, your client develops the habit of analysing and profiting from set-backs. For example:

Carol struggled with an eating disorder and had periods of binge-eating. One evening she bought quite large quantities of her favourite foods, went home alone and consumed it, only spitting out chewed mouthfuls when she became over-full, but unable to stop eating. During this time she could not stop herself. Such an evening would usually have marked the beginning of a significant decline. She would have woken the next day feeling physically unwell and uncomfortable, she would have concluded that she was a hopeless failure and her mood would certainly have been depressed. As a 'hopeless failure' she would have felt powerless to resist the urge to comfort eat. However, on this occasion, she asked herself:

- *How can I make sense of this lapse? She realised that she had been feeling stressed at work for several days but had kept pushing herself in order not to think about her troubled relationship. In addition, she had begun to resume her old habit of starving throughout the day in an attempt to lose weight. Once she had reflected on her situation, she was then able to say: 'It's no wonder that I fell off the wagon. Not only was I stressed to breaking point but I set myself up for a binge by not eating during the day.'*
- *What have I learnt from it? 'I realise that, for me, it is dangerous to starve as a means of weight control – it backfires. Also, I need to keep a check on my stress level: when it gets too high I am vulnerable to comfort eating.'*
- *With hindsight, what would I do differently? 'Hard as it is, I would try to eat 'sensibly' and avoid starving. Looking back, I made a mistake in trying to pretend that I did not have problems in my relationship and then throwing myself into my work as a distraction. If I had that time over again I would acknowledge my problems, or maybe even talk to someone about them rather than ignoring them.'*

Not only does this give Carol a plan for coping in the future, but she has learnt more about her particular needs and vulnerabilities. With each set-back she will be able to continue to 'fine-tune' her understanding of difficulties and develop a wider and more individually tailored repertoire of coping responses.

The pioneers of relapse work in CBT are Marlatt and Gordon (1985), who first developed their model and strategies in the treatment of addictive behaviours. However, their understanding of relapse risk and management has proven to be relevant across psychological disorders. They identified several factors that rendered clients vulnerable to relapse. A particularly potent one was a dichotomous, or 'all or nothing', interpretation of a set-back. They observed that those who perceived themselves as *either* being in control *or* having failed tended to relapse at the first sign of difficulty: they flipped from feeling in control to feeling as though they had failed completely. Once in the 'failure' mindset, clients tended to be dominated by a sense of hopelessness which drove unhelpful behaviours such as continuing to drink for comfort. Instead, clients were encouraged to develop a continuous notion of being in control and slipping out of control, which could accommodate minor and even significant set-backs without the client automatically assuming failure (see Figure 6.2).

Holding onto this model of a *spectrum* of experiences between control and perceived failure increased the likelihood that a slip or a set-back would be perceived as a temporary aberration that could be corrected. To further encourage resilience, clients would be urged to consider the different stages along the continuum and to ask:

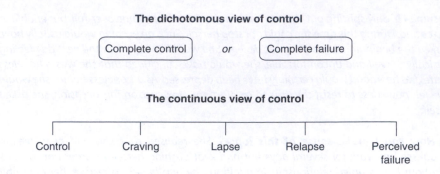

Figure 6.2   The dichotomous and the continuous view of control

- When will I be at risk of this happening?
- What are the signs?
- What could I do to avoid losing control?
- What could I do if I did lose control (damage limitation)?

In this way, clients can recognise 'early warning signs' and try to avert a lapse, whilst still having a well-considered back-up plan. Thus, a lapse can be construed as an anticipated event for which there is a solution.

What factors besides dichotomous thinking predisposes a person to relapse? Marlatt and Gordon identified a sequence of events that systematically increased the likelihood of relapse. These were:

- **Being in a high-risk situation**: for example, a depressed person being socially isolated, or someone with an eating disorder not having eaten for too long.
- **Having poor or no coping strategies**: for example, poor mood management skills or no helpful ideas for dealing with hunger pangs in a controlled way.
- **The sense of loss of self-efficacy**: for example, thinking: 'I'm hopeless. It's my fault that I'm depressed', or: 'There's no point in trying to resist: I just can't.' Such thoughts give a person 'permission' to let go or give in. This step can be exacerbated by substance misuse.
- **Engaging in unhelpful behaviours**: for example, withdrawing further or binge-eating.

In Marlatt and Gordon's view, the worst was still to come: they recognised that many clients who were striving to remain abstinent from problem behaviours became caught up in a powerful cycle of unhelpful thoughts and behaviours once they ceased to be abstinent. They called this the the 'Abstinence Violation Effect' (AVE) and saw this as marking true relapse – a state of not being able to break away from the problem behaviours because of compelling negative thoughts (see Figure 6.3).

An advantage of identifying the steps *en route* to the AVE is that they offer clear points for interventions which can interrupt progress towards relapse. As memory and performance are often impaired in distress, it is advisable to encourage your clients to write down their personal plan for minimising relapse. Below we lay out some strategies for each of the steps towards relapse:

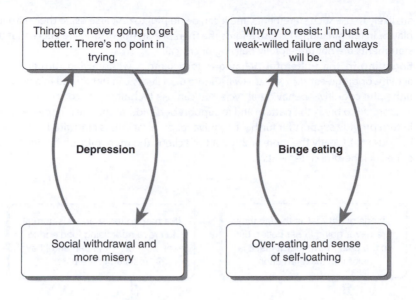

Figure 6.3   The relapse cycle

- **Being in a high-risk situation**: The key is to identify (through monitoring), predict and, where possible, avoid high-risk situations. For example, if a depressed person learns he is at risk of becoming miserable when socially isolated, he needs to strive to maintain social contacts; if a woman with an eating disorder is at risk of binge-eating when over-stressed or hungry, she needs to avoid getting into those situations. However, difficult circumstances are sometimes unavoidable, so vulnerable clients may find themselves in a high-risk situation. This does not make relapse inevitable, although it is more likely if the client has poor coping strategies or has grown increasingly ambivalent about change (in which case it may be helpful to try to remotivate clients by using a motivational interviewing approach: Miller and Rollnick, 1991).

- **Having poor or no coping strategies**: Clients are encouraged to develop appropriate cognitive and behavioural coping strategies and to plan how they would put the strategies into action. Although this is a routine part of their CBT, it is helpful for clients to keep reminders of what works for them. Someone prone to depression might list all the social activities and contacts that he could try if he felt vulnerable; the woman at risk of binge-eating might keep a reminder of the activities that curb her urge to binge.

- **The sense of loss of self-efficacy**: This is a very cognitive element in the course of relapse, and therefore CBT is well placed to help clients develop realistically hopeful and empowered self-statements. For example: 'It is my way of thinking that is bringing me down, but tough as it is I can "coach" myself out of it again. Furthermore, there are a lot of friends out there who want to support me,' or, 'I can resist. I have resisted in the past. I am not saying that it is easy but I know that it's possible for me.' Again, clients need to anticipate when they are likely to use such statements, and it can be helpful to rehearse using them either in role play or in imagination. This also affords the therapist an opportunity to check that the self-statements are not unhelpfully bullying or critical.

- **Engaging in the unhelpful behaviour**: for example, withdrawing further from social activity, or binge-eating. As you saw in Figure 6.3, clients can get locked in a powerful and unhelpful cognitive–behavioural cycle. You can use techniques of cognitive restructuring (Chapter 8) to break the pattern and to support behavioural change (Chapter 9), which will in turn provide support for further cognitive reappraisal. This is illustrated in the examples in Figure 6.4. Clearly the more ambivalent the client, the more difficult it might be to generate such helpful statements.

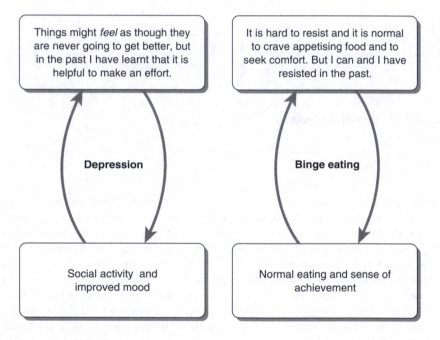

Figure 6.4   Breaking the relapse cycle

It is worth noting that ambivalence about change (which is discussed more fully in Chapter 11, on the course of therapy) can render a person even more vulnerable to lapses and relapse, and you need to keep track of your client's motivation to change.

'Self-help' reading (bibliotherapy)

Your clients' progress and maintenance can be enhanced by their reading relevant literature. Chapter 16 reviews different methods of delivery of CBT, amongst which is bibliotherapy. If you are intending to supplement CBT with such literature, do make sure that you have read the booklets or books yourself, so that you can evaluate the quality or demands of the text before you recommend them to clients.

Possible problems

Therapist maintains role of expert; client strives to remain a patient

First, discover what assumptions might be relevant to this problem: what makes sense of it? For example, perhaps you are thinking: 'I have to know more than the client in order be competent'; or the client believes, 'I can never help myself, so there's no point in trying.' The obvious next step is evaluating and challenging such unhelpful assumptions. Use supervision to help clarify and rectify this type of impasse.

Course of therapy not reflecting the learning cycle

Review your, and your client's, learning styles and preferences and, if appropriate, use supervision to discuss the possible impact on your work and ways of overcoming problems.

The client wants to be 'fixed' or 'parented'

Some clients do not readily take to the idea of collaboration and self-help. Sometimes, a few sessions of socialising your clients into the ways of CBT will be sufficient to shift his expectations of passivity or long-term care. However, there will be those who continue to find the goal of self-help unappealing, or even frightening. Try to uncover the assumptions which explain this attitude – assumptions which might have to be tackled before your client can engage in CBT. This can take some time, and you need to ask yourself if you have the time and the skill needed to do this (see Chapter 17 for more discussion of working with complex clients). In any case, an essential guideline is to review regularly. Clarify unhelpful patterns, and if it is not possible for you to help your client with CBT, then consider referral to a more appropriate therapy.

Relapse management is reserved until the end of treatment

Awareness of personal vulnerability and its management is relevant from the onset of therapy. Try to build this into early sessions by asking: 'When can you imagine struggling with this?' or, 'When do you see yourself being at risk of having a set-back?' If your client has a lapse, use the opportunity to review this *thoroughly* (setting aside enough time to do so), encouraging your client to learn from set-backs early on in your work together.

Therapist feels pressured and skimps on relapse management

Relapse management is an investment of time. If your client cannot see trouble coming or handle it when it arrives, then he will be vulnerable to relapse – even if he is otherwise skilled in cognitive and behavioural techniques.

Socratic Method

Introduction

Socratic questioning has been called 'the cornerstone of cognitive therapy' (Padesky, 1993). In this chapter we will look at why this approach is considered so invaluable and how you can develop your skill in using it.

The Socratic method derives from Socrates, a philosopher living in Athens around 400 BC. He spent his time in the marketplace encouraging the young men of Athens to question the truth of popular opinion. His unique approach was using questions to help his students reach a conclusion without directly instructing them. A Socratic question was one which the student had the ability to answer – although he might not yet realise it. Thus, Socrates encouraged students to make use of their own knowledge base, to form their own opinions, and to see new possibilities, which they act on.

In CBT, Socratic questioning affords the therapist and client the same opportunities: revealing what clients already know but what they have not yet considered, or have forgotten. Through sensitive questioning, clients are encouraged to use what they know, to discover alternative views and solutions for themselves, rather than the therapist suggesting them.

So, what is a good Socratic question? You have asked a 'good' Socratic question if

1. your client can work out an answer to it; and
2. if the answer reveals new perspectives.

A 'good' question draws the client's attention to information relevant to the issue being discussed but which might be outside his current focus. This can be helpful in clarifying the meanings of problems, and it can also be used to help the client make use of the new information in order to re-evaluate previous conclusions and to construct new plans.

However, what is a good Socratic question for one person at one time is not necessarily good for a different person, or at a different time. Take the question: 'What is a good Socratic question?' Clearly, this would not be useful if I asked it of a person who did not know the answer, but what if I asked it of a colleague who could come up with the answer? Would that make it good?

It would not be good if I asked a colleague who readily answered the question, but simply thought, 'So what?': she already knew the answer and so learnt nothing from the exercise. However, imagine that my colleague had lost confidence in her ability to teach CBT and had told me that she knew nothing of worth and could contribute very little to our training programme. In that context, answering the question might help her realise that she had specialist knowledge and could contribute to training. In this case, the enquiry provoked an answer that illuminated the issue.

Why choose Socratic questions?

Why do cognitive therapists strive to develop a repertoire of good Socratic questions? The answer lies in their effectiveness in encouraging a personal review of a situation and, where relevant, a shift in attitude, feeling and behaviour.

In his self-help book, David Burns (1980) wrote: 'Through a process of thoughtful questions, you discover on your own the beliefs that defeat you. You unearth the origin of your problems by repeating the following questions over and over: "If that negative thought were true, what would it mean to me? Why would it upset me?" *Without introducing some therapist's subjective bias* or personal beliefs or theoretical leanings, you can *objectively* and systematically go right to the root of your problems.' (p. 239).

Although didactic teaching has value in CBT, Socratic questions encourage clients to review data and draw their own conclusions – conclusions that are more likely to be memorable and convincing.

Socratic questions can be helpful in many areas of therapy, as we illustrate below.

1. Assessment and formulation

In identifying the cognitions, affect, behaviours and sensations pertinent to a client's difficulties, Socratic dialogue can elaborate something which might 'cross a client's mind' but which was not previously fully acknowledged. Simple questions such as: 'How do you feel?' or 'What went through your mind?' can help clients clarify and articulate feelings and thoughts. Other examples of useful assessment questions are:

What did you do when that happened?
What did it mean to you when you thought/did that?
When was the first time that this thought occurred to you?
Did you have any other feelings?

You can also further inform the formulation by asking questions that help you check out hypotheses generated by the preliminary formulation, such as:

And when that happens, how do you feel?
What goes through your mind when you feel like that?
What do you tend to do at those times?

This encourages further exploration, thus building and revising the formulation.

2. Education

An essential part of cognitive therapy is teaching the client the skills of CBT. Some of this is best achieved didactically: for example, teaching assertiveness skills and breathing techniques. However, the links between thoughts and feelings, and their impact on motivation and behaviour, is often better explored collaboratively using a Socratic approach. A standard approach in examining these links is to encourage the client to imagine the consequences of different thoughts. For example:

> *Imagine that you believed that dogs were dangerous and you saw a dog: what would go through your mind?*
> *How would you feel?*
> *What would you do?*
> *Imagine that you believed dogs were cuddly and safe.*
> *How would you feel?*
> *What would you do?*
> *What does that suggest about the links between thoughts and feelings, or thoughts and actions?*

This particular technique can be elaborated if necessary. Further questions can be added, such as: '. . . and what might happen if you did that?' thus encouraging the development of further scenarios which can facilitate further exploration of the linkages.

3. Challenging unhelpful cognitions

The Socratic method is an ideal tool for prompting clients to consider a range of possibilities that lie outside their current perspective and so construct alternative views of a situation or event. There are several types of question which can be used for this purpose:

- 'consequences of' questions
- 'evidence for' questions
- 'evidence against' questions
- 'alternative view' questions.

Enquiry about the consequences of holding a current view (and an alternative view) will elicit the pros and cons of current beliefs and can provide a rationale for change.

> *How helpful, or unhelpful, is it to hold this particular belief?*
> *What good, if any, comes of holding this belief?*
> *What is the downside of seeing things this way?*
> *If you see the world this way, how do you feel, how do others react?*

Questions which elicit evidence supporting the problem cognition are important in building up a balanced view of a situation; they also enable the client to see that 'it's no wonder that I have this thought' and therefore minimise the likelihood of self-criticism such as 'I am stupid for thinking like this'. Questions here include:

In your experience, what fits with this belief, what makes it seem true?
Why might any of us have that thought at some time?

In searching for evidence which is inconsistent with the problem cognition, you direct the client's attention to incidents or experiences that challenge the original belief, thus undermining the validity of unhelpful cognitions. You might ask:

Do you have any experience of this not being the case?
Is there anything that doesn't seem to fit with that thought?
How might someone else view the situation?
Is that so all of the time, or are there occasions when things are different?

Once clients have reviewed why they hold a belief (even though it might be unhelpful) and have looked at ways in which the belief might not stand up to scrutiny, then they can be guided towards generating alternative possibilities by questions such as:

Now that you have looked at the bigger picture, how would you view your original concern?
Given what you've just described, how likely do you think it is that the worst will happen?

In this way, you encourage the client to stand back and review the situation, reflecting on the bigger picture that has emerged. This is essential training in CBT if your client is going to become his own CBT therapist and is described in more detail in Chapter 8.

4. Problem-solving and working out solutions

You can guide your clients towards good problem-solving by using the Socratic approach to encourage first precision and then creativity.

So, just what is it that you fear will happen?
How might your friend try to deal with such a dilemma?
Given that you have identified avoidance as an obstacle to gaining confidence, how would you advise a friend to go about dealing with this obstacle?

This can then explore as many coping options as possible. You can also use the Socratic approach to tease out the pros and cons of a solution by asking your client to consider what might go well and badly, and you can prompt him to devise back-up or reserve plans.

What is the worst-case scenario if this solution does not work?
How would you prepare for that? How might you guard against it happening? What could you do if it did happen?

Thus you can guide him through the stages of defining the problem, generating as many solutions as possible, planning to put a solution into action, and devising contingency plans.

5. Devising behavioural tests

Once the client has a new perspective, he needs to take it forward and check its validity. Thus, the insights that Socratic questioning can generate often need to be followed by behavioural testing (see Chapter 9). For example, when working with a person with a phobia, we generally hypothesise that it will be helpful to face the fear. You can use the Socratic method to elicit the rationale for a behavioural experiment along these lines:

> *What do you think would happen if you held your ground and did not run away?*
> *What would go through your mind?*
> *And if you were able to remain in the situation, what would go through your mind?*
> *How would you feel? What would this mean to you?*

This can lead on to questions that shape the behavioural experiment, such as:

> *How might we set up a situation where this could happen?*
> *What would make it easier for you to take on the challenge?*
> *How will you gauge your success?*

In this way, experiments can be evolved collaboratively. Similarly, trouble-shooting can become a collaborative venture, for example:

> *What could go wrong?*
> *What is the worst-case scenario?*
> *How might you prepare yourself/deal with this if it happened?*
> *How might a friend prepare herself/deal with it if it happened?*
> *What would we learn from that?*

It is important that, as far as possible, experiments arise from the content of the session and are closely linked with the development of insight. Thus, if a client draws a new conclusion, for example: '*If I could stay in that situation, like I used to do, then I'll get back my confidence*', then you can ask, '*How might you check that out?*' Similarly, discoveries in session can be linked with behavioural change by asking the question, '*Given what we've covered today, how might you take things forward?*'

After experiments, Socratic enquiry can be used to prompt analysis of what happened, highlight problems and doubts and then move on to reconstruct new conceptualisations and further behavioural experiments.

6. In supervision

A final note regarding the Socratic method is that it can be as useful in supervision as it is in therapy. All the arguments for using it as a therapeutic tool stand when using it as supervisory tool: it enhances learning, fosters collaboration, tests hypotheses. (See Chapter 19 on supervision and CBT.)

When do we use Socratic enquiry?

A Socratic question is not the only 'good' question in CBT. Therapists have many tasks: establishing a collaborative relationship, gathering information, deriving a formulation, skills training, and so on. Different forms of question can yield different results, which can be useful at various points in therapy in achieving various goals. For example, information gathering might sometimes be best achieved through direct questions (e.g. 'Are you currently working?'), while establishing a warm and empathic relationship might merit a leading question (e.g. 'You seem distressed – is this too upsetting for you?')

Whatever type of question we choose, Beck et al. (1979) advise: 'Questions must be carefully timed and phrased so as to help the patient recognize and consider his notions reflectively – to weigh his thoughts with objectivity,' and they warn that a client: 'may feel he is being cross-examined or that he is being attacked if questions are used to "trap" him into contradicting himself.'

This reminds us that a good Socratic question is asked in the context of a good therapeutic relationship. Your aim is to communicate warmth, empathy and a non-judgemental attitude, whilst minimising client angst and hopelessness, so as to facilitate engagement, lateral thinking, creativity and recall. A client should feel that his perspective is interesting rather than 'wrong', and that his exploration of new possibilities will be valued and considered, rather than negatively judged. Clients need both the knowledge *and the confidence* to answer a question.

How is it done?

There is a common misconception that the effective cognitive therapist operates like a slick courtroom lawyer who never asks a question unless he knows the answer and, with two or three brilliant questions, reveals the 'truth'. It is interesting, therefore, that Beck has described the television detective Columbo as his role model. The gentle inquisitive style of the television hero – never pushy or omniscient – reflects a respectful and genuine enquiry. This attitude is crucial to 'good' Socratic questioning.

The style and purpose of Socratic questioning in cognitive therapy was most thoughtfully reviewed by Padesky (1993). She highlighted the important difference between using Socratic questions to *change minds* and using them to *guide discovery*. In summary, she argued that the therapist who 'changes minds' illustrates that the client's thoughts are illogical, while the therapist who 'guides discovery' reveals new possibilities. She argued that genuine curiosity was key to achieving the latter. Teasdale (1996), commenting on Padesky's view, has suggested that, at a psychological level, 'changing minds' invalidates specific thoughts or meanings, while 'guiding discovery' creates alternative mental frameworks. Thus, the cognitive therapist should strive to guide discovery not only by adopting a position of curiosity but also one of humility. Humility enables us to anticipate that we might learn from the client, rather than assuming that we always have (or should have) the answer. In this way, we can avoid falling into the 'changing minds' trap.

Metaphor and analogy can aid Socratic questioning. Each encourages your client to imagine a parallel situation so that the focus is temporarily shifted from his own view. By doing so, the strong emotion of the personal situation is tempered and the client may be able to think more productively. Clients can be encouraged to develop their own metaphors to help them discover more about their problems and solutions. For example:

> *You say that it feels as if you have a pigeonhole in your mind that collects and stores all the hurt and betrayal from the past. What would it mean if you also had a pigeonhole that collected memories of good relationships?*
> *How might we begin to build a pigeonhole for the positive memories?*
> *How might we try to ensure that you checked that pigeonhole regularly?*

Examining analogies can also prompt the client to stand aside from his own situation and consider a parallel one. For example, a question like: 'How would you advise your son, if he faced a similar dilemma?' can shift the client into a more hopeful and practical mindset which enables him to begin to generate new ideas for coping. Similarly, questions such as: 'How might a friend view the situation?' or 'How might a detective go about collecting evidence?' can help the client step into another 'mind set' and view things differently.

The skill of Socratic questioning is one that might come more naturally if you do not try too hard. In many social interactions you formulate hypotheses and ask questions which facilitate but don't lead and which permit flexibility and genuine responses. For example, imagine a man walking into a party and being greeted by an attractive, warm and friendly woman. He hypothesises: '*She is interested in me.*' His questions follow a line that enables him to collect information to support or refute his hypothesis and gives the other person an opportunity to feed back her intentions in greeting him:

> *Hello, I'm Billy – a friend of the host. And you?*

Depending on the responses that he gets, he might gauge the woman's romantic interest and ask further questions to clarify her interest and intentions. For example:

> *The band here is excellent, and local – do you ever go out and listen to them?*

Alternatively, he might discreetly realise that his initial hypothesis was not valid and he might revise it. For example:

> *She is a member of the host's family and is helping the party run smoothly. She is polite and sociable rather than interested in a date with me.* (Adapted from Westen, 1996.)

Downward arrowing

You might begin a line of enquiry with questions like:

> *Just how did you feel?*
> *What was going through your mind at the time?*

Such questions help clients focus on relevant cognitions and should be paced and phrased so that the client never feels interrogated, but rather that the therapist is taking genuine interest. The 'downward arrow' technique is an approach that is used to help clients 'unpack' or analyse further the meaning of unhelpful or distressing cognitions. The initial line of enquiry might be followed by further questions that help the client gently tease out the personal relevance of a thought or an image – questions such as:

> *I wonder what seems so bad about that?*
> *In your view, what does that mean?*
> *What does that say about you?*
> *What would that mean about your life/your future?*
> *What would others think of you?*
> *How would you label that?*
> *Can you describe the worst thing that could happen?*

Through such questions, you and your client can discover more about the belief system relating to a particular problem. These beliefs can then be examined and tested using cognitive challenging and behavioural experiment. You may also find out about more positive beliefs, such as: 'On the whole, people seem to like me' or, 'If I put in the effort, I can get things done' – beliefs which can enhance progress. For example, someone who believes himself likeable and capable is likely to engage well with you, can probably take on quite challenging social assignments and would be motivated to engage in homework tasks.

Through the downward arrow, the client's fundamental belief system is often revealed. This is sometimes referred to as 'the bottom line' (Fennell, 1999), although it is often more akin to a 'bottom triangle', comprising the elements of Beck et al.'s (1979) cognitive triad: beliefs about the self, others and the world, and the future. These elements relate to each other, and finding yourself going round the triangle is often an indication that the 'bottom line' has been reached:

Therapist:	*…and what might that say about you?*	
Client:	*That I am bad.*	*(Self)*
T:	*…and what would that mean to you?*	
C:	*That no one is going to want to know me.*	*(Others)*
T:	*…and if that were the case, what would that mean to you?*	
C:	*That I will always be alone and miserable.*	*(Future)*

In trying to determine whether or not the bottom line has been reached, ask yourself: 'Would anyone feel the way my client does if they held this view and believed it as much as he does?' If your answer is 'Yes', then you have probably uncovered a core belief.

It can take several sessions before the core-belief system is revealed, and sometimes it is simply not accessible. In fact, it is not always necessary to reach the bottom line (or triangle) in order to carry out effective CBT, and much productive work can be carried out with the rules and assumptions associated with core beliefs. However, there can be advantages in uncovering core beliefs. First, an understanding of core beliefs can aid a client in understanding persistent vulnerabilities: '*It's no wonder that I have no social confidence and am depressed if I feel bad and undesirable.*' Second identifying core beliefs paves the way for schema-focused work, *if necessary*, as core beliefs are a key component of many schemata (see Chapter 17).

There is always a danger that if you have a strong belief in a hypothesis you may use the downward-arrow technique simply to pursue its confirmation (to 'change minds'). It is crucial to remember that however well informed we might be, we are sometimes wrong. A great strength of Socratic dialogue, provided that it is coupled with curiosity and humility, is that it can lead us to conclusions that we did not anticipate. A useful rule of thumb when using the technique is to devise questions that might *refute* your hypothesis. When you think that you have confirmed your hypothesis, ask another question or two which is designed to disprove your theory. This both helps you refute an incorrect hypothesis and also guards against being too narrow in focus.

Stages in Socratic questioning

Padesky (1996) has defined four stages in Socratic questioning. These are the stages of:

1. Concrete questioning: structured, information-gathering questions which begin to inform your hypotheses about the client's difficulties. For example:

   How long have you felt low in your mood?
   How often do you binge?

2. Empathic listening: careful, non-judgemental attention both to what the client is saying and to how it is said. The client can communicate a great deal through tone of voice or facial expression, which can further impact on your hypotheses and influence subsequent questions.

3. Summarizing: feeding back a synopsis in order to check hypotheses, clarify information or reiterate a point. For example:

   You say that you have felt depressed for the past three months, but that for several years you have felt rather low.

   You seem to be saying that you probably binge every evening, but you are sometimes unsure whether or not you have actually binged.

4. Synthesising or analysing questions: these encourage either the development and expansion of an idea or a theme (synthesising); or the refinement of key information (analysing). For example:

   When we review the past few years, your lowest points seem to be: when you split up from Paul; after the birth of Karen; when you feel that your marriage is not going well. Is there anything that links these events? (Synthesising)

   Although there are many circumstances in which you binge, on what evenings are you most likely to? (Analysing)

Socratic enquiry helps the client review relevant evidence as widely as possible. You are more likely to obtain this 'bigger picture' by maintaining curiosity and not being too constrained by a hypothesis; and by continually asking 'and is there anything else?' If you get bound by rigid expectations, then you might terminate your enquiry before a wide enough data base has been uncovered. Consider the following example of different ways of approaching Jon, an anxious and miserable 14-year-old referred to the school psychologist because of poor performance in some subjects.

Approach 1: The psychologist asked about Jon's schoolwork and concluded that the issue was indeed study-related. She hypothesised that Jon was experiencing specific academic difficulties and her questions were focused on this hypothesis:

> *Tell me more about the subjects that you're not doing so well in …*
> *Maths and physics: have you always struggled with these topics? …*
> *So maths and physics have always been difficult for you, and now it's even harder to keep up. [Summary] …*
> *If a friend of yours was struggling with a subject, what would you suggest in order to help him out?*

In this way, the therapist efficiently progressed to her target of developing more efficient studying strategies.

Approach 2: This time the psychologist developed the hypothesis that Jon was experiencing specific academic difficulties and initially asked similar questions. However, she followed these focused questions with an exploratory enquiry:

> *I can probably help you with your study technique, and we'll talk through some of the strategies later – but first, I was wondering if there is there anything else on your mind when you find yourself struggling in class.*

It then transpired that Jon felt judged by the maths and physics teacher, Mr Smith. The psychologist focused her enquiry, finding out more about the relationship with the teacher. It became clear that Jon struggled in class because he felt especially anxious and self-conscious with this particular teacher. The psychologist then constructed a new hypothesis, that Jon had specific interpersonal difficulties with Mr Smith. Again she asked more exploratory questions ascertaining the nature of their relationship:

> *How do you imagine Mr Smith views you? What goes through your mind?*

Jon then revealed that he believed that this particularly conventional and religious teacher was blaming him for his parents' impending separation. Jon blamed himself for his parent's marital problems and felt guilty, even sinful.

The formulation was now quite different from the initial hypothesis. Jon was insecure and distressed because his parents were going to separate. Increasingly, he felt responsible for this, but he also felt isolated and could not discuss it with his parents. Shame inhibited him from sharing his troubles with his friends. He soldiered on. In lessons with Mr Smith, however, he felt judged and was reminded of his guilt. This interfered with his ability to perform in the class.

Having too narrow a focus is not necessarily a therapeutic disaster, as the limitations of the intervention will become apparent and you can reformulate. However, there are advantages to building the bigger picture as early as possible, as it communicates empathy – the therapist really 'gets it'– and this can inspire hope. Also, the formulation will be better informed and will lead to more relevant interventions or more sensitive prioritisation of issues.

Cautious and compassionate Socratic enquiry

A skilled therapist can become increasingly adept at 'unpacking' cognitions and identifying key, fundamental beliefs. However, this can become anti-therapeutic if you become overly focused on getting to the bottom of a problem without empathic pacing, a practice that has been called 'psycho-bulldozing'. It can leave the client feeling that you are insensitive and can result in your missing opportunities to teach the client about the role and management of cognitions. There is useful material to be worked with en route to the 'bottom line', and it can help the therapeutic dialogue if exploration is sensitively paced and punctuated by summaries.

Below is the case example of Neil, a depressed, 30-year-old divorced man who, despite an impressive academic background, had never remained employed for more than a few weeks. He tended to start jobs with great hope and enthusiasm but never sustained them. He was well defended emotionally and tended to minimise his emotional responses, often appearing rather superior and arrogant. However, the downward-arrow procedure distressed him unless it was paced very carefully. Because of this fragility, his therapist did not proceed directly down to the bottom line. In such cases, it is helpful to ask:

Is it alright for me to continue with these questions?
Do you need a bit of a break? Let me know if you do.

Clients like Neil may have spent a long time trying to avoid the pain that is provoked by a core belief, and a therapist must not underestimate the fear and distress that uncovering it might elicit. In summary, this is the course that his therapist followed:

Therapist:	*Why did you give up the project?*
Client:	*I was not good enough.*
T:	*And that means?*
C:	*There was no point. I have to be the best, or else I've achieved nothing.*
T:	*Can you tell me more about the importance of being the best?*
C:	*If I'm not superior, I'm wasting my time*
T:	*What is so bad about wasting time?*
C:	*Time wasting is failure.*

T:	Let's imagine that you did waste time and you felt like a failure. What would that mean to you?
C:	If one is a failure, one is pathetic.
T:	Are you able to tell me what that means to you personally?

At this point, Neil revealed a core belief about himself. Before this, however, many assumptions, ripe for further exploration, had been revealed. The assumptions that Neil disclosed gave opportunities to address thinking biases; to look at the pros and cons of holding a particular assumption; to construct vicious circles explaining the maintenance of the assumptions; to look at evidence for and against them; to challenge beliefs; to set up behavioural experiments; and to introduce techniques such as continuum work (see Chapter 8 for descriptions of cognitive techniques). For example, the statement: '*There was no point. I have to be the best, or else I've achieved nothing*', gave an opportunity to highlight dichotomous thinking and unrelenting high standards and to explore the behavioural, emotional and occupational consequences of having such thoughts.

When Neil disclosed his painful core belief, he was tearful and it was clearly a brave and difficult thing for him to say. His worst fear was that he would be revealed as the 'candy floss' that he believed he was. As it was not obvious why this might be so upsetting, the therapist asked him to describe a person who was 'candy floss'. He reported that this was his family's term for the most despicable sort of character: soft, vulnerable and sensitive. As he elaborated, he completed the triangle when he said that 'candy floss' people end up despised, rejected and lonely. Interestingly, as he said this, he became less upset. The words 'soft, vulnerable, sensitive, despised, rejected and lonely' did not provoke the emotion that was triggered by 'candy floss'. This is a reminder of the importance of uncovering the idiosyncratic meaning for the client: the word or phrase that carries the distress and helps him make sense of the problem.

It might seem obvious, but the tone you use when posing Socratic questions will communicate messages to the client. Consider the commonly used downward-arrow phrase: 'What is so bad about that?' If delivered in a brusque manner, a client might infer that you are suggesting that he is making a fuss about nothing, thus compromising the therapeutic relationship. If you pose the question in a gentle, inquisitive manner, perhaps prefaced with '*This might sound like a silly question, but …*', then it is more likely that the client will feel able to respond without fear of being criticised or judged. Gilbert (2005) has studied the role of the 'compassionate voice' in cognitive therapy and argues for the advantages of clients developing a compassionate inner voice. You can be a good role model for promoting this voice. By using phrasing and a tone of voice that communicate support and non-judgement, you are leading by example.

Socratic questions and self-help

Ultimately, clients must become both Socrates and his pupil. They need to stand back, review and develop new perspectives. An invaluable aid in learning to do this is the daily thought record (DTR) (see Chapter 8). This record of key events guides the user through the stages of identifying key emotions/cognitions, exploring the validity of the cognitions and then synthesising a new perspective. With rehearsal, this procedure can become second nature.

Some authors have produced annotated DTRs that prompt the user with salient Socratic questions at each stage in the log's completion (Greenberger and Padesky, 1995; Gilbert, 2005). For example:

What is going through my mind and how much do I believe it?
What supports this?
What contradicts my conclusions?
How might someone else view this situation?
What would I advise someone else?
What evidence is there to support alternatives?
What thinking biases can I identify?
How does my thinking help or hinder my achieving my goals?
What effect would believing an alternative have?
What's the worst thing that could happen?
How would I cope?
Can the problem situation be changed?
What can I do differently?
How can I check this out?

Others have produced lists of key questions for clients to use as prompts (Fennell, 1989), and clients can be encouraged to keep their own log of questions which have been particularly productive for them, such as:

What line of enquiry has helped me in the past?
What do I imagine a therapist asking at this point?

Problems when using Socratic questions

Here are some of the more common difficulties in Socratic questioning, with suggestions for managing them.

1. The client cannot access the key thoughts or images in the session

Encourage clients to record relevant cognitions at or near the time of the problem occurring. It can also be useful to discuss a recent experience, using imagery or role play if necessary, in order to evoke the emotional state related to key cognitions: stronger emotions are likely to make relevant cognitions more accessible. As suggested in Chapter 8, it is also helpful to look out for clear changes in emotions within the session, as these can reflect 'hot cognitions' which might be relevant, and which can be explored very close to the event.

2. The client is avoidant of distressing cognitions

A good starting point is working on your therapeutic relationship. Discover what your client needs in order to feel 'safe' and try to identify his fears. Take things slowly and make clear the rationale for unpacking cognitions. Encourage exploration of affect (How do you feel emotionally?) and/or sensation (How are you feeling in your body?). Be aware of the client who invalidates key cognitions as they emerge in order to avoid experiencing the 'hot thought': '. . . *but I know that is silly*', '. . . *although I am sure that I'll be fine*', '. . . *but that doesn't upset me.*' Acknowledge this pattern and try to uncover the client's fears about staying with an emotionally laden thought or image. Such fears will have to be addressed before you can move on in therapy. Behavioural experiments (see Chapter 9) can help your client test out the negative predictions underlying the avoidance.

3. Key cognitions are fleeting in nature

Some clients find it difficult to identify important cognitions because they seem inaccessible or 'slippery' and easily forgotten (see Chapter 8 for a full description of the nature of cognitions). You can help by encouraging clients to carry a DTR or thought log so that they are better able to catch key cognitions as they arise. Again, attend to mood shifts in session, as these can give insights into thoughts and images relating to the problem. And again, try evoking a recent experience so that the relevant cognitions might be accessible in the session.

4. Crucial meanings are held in a non-verbal form

When clients seem to be unable to express key meanings verbally, try exploring sensations: 'Where is it in your body, does it have a shape or texture? Colour? Temperature?' 'Can you picture it in your mind's eye?' This might provoke descriptions such as: 'It's red and it is a hard ball in the pit of my stomach' and 'It's a soft, purple sensation, that gradually spreads throughout my body.' Accept that some non-verbal meanings are going to be metaphorical rather than literal, for example: '. . . *my body is full of red, boiling jelly with metal shards cutting through my skin*' [pain] or '*I feel nausea, and a black tidal wave inside me is pulling me away*' [disgust]. It is still possible to incorporate this information into a formulation and to work towards developing alternative meanings.

5. The client invalidates new perspectives

Some clients seem to collaborate with guided discovery only to dismiss new conclusions with a 'yes but'. This might indicate that you have slipped into giving advice rather than posing Socratic questions: self-monitor to see if this is true. Alternatively, the client might need to substantiate his new perspective by engaging in behavioural change. Behavioural experiments are effective in achieving 'gut-level' changes in beliefs. 'Yes buts' might also indicate that a robust belief system is at work, which can be revealed through further Socratic enquiry. Sometimes such a belief system reflects a problem schema and schema-change interventions might be appropriate (see Chapter 17).

6. The therapist questions without direction, or in an unfruitful direction

Although the importance of curiosity has been stressed, Socratic enquiry should remain hypothesis-led and guided by a formulation. Without this underpinning, you might well collect information but be unable to structure it, struggle to remain focused on the presenting problem or find yourself in blind alleys, hopping from one topic to another without getting closure on any. In each of these situations, referring back to a working formulation will provide the necessary structure to make sense of new information and to keep you on track. Having said that, blind alleys can sometimes provide useful further information about a problem, provided there exists a conceptualisation that can incorporate it.

7. The therapist lectures

It is possible to lapse into lecturing, particularly if you have a clear idea of where you want to lead the client or what you think the client should know. The need for collaboration, curiosity and humility have already been discussed, and session tapes can help you identify when you lose these qualities. It is important to identify a lecturing style early on, before the therapeutic relationship is put at risk. On occasion, you might find yourself unable to sustain a 'good' Socratic style because of tensions in the therapeutic alliance. It is important to keep the therapeutic relationship in mind and to address problems swiftly.

8. The therapist explores but does not synthesise and draw conclusions

Although the importance of curiosity has been stressed, Socratic enquiry should remain hypothesis-led and should aim to inform the formulation. Therapy should be regularly punctuated by summaries which draw together information and which link it to the case conceptualisation. You might need to devise a reminder to summarise regularly, or to ask a client to synthesise new conclusions, say every ten minutes. It can be helpful to ensure that a copy of the working formulation is always accessible for reference – better still, actually on view during the sessions, so that it is constantly there as a structure to help both you and your client.

Cognitive Techniques

Introduction

This chapter introduces a range of cognitive techniques which are used to review and reappraise thoughts and images relevant to the client's problems. As with any of the interventions used in CBT, their use must be part of a coherent plan and they should not be introduced without a genuine rationale. Even when following an empirically based treatment protocol, it is essential that you continue to ask: 'Is this an appropriate intervention for this client at this time? Given the formulation of this person's problem, can I justify introducing this intervention?'

Remember that not all distressing thoughts are inappropriate. For example, a client might attend a session feeling tremendously upset because he has to take exams in a day or two and is not fully prepared. He might believe that his chances of failure are high, and that he will therefore lose a postgraduate position. These thoughts *might* be realistic, and if so, your job is not to introduce unrealistic positive thoughts. Instead you might help him use problem-solving skills to minimise the likelihood of failing, or you might help him look at the *meaning* of losing his position and how he could cope with it.

Timing is also important. For example, Beck et al. (1979) caution that, 'many depressed patients are so preoccupied with negative thoughts that further introspection may aggravate the perseverating ideation' (p. 142). Beck and colleagues advocate focusing on goal-directed activities that change the negative estimates of capability, before directly focusing on the cognitions associated with depression. We are again reminded that a cognitive intervention is part of a larger cognitive-behavioural treatment plan.

Presenting a rationale for cognitive work

Clients need to understand the rationale for cognitive work, because you will often be asking them to focus on the most frightening, most depressing or most shameful aspects of their lives and on cognitions that have been ignored or avoided for years. Fundamentally, that rationale rests on your client's individual formulation, which demonstrates the links between his individual thoughts and his feelings and behaviours. Your client also needs to know that you are not going to require him immediately to share the worst thing he can imagine and to dwell on it. Although he is likely to need to face difficult-to-tolerate thoughts or images eventually, this will be in the context of a respectful, collaborative relationship and will be taken at an appropriate pace.

It might sound obvious, but it is also important that your client understands what is meant by the term 'cognition'. Beck et al. (1979) describe a cognition as 'either a thought or a visual image that you may not be very aware of unless you focus your attention on it' (p. 147). This description nicely introduces the idea that cognitions can be ephemeral and that the client might have to work quite hard to identify them. It also reminds us that images are as relevant as thoughts.

You must guard against your clients identifying unhelpful cognitions as 'wrong' or 'irrational'. This can feed into negative beliefs such as 'I'm stupid' or 'I always get things wrong'. Even if a belief is currently unhelpful, that might not always have been the case. For example, the firmly held belief that 'It is dangerous to trust' might have been a helpful and adaptive belief for an abused child, even though in adulthood and away from an abusive environment, it might be unhelpful.

Identifying cognitions

A fundamental task of the cognitive therapist is helping clients observe and record the thoughts and the images that run through their minds. It is not uncommon for clients to struggle with this, sometimes reporting that they do not have cognitions or confusing thoughts and feelings. You cannot assume that you can leap in with a couple of well-constructed Socratic questions and discover the cognitive essence of a problem. Your first step will be to help your client learn to 'catch' relevant reactions, to discriminate between feelings and thoughts and then to link them so that feelings become a cue for cognitive exploration. Table 8.1 gives some examples.

As the table illustrates, a good general rule for distinguishing thoughts and feelings is that feelings can often be expressed – at least crudely – by a single word, whilst cognitions demand a lengthier description. Clients often find it easier to notice feelings first, rather than thoughts or images. This can provide a useful stepping stone for accessing thoughts. If you encourage clients to begin by focusing on feelings, exploring and elaborating them, you will find that they tend to 'drift' into identifying cognitions.

Cl: *I don't know what was going through my mind.*
Th: *Can you see yourself back there? Get a picture in your mind's eye?*

Table 8.1   Feelings with commonly associated thoughts

Feeling	Thoughts
Depressed	I am hopeless; the future is bleak and I can't change it.
Anxious	I am in danger. Something bad is going to happen. I cannot cope.
Angry	I have been disrespected. People are mean to me and I won't stand for it.

Cl: Yes.

Th: *Can you now try to remember how you felt at the time?*

Cl: *Yes – physically sick. Tense.*

Th: *Stay with that image and those feelings and see if you can tell me more about your experiences that evening.*

Cl: *Well I felt really tense, anxious. My heart was pounding and I was scared, really scared that he would come back and hit me. I thought that he was going to attack me.*

In this example, the client first tapped into his physical state, then identified his mood and finally clarified his cognitions. Clients who have difficulty in verbalising cognitions, or claim to have none, can often be helped by focusing on physical sensations.

'Hot' cognitions

Beck et al. (1979) emphasised the importance of capturing *hot cognitions*, i.e. those which seem to be most directly linked to the client's most significant emotions. Cognitive interventions will be most effective if they target these hot thoughts. When trying to uncover these key cognitions, it can be helpful to ask: 'Would anyone feel as bad as my client does if they had that thought and believed it as much as he does?' If the answer is 'Yes' then you might well have found a hot cognition.

Diary-keeping

Records of cognitions are most likely to be accurate if they are made at or near the time the thought occurs. The records can range from simply counting thoughts, perhaps using a golf counter, to quite complicated thought and/or image records (see Chapter 5).

When we ask clients to keep records, we are not simply asking them to collect useful examples: we are also introducing a basic skills training exercise. We are encouraging the client to tune into relevant thoughts, stand back from them and, ultimately, evaluate them. That is a challenging task: just as foreign vocabularies are best learnt by repeatedly writing them out, or piano-playing skills developed by playing arduous scales over and over, this fundamental skill of cognitive therapy is learnt through practice.

Such records are not filled in at random. You should ask clients to record cognitions at times that will cast light on their problems. For example, the following might prompt thought recording:

- The urge to self-harm
- A depression rating of more than 6 on a 10-point scale
- An urge to check
- A binge-eating episode
- A self-consciousness rating of more than 6 on a 10-point scale
- A contentment rating of more than 6 on a 10-point scale
- Specific times of the day
- Particular environments.

Remember that such records need to be tailored to the individual. Although some excellent thought-record templates exist (Beck et al., 1979; Greenberger and Padesky, 1995), and an example of a thought record is given below (Figure 8.1), it is crucial that any record you use reflects (a) the client's ability to gather information and (b) the type of information that you and the client need in order to understand the problem better. It is also crucial that the client fully understands *how* to fill in the record. It is advisable to carry out a dry run in the session, when the client can reflect on a recent example and fill in the form with you.

Below you will meet Judy, who struggled with feelings of panic; this is her therapist's introduction to the assignment of diary-keeping:

It seems that we have two tasks immediately ahead of us. First, we need to get a better idea of just what is happening for you when you feel so uncomfortable – and keeping this record of events at the time will help us to do this. Second, you described the panicky feelings coming out of the blue and we agreed that we need a way to help you become more aware of what triggers the panic, and feel less overwhelmed by it – tracking your feelings using the diary should help you start to achieve that. But remember, this is our first trial, so we are experimenting really – see how it goes and we'll see if we have to modify the task at all. Why don't we run through it now, using the example that you described at the beginning of the session and see how that would fit in?

Figure 8.2 is an example of Judy's first thought record, which she completed as a between-session assignment. This was drawn up with her in the session where it had become clear that she could readily articulate her thoughts if she 'anchored' herself in the way she was feeling. For her, reflecting on her feelings served as a powerful reminder of the time at which she was distressed, and her thoughts became accessible. She was also able to evaluate her experiences and put a rating on the severity of both her feelings and thoughts. Had she been very apprehensive about using a rating scale, the thought record could have omitted this and incorporated it later when she felt more confident. Had she not been able to access thoughts, the record could have comprised columns 1 and 2, with column 3 being introduced as she became able to catch her automatic thoughts. Had she found the thought of diary-keeping overwhelming, she could have started by simply keeping a tally of the times she felt panicky each day. If clients are to gain confidence in therapy, it is important that they feel capable of the task that you negotiate with them.

The advantage of rating the degree of physical, emotional or cognitive response was that it helped Judy develop a better ability to discriminate key reactions and it provided a method of quantifying changes over time.

It goes without saying that you must review clients' diaries. Although some clients find diary-keeping fascinating, to others it can be tedious or distressing. Without a sense of achievement or progress, the client can easily stop completing records, so it is particularly important that you pay attention to them. Record-keeping is another therapeutic task that you should set up as 'no lose'. If the records are completed, then you have useful

Date and time	Emotion(s)	Thoughts
	What emotion(s) did you feel? Also rate the strength of the feelings from 0 (none at all) to 100 (the strongest possible)	What went through your mind?. Also rate how much you believed the thoughts *at the time you had them*, from 0% (did not believe at all) to 100% (absolutely sure they were true)

Figure 8.1 Example of a daily thought record (DTR)

1. Situation	2. Feelings	3. Thoughts
Tuesday lunch break: I was at the check out, waiting to pay. It was a large shop with many customers milling around.	Hot and a bit jittery. Light-headed and it felt as though my heart was racing. **Discomfort:** 8/10	I am going to have a panic attack and all these eyes are upon me. They will think I'm crazy. **Belief in these thoughts:** Panic attack 7/10 Everyone is looking 9/10 Think I'm crazy 9/10
Saturday morning: filling car with petrol	Nervous, dizzy, hot, shaking **Discomfort** 9/10	People on the forecourt are noticing that I'm a wreck. I am a wreck. I'm going to have a panic attack. **Belief in these thoughts:** People looking 9/10 Panic attack 9/10

Figure 8.2   Judy's first thought record

information to work with; if the records are not fully completed, then you can explore and work with what stopped them.

Turning questions into statements

It is not uncommon for clients' thoughts to take the form of questions. These can be in the form of rhetorical questions such as: 'Why am I so stupid?', or they might be phrased as 'What if' questions: 'What if I fail?', 'What if it's bad news?' Questions do not lend themselves to reappraisal and testing, so they should be turned into clear statements, with associated belief ratings. Thus, 'Why am I so stupid?' might lead to your asking 'How would you answer that?' The reply might be: 'Why am I so stupid? Because it's my nature, it's what I am. I am very stupid.' Now we have identified a definite statement that can be rated for belief and eventually challenged.

Similarly, you can explore 'What if' questions with an enquiry such as: 'What if that did happen – what would be the consequences?'; or, 'What would be the worst answer to that question?' A typical reply might be, 'If I failed, then I would never get a proper job and I wouldn't be able to make a living', or 'If it's bad news then I won't be able to cope – I'll go to pieces.' You can then explore these statements further in order to make sense of your client's fears.

Sometimes clients are reluctant to answer their own questions because the question feels less distressing to them than the statement that lies beneath it. This is a form of cognitive and/or emotional avoidance and, it goes without saying, unpacking this distress needs to be done sensitively.

Enhancing recall through imagery and role play

Not everyone is as able as Judy to catch their automatic thoughts. For others, it may be helpful to use evocative interventions such as imagery and role play in order to recreate a key situation vividly enough for thoughts to become accessible. Possibly the most widely used technique is asking a client to recount a recent experience of the problem in detail (or, if the focus is a unique experience, to recall that specific event). The vividness of recall can be enhanced by asking questions such as: 'Try to see this in your mind's eye: can you describe to me what is going on around you, what you felt, how you reacted?'

Judy had some difficulty describing her experiences verbally when she first came to therapy, and imagery helped her to appreciate why she experienced such powerful reactions.

Th: *Can you recall when you last felt panicky?*

Judy: *In the waiting room here, just a few minutes ago.*

Th: *Perhaps we could explore that further. Can you imagine yourself back there for a moment? Can you see it in your mind's eye?*

Judy: *Yes.*

Th: *If you can, stay with that image and tell me as much as you can about the way you felt. Just focus on that feeling of being there and observe as many of your reactions as you can. See if you can describe things in the present tense.*

Judy: *I am okay but then another person joins me. I feel myself flush and I feel tense and a bit dizzy. I'm thinking that she reckons I'm a lunatic sitting in this place. I get hotter and I know that she's looking at me and I know that I am going to make a spectacle of myself. Then she gets up and walks out – she can't bear to be in the same room as such a weirdo.*

Judy was asked to describe things in the present to increase the chance of catching the hot thoughts that make sense of her panicky feelings. Earlier in the session it had been difficult to target the hot thoughts because Judy rationalised them with phrases like: '… I thought that she was looking at me but she might have been thinking of something else.' Although this is a useful perspective for challenging her NATs, at this point it does not help us explain Judy's extreme reaction.

Imagery work can be a particularly important intervention with adult survivors of trauma who suffer from flashbacks or other unwanted mental intrusions, whether this relates to adult or childhood trauma (for example, Ehlers & Clark, 2000; Arntz & Weetman, 1999).

Imagery need not be confined to visual images: 'visceral' or 'felt sense' reactions can also be relevant. For example, a woman with restrictive anorexia might not be able to put into words why she cannot eat an objectively small amount of food. However, questions prompting her to imagine eating might reveal that, although her mind was aware that she would not gain weight, she experienced a rapid sensation of bloating and feeling fat that made eating aversive.

The use of imagery can be a very powerful technique, and for some it can be *too* evocative. For example, a person who has been through a very traumatic experience might not be able to use imagery without being overwhelmed by traumatic memories. In such cases, it can be prudent to gradually work towards using imagery. The first step would be to discuss the reasons for considering imagery work, then to establish the client's resilience. An alternative to using the first-person, present tense for recall is to begin with a third-person account in the past tense and gradually move towards capturing a more personal 'here and now' account as the client becomes more robust (Resick and Schnicke, 1993).

Role play can also be used to evoke key feelings and cognitions. Judy had recently felt panicky when she tried to pay for petrol, but she could not pinpoint what made sense of these feelings. When her therapist took on the role of cashier and Judy re-enacted the scene, she was able to identify the thoughts: 'I'm going to do something that makes me look stupid; she's going to think that I'm stupid; everyone will see that I am stupid.'

Using mood shifts during sessions

Therapy sessions can be a useful source of hot cognitions, so monitor changes in the client's position, facial expression and tone of voice that may indicate negative thoughts.

Judy, for example, presented as a jovial and humorous character, but there were moments in sessions when her face grew serious and her posture stiffened. Asking: 'What happened just then? Did something go through your mind?' frequently resulted in her identifying frightening hot cognitions. In Judy's case, it was crucial to catch them quickly, as otherwise she tended to trivialise and dismiss them.

Another client, John, had the occasional brief moment of losing concentration and disengaging from the session. Asking what happened at this time revealed that he was experiencing flashbacks of a childhood trauma.

Opportunities for catching hot cognitions during a session are significantly enhanced when using imagery, role play or in-session behavioural experiments.

Clarifying global statements

Negative thoughts are often not very specific, which makes them hard to evaluate. In such cases, it will be useful to ask your client to specify what he means by a particular word or expression. Take, for example, a student who states: 'I am useless'. This invites questions such as:

> *In what way 'useless'?*
> *What sort of things do you feel that you cannot accomplish?*
> *What sort of things can you achieve?*
> *How do you assess your success?*

By reflecting on such questions, this student might realise that, rather than being globally 'useless', she is achieving in many areas of study but has not been able to achieve her rather high standards in English language.

In response to someone who believes: 'It always goes badly for me', you might ask such questions as:

Can you tell me more about the incident that prompted that thought?
What else ran through your mind at that time?
Have there been times when, in a similar situation, things have gone smoothly?

It might become apparent that, although this person felt profoundly pessimistic, things were going reasonably well in many ways. However, with regard to relationships, he did seem to have difficulties, and each time a problem arose, he was beset by memories of other failed relationships and felt overwhelmingly negative.

Distraction

This very basic cognitive strategy rests on the idea that we can only concentrate on one thing at a time, so that if we focus on something neutral or pleasant, we can avoid getting caught up with negative thoughts and urges. This can serve two purposes:

1. Breaking unhelpful cycles of thought that might otherwise result in negative moods, increasing preoccupation.
2. Changing attitudes towards negative cognitions. Instead of getting caught up in them, distraction can help the client achieve distance from them and to see them as 'just thoughts' rather than convincing truths about themselves or the world.

Research suggests that distraction is more effective than thought suppression in reducing unwanted cognitions (Wenzlaff & Bates, 2000) and that it is more effective when clients devise a positive distraction which is unrelated to their unwanted thoughts (Wenzlaff et al., 1991). Thus, thinking about something positive is more distracting than trying *not* to think about something negative. Distraction techniques that clients can practise include:

*   Physical exercise: This is particularly useful when a person is so preoccupied that it is very difficult to come up with mental challenges, or with children and adolescents who might be more physically predisposed than psychologically minded. Physical activities can be overt (e.g. going for a run), discrete (e.g. pelvic-floor exercises), challenging (e.g. difficult yoga exercises), mundane (e.g. household chores). The important thing is that they are engaging for your client.
*   Refocusing: This usually means paying attention to the external environment, and objects or people within it, rather than one's internal world. Clients are encouraged to describe to themselves qualities of the surroundings such as shapes, colours, smells, sounds, textures and so on. The more detailed the description, the more distracting the task will be.
*   Mental exercise: Mental exercises include counting backwards in 7s from 1,000, or reciting a poem, or reconstructing in detail a favourite piece of music or scene from a movie. Another effective distraction is a self-created mental image of a place where your client would like to be – a beach, a beautiful garden, a ski slope – whatever appeals to your client. In order for this to be an effective distraction, the image should be attractive, filled with sensory details and well rehearsed.
*   Simply counting the thoughts can help clients get a distance from them – not paying any other attention to them, just counting them, with the same attitude one might have to spotting how many pigeons there are in one's neighbourhood:'There's one …and another.…oh, and there's another'!

When devising distraction exercises with clients, remember:

- The exercise must suit the client: mental arithmetic and a beach image would not be effective for a person who hates mathematics and is allergic to sand. Your client will only be able to engage in distraction if the exercise is readily accessible and attractive. Build on your client's interests and strengths.
- Clients might need several techniques to use under different circumstances. For example, tasks need to be discrete in a public place, whilst in private they can be more overt; physical strategies can be most accessible when highly preoccupied, and mental strategies more usable at lower levels of preoccupation.
- Distraction can be used in behavioural experiments to test predictions such as: 'I can't stop thinking about x,' or, 'I cannot get the worries out of my head.'
- Distraction will be counter-productive if used as a long-term avoidance or safety behaviour.
- Distraction does not fundamentally change the unhelpful cognition, so is not usually a good strategy for the long term: hence the need for the other strategies described in the remainder of this chapter.

Identifying cognitive biases

As clients become adept at identifying relevant images or thoughts, they can usefully learn to look out for cognitive biases (see Table 8.2). These are exaggerations of thinking errors that we all experience from time to time when we are emotionally aroused. They reflect normal fluctuations in our information-processing styles, and they only become a problem when the bias is chronic or too extreme. For example, the first bias in the list below is 'dichotomous thinking' – an 'all or nothing' style which fails to incorporate the possibility of shades of grey. This type of information-processing style increases with stress levels (Kischka et al., 1996), and, indeed, it may be appropriate when we are under threat. If a car swerves towards mine, it is appropriate that I think 'life or death!' and swiftly manoeuvre out of the way – it would be inappropriate for me to lose valuable time considering the many less dramatic options. If, however, this was my habitual way of responding to moderately stressful situations, I would probably very quickly develop an anxiety-related problem.

Table 8.2 contains four groups of cognitive biases: extreme thinking, selective attention, relying on intuition and self-reproach. Note that the specific categories within these groups are not mutually exclusive.

Judy was given a copy of the summary of cognitive biases in Table 8.2, and she smiled and said: 'I can achieve something: I can tick all these!' Like many clients, she readily recognised a tendency towards cognitive biases or 'crooked thinking' (Butler and Hope, 1995). Her amusement at realising this helped her to stand back or 'decentre' (see next section), and, as it was difficult to maintain a fearful 'mindset' when she laughed, she was much better placed to see alternative, more positive possibilities. Table 8.3 (on p. 117) is an extract from her diaries, identifying the cognitive biases pertinent to her.

Table 8.2   Common cognitive biases

1	Extreme thinking
Dichotomous thinking	Viewing things in 'all or nothing' terms without appreciating the spectrum of possibilities between the two extremes. Things are 'good *or* bad', 'successes *or* failures'. Typically, the negative category is more readily endorsed. Example: ***Nothing is ever going to go right for me. I can trust no one. I am a total failure.***
Unrealistic expectations/ high standards	Using exaggerated performance criteria for self and/or others. Using 'shoulds', 'oughts', and 'musts'. Examples: ***Unless it's the best, it doesn't count. I should get full marks. Mistakes are unacceptable. I must please everyone***.
Catastrophisation	Predicting the very worst, sometimes from a benign starting point. This may happen very rapidly so that it seems that the client has immediately leapt to the most awful conclusion. Examples: ***I made a mistake; my boss will be furious; my contract won't be renewed; I will lose my job; I will lose my home; my wife will leave me; I will be poor and lonely***.
2	Selective attention
Over-generalisation	Seeing a single negative event as an indication that *every*thing is negative. Examples: ***I have failed an interview – I'll never get a job. This relationship is going badly – I'll never find a partner. She let me down – I can trust no one.***
Mental filter	Picking out and dwelling on a single negative feature without reference to other, more benign events. Focusing on the one thing that went badly in an otherwise successful day. Forgetting achievements and compliments but dwelling on a single criticism. Example: ***One of my exam marks is low – this is terrible – I'm really no good at anything.***
Disqualifying the positive	Rejecting, down-grading or dismissing as unimportant any positive event. Examples: ***He is only saying that to be nice. She is probably trying to get something out of me. This was a small achievement – others do better.***
Magnification and minimisation	Exaggerating the importance of negative events and under-estimating the importance of positive events. Example: ***What a mess up I made of that deal. Yes, I got the terms that my boss wanted but I didn't handle it well.***
3	Relying on intuition
Jumping to conclusions	Making interpretations in the absence of facts to support them. Examples of jumping to conclusions divide into two categories: i. Mind-reading: ***I just know that they were all laughing at me behind their friendly faces.*** ii. Fortune-telling: ***when I meet him, he will dislike me.***
Emotional reasoning	Assuming that feelings reflect fact. Examples: ***I feel as though I can't cope, so I'll have a couple of drinks first. I feel awful when I get angry, so it must be bad to get angry. I feel unattractive so I must be.***

Table 8.2   *(Continued)*

4		Self-reproach
Taking things personally		Assuming responsibility if something (perceived as) bad happens. Examples: ***The dinner party did not go well: it was my fault for being tense and cause others to feel uncomfortable. Two students left my lecture early: I must have been boring.***
Self-blame or self-criticism		Seeing oneself as the cause of a bad event or criticising oneself without cause. Examples: ***I feel ill: I must have brought it on myself.*** ***I can't catch up with my work: I must be stupid and lazy.***
Name-calling		Attaching harsh and demeaning names to oneself. Examples: ***Idiot! I am so stupid. What a fool I am.***

In summary, so far we have outlined the need to help the client:

- understand and identify cognitions, using Socratic enquiry coupled with imagery and role play if necessary.
- record cognitions.
- link situation, thoughts and feelings, so that you are both able to say: 'It's no wonder that …'.
- use distraction for short-term coping.
- become aware of cognitive biases.

Now your client is ready to appraise the automatic thoughts and images that are giving rise to problems.

Appraising automatic thoughts and images

Taking a step back, or 'decentring'

Beck et al. (1979) described decentring, or the ability to view cognitions as mental events rather than as expressions of reality, as a core component of cognitive therapy. Rather than buying into the emotionally laden content of a cognition, the client stands back and observes it, recognising that a thought is an opinion, not necessarily a fact. Decentring is also termed 'meta-cognitive awareness', meta-cognition being defined as any knowledge or process that is involved in the appraisal, monitoring or control of cognition (Flavell, 1979). Clients may be able to achieve this if they are able to label the thinking *process* rather than dwell on the content. You might hear phrases like: 'There's my all-or-nothing thinking again', or 'I'm catastrophising here,' or 'It's my abandonment fear kicking in.' Such responses indicate that your client has achieved meta-cognitive awareness. The past decade has seen decentring playing an important part in CBT since the introduction of mindfulness meditation into CBT practice – see Chapter 17, which reviews such developments.

Understanding the origin of a cognition

When clients are learning to view their cognitions objectively, they can easily label themselves as 'stupid' or 'silly'. You need to let them appreciate why it makes sense that they

Table 8.3   Judy's extreme thinking

Thoughts	Cognitive Biases
I am going to have a panic attack and all eyes are upon me.	Catastrophising Jumping to conclusions
They will think I'm crazy.	Mind-reading
People on the forecourt are noticing that:	Mind-reading
I'm a wreck.	
I am a wreck.	Name-calling
I'm going to have a panic attack.	Catastrophising

have such unhelpful thoughts, or why it made sense at some time in their lives. One way of doing this is to ask them to consider the evidence or experience that supports a hot thought. Problem cognitions rarely, if ever, come out of the blue. There is usually an earlier experience that renders them understandable. Aim to help your client recognise that there might be a reason why they drew certain conclusions, so that they can begin to conclude: 'It's no wonder that . . .' or 'I can understand why . . .' when they review their automatic thoughts.

The student in the earlier example, who believed 'I am useless', had attended a very demanding school where the children had been encouraged to excel in all subjects. Holding high standards at that time both helped her to cope with the culture of the school and, because she was academically able, to achieve and gain a great deal of reinforcement for doing so. Later, at a different time in her life, these same high standards proved stress-provoking and often unattainable, thus promoting the belief 'I am useless'.

The young man who felt that 'It always goes badly for me', had indeed had a number of broken relationships, so it was understandable that he might be pessimistic. He believed that he could protect himself against major hurt by anticipating the break-up of a relationship, and so it was not surprising that he had maintained a pessimism within relationships. However, he now discovered that this attitude diminished his enjoyment of, and commitment to, relationships.

Below are Judy's explanations for her automatic thoughts. When appraising 'They will think I'm crazy', the therapist asked:

Can you recall a time when you did not feel like this, when getting panicky did not make you assume that others would think that you were crazy?
Can you recall when you began to hold this view?
Can you be more specific?

It transpired that Judy's attitude had very much been influenced by her mother telling er not to show emotions publicly, lest people assume that she was weak and strange. (See T. le 8.4.)

Table 8.4 Judy's automatic thoughts

3. Thoughts	4. Why I draw this conclusion
I am going to have a panic attack and all these eyes are upon me. They will think I'm crazy. **Belief in these thoughts**: Panic attack 7/10 Everyone is looking 9/10 Think I'm scrazy 9/10	I can understand why I anticipate having a panic attack – I've had them in the past. It is no wonder that I think everyone is looking at me because that is what it *feels* like. If I saw someone having an panic attack and I didn't know what was happening, I might think they were weird, especially as my mother has indoctrinated me over the years.
People on the forecourt are noticing that I'm a wreck: I am a wreck. I'm going to have a panic attack. **Belief in these thoughts**: People looking 9/10. Panic attack 9/10.	It is no wonder that I think everyone is looking at me because that is what it *feels* like. No wonder I *feel* like a wreck, I'm so distressed. I can understand why I anticipate having a panic attack – I've had them in the past

Weighing up pros and cons

In cognitive therapy, we look for the reasons why an unhelpful reaction or response makes sense. This is one reason why we ask clients to consider the *advantages* of holding cognitions that are, ultimately, not in their best interests. It is useful to consider the pros (and cons) both in the short and the long terms, as some cognitions might only have advantages in the short or in the long term. For example, permission-giving thoughts like 'I'm useless so I might as well give up' give a good deal of short-term relief but may compound problems in the long term; in eating disorders, the thought: 'I am not giving into the hunger pangs' might create short-term discomfort but can confer a sense of control in the long term. The advantages of negative thoughts are often perceived protection, e.g. 'If I anticipate having a panic attack, it won't take me by surprise' or 'If I expect the worst from people, I won't be disappointed.' When these assumptions are considered, the resilience of a negative thought becomes more understandable. Although there may be a grain of truth in such assumptions, it is often exaggerated.

Next, we enquire about the *disadvantages* of having the thoughts or beliefs (again in both the short and long terms). This step helps loosen up a conviction and can sometimes improve the client's motivation to change. In Judy's case, the disadvantages of predicting that she would have a panic attack were that she increased her physical discomfort, she made it more likely that she would have a panic attack, and she was always miserable in challenging situations. The disadvantages of assuming that others judged her negatively were again that she was always distressed in challenging situations, and she was inhibited about doing many things that she might otherwise enjoy.

Sometimes referred to as a cost–benefit analysis, balancing pros and cons is an approach that encourages a widening of the client's perspectives, which is particularly useful when it is not possible to conclude whether something is true or not but, rather, what is most useful on balance.

Another related strategy is 'reframing', which facilitates the development of a wider perspective by requiring reflection about the other side of the coin. For example, the ambitious father who spends most of his evenings at work is missing out on time with his children: thus, the uncomfortable prospect of reducing his workload could be reframed as making more time for his children. The extreme dieter who is striving for control of her weight and shape might realise that she is losing control in her social and work life through her focus on dietary restriction: she could reframe the apparent benefit of dieting as the enemy of her work and social life.

When exploring the pros and cons, you should, of course, be non-confrontational, empathic and collaborative. Such exercises are aimed at enabling and enlightening your client rather than illustrating how wrong they might be. Carried out in this way, this approach is a particularly helpful one in engaging and motivating clients who are ambivalent about change (Miller and Rollnick, 1991).

What is the worst thing and how would you cope?

Although a difficult prospect for the client, 'What is the very worst thing that could happen?' can be an extremely valuable question. It prompts the client to name the fear (which cannot otherwise be tackled), and the answer clarifies the ultimate problem that needs to be resolved. The corollary question, '. . . and how would you cope?' then kicks off the process of problem-solving. When a solution for the worst-case scenario has been devised, it often takes the heat out of catastrophic predictions.

Judy's worst fear was that she would have a panic attack in public. The enquiry about how she might cope was, in itself, a revelation to her. She had never contemplated coping, and she had never viewed the panic attack as having an end – her projected fear had been too vague. Now, with the help of her therapist, she was able to generate some ideas for managing the situation: she would try to find somewhere discreet, she would try to talk herself through the experience, and she would rehearse a statement to explain her predicament to anyone who approached her. Through this exercise, Judy became more confident that she could cope with the worst outcome, and it frightened her less.

Identifying cognitive themes

It is usual to find themes of either process or content running through thought records. Process themes might include dichotomous thinking as the most prominent form of information-processing, or withdrawal as the reaction to perceived interpersonal conflict. Themes reflecting the content of cognitions might include rejection, threat, shame, anger and so on. Some themes are more common in particular disorders: for example, the need for control and perfectionism is often associated with eating disorders, loss and shame with depression, threat with anxiety disorders. The value of identifying such themes is twofold.

First, recurrent themes can be challenged thematically – that is, developing a repeatable challenge for addressing the pervasive shame or recurring sense of loss. This is much more efficient than having to generate a novel challenge for each problem cognition. Second, themes can give insight into pervasive core beliefs. Studying Judy's diaries revealed two dominant themes, one concerning the self (I am crazy) and one focusing on others (They are judgemental). Managing the latter core belief is illustrated below in this chapter.

In summary, by now the client has learnt to:

- identify unhelpful cognitions;
- identify cognitive biases;
- stand back from them and view them as unhelpful but understandable thoughts;
- question their utility and validity;
- consider the worst outcome, and develop solutions for this.

Thus, your client can develop a more objective and wider perspective on his negative thoughts and beliefs.

Developing new perspectives

The groundwork done, now it is time to reflect on problem cognitions and reappraise them: the notion of there being alternative, less-discomforting possibilities can be entertained. There are several techniques that can help your client develop new perspectives.

Reviewing evidence for and against: getting a balanced view

Armed with an enhanced perspective on the situation, your client can now review what supports, and what undermines, his initial conclusion. This is illustrated in the example from Judy's diary below (Table 8.5), where she reviews why it is understandable that she draws a negative conclusion but then balances this with evidence that does not support that conclusion.

A useful strategy for gathering evidence to inform a more balanced view is an elaboration of decentring, in which you ask your clients to distance themselves from the thought or image enough to imagine a number of different perspectives. This can be prompted by questions such as:

If someone you cared about had this thought, what would you want to say to them?
If someone who cared about you knew that you had this thought, what might they   say to you?
If someone you knew had this thought, or struggled with this situation, what might they say to theselves? How might they cope?
Have you been in similar situations and not felt or thought like this?
Have there been times when you have felt like this and coped?
When you are away from this situation, what do you think?
If you 'fast-forwarded' five years from now, how would you view this situation?

Table 8.5   Judy's diary

3. Thoughts	4. Why I draw this conclusion	5. What conflicts with my conclusion
I am going to have a panic attack and all these eyes are upon me. They will think I'm crazy. **Belief in these thoughts**: Panic attack 7/10 Everyone is looking 9/10 Think I'm crazy 9/10.	I can understand why I anticipate having a panic attack – I've had them in the past. It is no wonder that I think everyone is looking at me because that is what it *feels* like. My mother has indoctrinated me over the years.	Feeling as though I will panic does not mean that I will – I've felt like this and not had a panic attack before. I know that calming myself helps. Even if I panic it won't last for ever and I have some ways of coping. **Belief in this thought 9/10** My *feeling* that others are looking does not make it fact. **Belief in this thought 10/10** Even if I had a panic attack, it is unlikely that people would think that I was crazy. Even if they did so what? They don't know me. **Belief in this thought 10/10**
People on the forecourt are noticing that I'm a wreck: I am a wreck. I'm going to have a panic attack. **Belief in these thoughts**: People looking 9/10 Panic attack 9/10.	It is no wonder that I think everyone is looking at me because that is what it *feels* like. No wonder I *feel* like a wreck, I'm so distressed. I can understand why I anticipate having a panic attack – I've had them in the past.	My *feeling* that others are looking or that I am a wreck does not make it fact. **Belief in this thought 10/10** Feeling as though I will panic does not mean that I will – I've felt like this and not had a panic attack before. I'm only here for a minute or two, so I'll be fine. **Belief in this thought 9/10**

This sort of prompting can elicit coping statements and even plans for action. When Judy was asked these questions in therapy, she readily generated helpful self-statements (see her diary, Table 8.5) as well as strategies such as self-calming. She remembered that a friend had once told her that adopting a Pilates posture helped her to combat stress. Judy had attended Pilates classes but then neglected her practice – she decided to revise them and found it helpful. This reminds us that familiar, comfortable strategies that have validity for the client will be most readily adopted and maintained.

Addressing cognitive biases

Dichotomous thinking is readily moderated by introducing the notion that there is a *range* of possibilities between the extremes. Encourage your clients to generate examples that illustrate different points on the spectrum. Judy tended to assume that she felt calm *or* panicky (which meant that a panic attack was imminent). She was later able to recognise different stages in growing panicky:

1	2	3	4	5	6	7	8	9	10
Calm		Mildly nervous				Panicky but not			Panic
		Might even be excitement				actually panicking			attack

This exercise was helpful in several ways. It illustrated the range of possibilities, which curbed her tendency to jump to the most catastrophic conclusion; it provided reassurance that she could feel panicky without progressing to a panic attack; and, in discussing the variations in her feelings of nervousness, she realised that she might misinterpret excitement as the warning signs of panic.

Selective attention to the worst possibilities can be tackled by prompting your client to search for other possibilities by asking himself questions such as:

> *Are there other ways of looking at this?*
> *Do I have strengths / assets / resources that I am ignoring?*
> *What other possibilities might a friend see?*
> *Am I missing something?*

Relying on intuition can be curbed if a client accepts that feelings or unsubstantiated beliefs do not necessarily represent reality. There are many examples that clients can consider to support this idea: for example, children's belief in Father Christmas does not mean he is real; our ancestors' belief that the world was flat did not stop it being spherical; an emotionally deprived child's feeling that he is bad does not mean he IS bad; and 'feeling ten feet tall today' does not mean that you need to duck when you go through doors! Whether mind-reading, fortune-telling or assuming that a feeling reflects a fact, clients can begin to question the truth of such intuitions and ask '… is this supported by some evidence?' or '… do I have experiences which suggest that this is the case?' or simply '… how do I know?' One simple strategy that Judy worked out for herself was *asking* friends what they felt or what they intended by a remark, instead of ruminating on what her friends *might* feel or think.

Self-reproach can be very undermining – just as it would be if severe criticism came from someone else. However, it can be moderated by prompting the client to ask questions such as:

> *Is it really so bad?*
> *Am I blaming myself unfairly? Who else might be responsible?*
> *Whose voice is this? … and are they an expert?*

When Judy reflected on her thought: 'They will think that I am crazy', she realised that this was the voice of her mother, who restricted emotional expression within the family and warned her children that others would view them as weak and silly if they were not in control of their emotions. She quickly realised that her mother was not an expert in social psychology and that her view was extremely unhelpful. As a result, Judy was able to dismiss this thought altogether.

Another client, Jeff, had for years blamed himself for being bullied at school, assuming that he had brought it on himself by being 'geeky and weak'. In therapy, he considered who (or what) else might have contributed to the bullying. He came up with quite a list: the particular girls and boys who chose to pick on him; the schoolteachers who did not notice or help him when he tried to ask for help; the school itself because it supported a culture of brutality amongst the children; his parents for never offering him a shoulder to cry on. By the time he had compiled this list, his own role in the bullying had diminished and he was more compassionate towards himself.

Using imagery and role play

As in identifying thoughts, the more experiential strategies of imagery and role play can be invaluable in shifting unhelpful cognitions.

Rehearsal of new possibilities can be carried out in imagination: for example, Judy imagining herself walking into a public area and feeling calm; a person with a fear of flying imagining himself travelling by plane.

Transforming problem images can also be helpful. The horror of recurrent nightmares can be diminished through repeatedly imagining a new ending (Krakow et al., 2001); traumatic memories can be rescripted (Layden et al., 1993); a hostile self-image can be transformed into a compassionate one (Gilbert, 2005).

As well as constructing a new narrative and/or visual image, you can help clients to overcome problem images via image manipulation techniques such as imagining the unwanted image on a TV screen and then manipulating the image by changing the volume, fading the picture and so on or 'morphing' characters in the image to make it more tolerable. Judy had an unhelpful image of people looking at her judgementally, but she reduced its impact by shrinking the onlookers in her imagination.

An approach recently advocated by Padesky (2005) is to ask clients to create a vision of how they would *like* things to be. They are encouraged to make this mental picture as vivid as possible and to identify the assumptions that they would have to live by in order to realise the vision. For example, Judy's image might be walking into a public area and feeling calm. The assumptions that would facilitate this might be 'People who know me accept that I am basically OK, and strangers are not that interested in me.' Behavioural experiments can then further establish confidence in the new image.

Imagery can be incorporated into role play. Beck et al. (1979) described client and therapist taking on critical and supportive inner voices and creating a dialogue to strengthen the supportive voice; Padesky (1994) described using 'historical role play' or 'psychodrama' to rework earlier unhelpful interactions; Gilbert (2005) advocated using the Gestalt two-chair technique as the basis for building up a compassionate self and diminishing the inner critic. When Judy realised just how unhelpful her mother's influence had been, she felt less anxious, but she was angry and these feelings were uncomfortable. She resolved them in session by first imagining her mother in an empty chair. She then 'told' her mother of the consequences of her mother's attitudes and the anger that she now felt. In this exercise, she also agreed to take on the role of her mother responding to Judy's statement. In this role, 'her mother' explained that she had been trying to protect Judy from being victimised as she once was. This was the first time that Judy had considered her mother's perspective and it helped her to dissipate her anger.

Drawing new conclusions

At this point, the client has viewed the original negative thoughts from several angles, has built up a wider perspective and has entertained new possibilities. Now it is time to condense this awareness into pithy, memorable and *believable* new conclusions. Judy's new conclusions are shown in Table 8.6, along with her ratings of belief in each statement.

Table 8.6   Judy's conclusions

6. New conclusion
Feeling as though I will panic does not mean that I will have a panic attack – I've felt like this before and not had a panic attack.
Belief in this conclusion 8/10
My *feeling* that others are looking does not make it fact.
Belief in this conclusion 10/10. (I *know* this but I don't know if I will feel confident when I'm outside).
Even if I had a panic attack, it is unlikely that people would think that I was crazy. Even if they did, so what? They don't know me.
Belief in this conclusion 10/10

It is interesting that the predominantly intellectual task of analysing her cognitions had resulted in her developing a 100% belief that feeling was not fact, and that it was unlikely that others would think that she was crazy; however, her belief that the sensations of panic would not lead to a panic attack was not so compelling (80%). It is also interesting that, although she developed a new belief ('My *feeling* that others are looking does not make it fact'), which she believed in the session, she was not wholly confident that she would be so convinced when in a challenging situation.

This reminds us that therapy does not end with the intellectual achievement of shifting beliefs. There is also scope for behavioural testing both to establish their veracity and to consolidate realistic new attitudes.

In summary, in reappraising cognitions and developing new perspectives, we encourage clients to:

- de-centre, standing back from the emotionally loaded cognition;
- address cognitive biases through tackling extreme thinking, selective attention, relying on intuition and self-reproach;
- use imagery and role play to enhance this process;
- draw new conclusions, which can then be reality-tested.

Testing automatic thoughts and images

The importance of testing out new possibilities or perspectives is elaborated in Chapter 10, which describes the role of behavioural experiments in cognitive therapy. The validity of a new cognition is usually enhanced if it stands up to 'road testing'. In addition, the new possibility will be more memorable if a client takes it from a conceptualisation through to an active experience.

Judy decided to 'research' her new conclusions by collecting information that could confirm or disconfirm them. With regard to her new prediction that the feelings of panic would not necessarily herald a panic attack, she planned to provoke panicky feelings and record what happened. She had begun to appreciate that panic was not 'all or nothing', and she devised a scale of her panicky sensations to assess degree of change. She also planned to involve her friends in her research, for example by asking them to observe the reactions of others and to note if Judy was the subject of much attention.(See Table 8.7.)

Modifying core beliefs

There is some confusion in the literature between 'core beliefs' and 'schemata'. The terms are not interchangeable, because a schema is generally considered to be more complex than a core belief, but the latter can reflect a 'summary label' for a schema. For example, the core belief 'I am stupid' is a useful cognitive label that summarises the thoughts, feelings and physical sensations associated with believing that one is truly stupid. This section will focus on core beliefs; in Chapter 17 we discuss the nature of schemata.

We should not assume that core beliefs are always difficult to identify, as they may be expressed as automatic thoughts. In the earlier example, the student readily identified 'I am useless' as a key cognition which might well be a core belief. If a core belief is not expressed as an automatic thought, then guided discovery and the downward arrow technique can often uncover it.

It is also important not to assume that a core belief is necessarily resistant to change. Judy rapidly shifted a long-standing core belief ('I am crazy') when she realised that her mother was not an expert in character analysis; it is not uncommon for core beliefs to shift as a

Table 8.7   Judy researches her new conclusions

6 New conclusion	7. Researching it
Feeling as though I will have a panic attack does not mean that I will – I've felt like this before and not had a panic attack.	I will go into difficult situations and instead of focusing on the times that I feel panicky and anticipating having a panic attack, I'll start to note the times that I move along my 'panic' spectrum without having a panic attack.
My *feeling* that others are looking does not make it fact.	I will ask my friends to check this out for me when I feel panicky. Then I'll see if there is justification for my thought.
Even if I had a panic attack, it is unlikely that people would think think that I was crazy. Even if they did, so what? They don't know me.	I will ask friends if they think that panicking people are crazy people. However, since I realised where this thought came from, it really does not bother me anymore.

consequence of therapy that targets automatic cognitions (Beck et al., 1979). However, some belief systems are more rigid, and augmented techniques have developed to specifically target them (see Chapter 16).

In their self-help book, Greenberger and Padesky (1995) describe a collection of strategies (see Box 1) aimed at modifying *core beliefs*. They emphasise that, because core beliefs can be robust, these strategies are likely to have to be used over several months before they have significant impact. They therefore need to be negotiated carefully with clients so as to avoid disappointment and demoralisation. The strategies include:

BOX 1

- Carrying out behavioural experiments to test the predictions of core beliefs.
- Recording evidence that a core belief is not 100% true.
- Identifying alternative (more helpful) core beliefs.
- Carrying out behavioural experiments to test the predictions of *alternative* core beliefs.
- Recording evidence that supports an alternative core belief.
- Historical tests of new core beliefs.
- Rating confidence in new core beliefs.

Judy felt that she needed to work on a core belief that others were judgemental. The behavioural experiment that she devised was a data-collection task. Over several weeks she asked friends what they thought of people who had made a mistake or appeared 'silly' to her. Her prediction was that her friends would judge others badly. Table 8.8 shows two examples from her record.

Judy then made a log of such findings, which she headed: 'Evidence that my belief is not 100% true.' On occasion, her opinion polls supported her prediction, but she was now able to put this in the context of the data that showed that this was not true *100%* of the time. Of course, you might discover that your client's prediction is repeatedly confirmed. If so, it merits investigation: is your client only mixing with like-minded people? Is your client filtering out disconfirming evidence before it can reach the page? You might consider that schema-focused techniques could be more helpful in such instances (see Chapter 16).

Table 8.8   Judy collects data

Incident	Incident	what happened
Harry got rather drunk at the department party and was over talkative and danced too much.	Others will think that he is a weak and silly person and his authority in the department will be undermined.	Sue thought that it was endearing to see him a bit tipsy; Ron said that he was pleased that Harry could let his hair down because he was too serious about his work.
A middle-aged woman in the street fell and became quite hysterical even though she did not seem to be hurt.	Sue (who was with me) would think that she was silly and attention-seeking.	Sue said that she felt concern for this woman and wondered if she had injured herself internally.

Judy, however, reviewed the responses that she had collected, and concluded:

It is true that some people are judgemental, but most of my friends are actually quite gener-ous in their opinions of others. Furthermore, I find that those who are more judgemental are not amongst the friends that I most value and I tended to dismiss their harsh appraisals.

She was then able to identify a new core belief: *Some are harshly judgemental but most people are generous.* At first, she believed this at a 50% level. In order to strengthen this new, more comfortable belief, she began a log of evidence that supported her new belief. She was diligent in maintaining this log, and after a few weeks, her rating of her conviction in the new statement was 98%.

In order to strengthen a new core belief that is counter-balancing a less helpful one from the past, Greenberger and Padesky (1995) advocate the use of a historical test of the new core belief, where the client reviews his life history looking for evidence which is consistent with the new belief. Although Judy was already successful in developing a new fundamen-tal belief, she was keen to reinforce her progress and chose to carry out this retrospective analysis. She was, by now, much more able to 'see' the evidence that supported her new belief and found that many of her earlier experiences strengthened her new conviction.

A final note

This has been a lengthy chapter because the cognitive techniques of CBT are both crucial and diverse. In summary, we have seen that there are techniques for observing key cogni-tions and for distracting from them; and for analysing them and synthesising new possibil-ities that can be evaluated through behavioural experiment. We have seen that interventions can be verbal, visual and experiential and can focus on cognitive content or cognitive process. Although the predominant focus is in the present, we have also seen that some cognitive strategies review or even confront the past.

Despite this diversity, your aim as a therapist is simple: to help your client achieve enduring respite from the distress caused by problem cognitions. The art of this is in knowing which of the cognitive approaches will be most relevant at a particular time. Achieving this relies on the skill of formulating your client's situation and keeping that formulation dynamic.

Problems

The client seems to avoid exploring cognitions

Sometimes a client simply wants to talk about feelings. In some such cases, supportive counselling may be more appropriate. For instance, when people are first coming to terms with loss or trauma and realising the scope of their problems, they may need time just to talk them through. Alternatively, clients who are ambivalent about therapy might need 'motivational interviewing' (Miller & Rollnick, 1991).

Other clients focus on exploring feelings because they believe that this is the best use of therapy, so they may need to be reminded of the method and strengths of CBT and how this approach differs from other forms of psychotherapy.

Avoidance of exploring cognitions also occurs when clients are afraid of the content of their thinking. Sometimes the cognitions are never properly reviewed, but the sufferer has a sense of their awfulness or is reluctant to revisit cognitions that trigger other painful feelings – the shame of the sexual-abuse victim, for example. In these instances, you need to invest time in creating a sense of safety in the sessions that will allow your client gradually to confront distressing thoughts.

The cognitions are so fleeting that the client has difficulty identifying them

This is not uncommon and it is helpful if the client realises that it is in the nature of NATs to be elusive. Behavioural experiments, done to provoke negative thoughts rather than to test them, can be useful in making the thoughts more obvious (see Chapter 9).

Some thoughts don't readily map onto language and are better described as a visceral 'felt sense' (Kennerley, 1996). For example, clients with body dysmorphic disorder might report 'feeling' disfigured, a person with OCD might describe 'feeling' dirty, or someone with disgust-based PTSD might 'feel' this physically. Such felt senses can be worked with, but most cognitions can be verbally articulated, given encouragement and time.

Challenging has little or no impact

In such cases, the first question you must ask yourself is: 'Is the focus of therapy correct?' This will require revisiting the formulation and revising it if necessary.

It is also important to check out with your client what keeps him believing the old thoughts, or what *stops* his believing new alternative thoughts. There may be pieces of evidence, safety behaviours or other blockages which have not been fully dealt with. Or you may not be focusing on the 'hot' thought. Behavioural experiments can often be critical in ensuring that new learning is felt at a gut level rather than just heard intellectually.

A final possibility is that the problem is driven by a particularly rigid and inflexible belief system and so a more schema-focused approach is called for.

Behavioural Experiments

At the 2004 conference of the European Association for Behavioural and Cognitive Therapies, there was a symposium entitled 'Where is the B in CBT?' This chapter will outline an answer to that question, i.e. the place of behavioural methods in current CBT. We shall focus on one specific area where behaviour change is crucial: *behavioural experiments* (BEs), a CBT strategy which can be used to great effect in most if not all problems. Another common behavioural technique in CBT, *activity scheduling*, is described in the chapter on depression (Chapter 12), because that is where it is most widely used.

What are BEs

The following discussion of BEs draws heavily on the recent volume devoted to the use of BEs in CBT, to which all three of the present authors contributed (Bennett-Levy et al., 2004). We shall adopt Bennett-Levy et al.'s operational definition of BEs:

> Behavioural experiments are planned experiential activities, based on experimentation or observation, which are undertaken by patients in or between cognitive therapy sessions. Their design is derived directly from a cognitive formulation of the problem, and their primary purpose is to obtain new information which may help to:
>
> - test the validity of the patients' existing beliefs about themselves, others, and the world;
> - construct and/or test new, more adaptive, beliefs;
> - contribute to the development and verification of the cognitive formulation.
>
> (Bennett-Levy et al., 2004, p. 8)

This means that BEs are designed, like experiments in science, to generate *evidence* that will help us decide what hypothesis is best supported. But instead of testing scientific theories, BEs in CBT are designed to gather evidence that will help patients test the predictions that follow from their unhelpful cognitions or to test elements in a formulation. Chapters 7 and 8 have already addressed verbal methods for exploring cognitions and expanding the range of evidence that the client considers. BEs offer us a way of taking this a step further, by exploring beliefs through action and observation rather than just through verbal discussion and by helping the client generate *new* evidence. BEs are therefore often used to follow up verbal discussion. Having explored a particular negative cognition and generated possible alternative views during a session, BEs may offer a useful way of testing out and consolidating these conclusions. They can help the client gather more cogent evidence as to whether the original negative cognition or the new alternative offers the best (most accurate or most helpful) view of a situation.

> *A client with social anxiety had the belief that he looked 'peculiar' (and that others would therefore disapprove of him). One piece of evidence for this belief was that he noticed when he went into the canteen at work that other people 'stared at' him. His response was to look down so as to avoid their gaze, sit and eat alone and focus closely on his plate. During CBT sessions, an alternative account was developed, namely that perhaps people tended to look at anyone who entered the canteen, because they were curious, rather than this behaviour being exclusive to him and due to his 'peculiarity' and, furthermore, that maybe his subsequent avoidance of looking at other people meant that he had no opportunity to observe whether this was true. This discussion led on to a BE designed to gather evidence about which account was most convincing. It was agreed that he would enter the canteen as usual but this time try to keep looking up and count roughly how many people looked at him. Then after he sat down, he would make an effort to continue looking around and to count how many people looked at anyone else who entered the canteen. He was able to do this and, somewhat to his surprise, found the new alternative belief amply supported. Some people in the canteen seemed to look up at anyone who entered, and there was no evidence that he attracted more curiosity than anyone else. He found this helpful in beginning to question the belief that he was 'peculiar'.*

> *Another client with social anxiety was worried about the consequences of blushing during social interactions. She believed that if she blushed, other people would be bound to make negative judgements about her: that she was silly, or abnormal. Although she had occasionally been teased about her blushing, no one had ever actually expressed a negative evaluation because of it, but she tended to dismiss this on the grounds that they were just being kind to her. This client found it helpful to do a survey experiment. A question about reactions to people blushing was carefully constructed so that both she and the therapist agreed that it was reasonably unbiased (i.e. not obviously expecting either negative or positive responses – for example, not starting off with 'Would you think badly of such a person?', but a more neutral 'Would blushing have any impact on your opinion of such a person?'). Then the therapist distributed the question sheet to a number of work colleagues and friends to collect their responses – for this client, it was important that the people surveyed did not know her and were therefore less likely to be 'kind' in their answers. She found that most people thought blushing was quite charming and that the worst anyone thought was that someone blushing might be anxious and that they would therefore tend to feel sympathetic.*

Behavioural experiments compared to behaviour therapy

BEs are derived from CBT's behavioural legacy, and some BEs may look like traditional behavioural methods such as exposure *in vivo* to anxiety-provoking situations. However, it is important to remember that the aims of, and the conceptual framework surrounding, BEs are quite different from traditional behavioural therapy. In the latter, the most common conceptual model is of *exposure* leading to *habituation*. To put it in very crude terms (with apologies to learning theorists, whose ideas are actually far more complex than this) the idea is that exposure to anxiety-provoking stimuli leads to the anxiety response gradually dying away as the person gets used to the situation. An analogy sometimes used is that if I suddenly make a loud noise, you will probably be startled, but if I repeatedly make a loud noise every 10 seconds for the next 10 minutes, then you will probably gradually stop being startled and react less.

In contrast to this model, BEs in CBT are quintessentially a *cognitive* strategy, explicitly aimed at generating information and/or testing out beliefs, not at promoting habituation of anxiety responses. If we consider the treatment of someone with agoraphobia and panic who fears supermarkets, both traditional behaviour therapy and CBT might suggest that it would be useful for the client to visit a supermarket, but the goals and thinking behind the strategy (and hence the exact procedure to be followed) would be quite different:

- Behavioural *exposure* would aim for the person to learn a new response to supermarkets, which would involve staying in the situation long enough (and repeating exposure often enough) for the anxiety response to die away. No particular attention would be paid to thoughts or beliefs; all that would be thought necessary is for a client to overcome his avoidance for long enough for habituation to occur. In order to assist this, exposure would usually be graduated, i.e. working up a hierarchy of increasing levels of anxiety, trying to make sure that he was not too anxious at any point (although there is also a form of exposure known as *flooding*, in which clients are exposed to the most fear-provoking situation from the beginning).

- If using a behavioural *experiment* within CBT, the visit to a supermarket would follow a cognitive understanding of the person's negative predictions about what might happen. The primary goal of the visit would be to help him test out these negative beliefs by seeing whether what he fears actually happens: does he actually collapse / die / pass out, or whatever it may be? His level of anxiety, although of course an important clinical concern, would not be the primary focus during the experiment – or at least not unless being anxious played a part in his negative beliefs (e.g. 'If I become very anxious I will lose control and go mad'). In the latter case, it might actually be important to an adequate BE that he *did* become very anxious, in order to test out this belief. Therefore, although it still might be clinically necessary to tackle the situation in a graded way, neither this nor repeated exposure is essential to a BE: the heart of the matter is simply to test out thoughts and beliefs as thoroughly and convincingly as possible, and this can sometimes happen with just one experiment.

Part of the appeal of BEs in CBT is that they offer a possible way of getting around a common problem in interventions that depend primarily on verbal methods, namely responses like, 'Well I can see intellectually that this is a more logical way of looking at it, but it still *feels* like my negative thought is true.' By testing out thoughts and beliefs in action, rather than just through words, BEs can help to develop a more 'gut feel' kind of learning. They are also useful in almost every kind of psychological problem, in contrast to exposure, which is focused on anxiety problems.

Types of behavioural experiment

We can usefully distinguish two dimensions along which BEs may vary: hypothesis-testing versus discovery BEs; and active versus observational BEs (Bennett-Levy et al., 2004). Putting these together, we have a diagram of possible BEs (Figure 9.1).

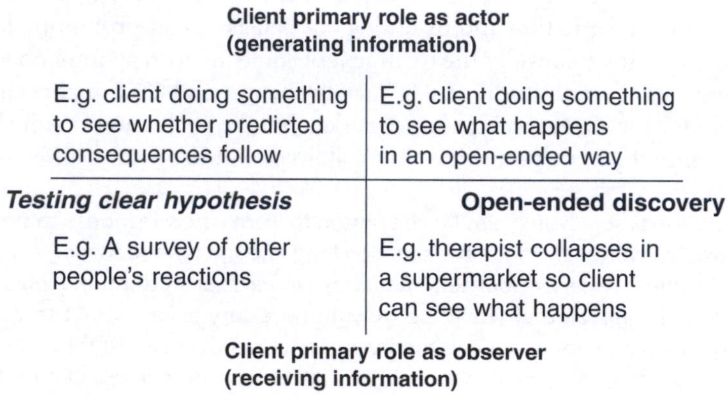

**Client primary role as actor
(generating information)**

E.g. client doing something to see whether predicted consequences follow	E.g. client doing something to see what happens in an open-ended way
Testing clear hypothesis	**Open-ended discovery**
E.g. A survey of other people's reactions	E.g. therapist collapses in a supermarket so client can see what happens

**Client primary role as observer
(receiving information)**

Figure 9.1   Types of behavioural experiment

Hypothesis-testing versus discovery

Hypothesis-testing BEs are perhaps the closest to the classical scientific experiment. In such experiments, we either start from one hypothesis, or from both of two relatively clear hypotheses – often known as Theory A and Theory B. Theory A is the client's initial belief or explanation, for example 'People look at me because I look peculiar.' Theory B is the new, alternative belief, often based on the CBT formulation or perhaps worked out during a CBT session between client and therapist, e.g. 'People look at *anyone* coming into a room, out of curiosity – there is nothing special about me.' When we can state at least one of these hypotheses reasonably clearly, then we have the necessary conditions for a BE in which the aim is to find some clear evidence bearing on the hypothesis. We may either test Theory A or Theory B alone (the question to be tested is then 'Does this theory correctly predict what happens in this situation?'); or we may compare the two theories to see which one works best in predicting the observed outcomes – as in the canteen experiment above. The aim is to find some predicted consequence of the hypothesis that is in principle observable so that the client can tell whether his prediction comes true.

Hypothesis-testing experiments are the most common, and often the most useful, but clients sometimes have no clear hypothesis to test, perhaps because they have not yet worked out a clear statement of their negative cognitions or because they can't yet even conceive of an alternative. In such cases it may be useful to do *discovery BEs*, aiming to explore in a more open-minded way 'What would happen if I did X?'. For example, 'What would happen if I were to talk a bit more openly about myself to other people? How would I feel? How would they react? Perhaps I can find out . . .'.

Active versus observational

The second distinction is between:

- BEs in which the client is an active participant, in the sense of going out and actively doing something to generate information – often something different to his usual behaviour.
- BEs in which the client is observing events or gathering already available evidence rather than actively doing something different.

The canteen experiment is an example of an active experiment; the blushing survey is an example of an observational experiment.

Observational experiments can include therapist modelling, where the client observes the therapist doing something, so that he can see what happens without too much 'risk' to himself:

For example, a client who fears collapsing in a supermarket might find it useful to observe what happens. After identifying what the client's negative predictions are, therapist and client can go to a supermarket together, the therapist can pretend to collapse, and the client can observe what actually happens.

Many other kinds of information-gathering are possible:

A client with social anxiety was worried about not having anything important or clever to say. He found it useful to observe how other people carry on conversations, which led to his realising that most ordinary conversations are pretty mundane, not necessarily containing profound topics or deep thoughts.

It may also be useful for the client to gather information from books or the Internet.

A client with claustrophobia found some detailed information on the Internet. About the risks of suffocation in confined spaces, including a calculation of how long one might survive in an airtight room!

Most classic behavioural experiments fall into the top left quadrant of Figure 9.1 (Theory A), but there are useful examples in the other quadrants as well. See Bennett-Levy et al. (2004) for a comprehensive collection. Using one or more of these approaches, the aim is to work out something the client can do, in or between sessions, that will help him generate or gather more evidence relevant to his negative cognitions.

Planning and implementing behavioural experiments

Planning

Careful planning is a crucial preliminary to most successful BEs. There are several essential components:

- Ensure that both you and the client clearly understand the purpose and rationale of the experiment and always plan experiments collaboratively. BEs should not be unilaterally assigned by the therapist in the last two minutes of a session, nor should they be done just because a protocol says you should be doing them! They should grow out of the session as a logical way to move things forward. Remember, it is desirable to involve the client in thinking about BEs and homework: 'Given what we've been discussing in this session, what do you think might be useful to take this further between now and the next session?'

- Particularly for hypothesis-testing experiments, spend time getting clear about what cognition(s) are to be tested and the client's negative predictions about what might happen. This step is crucial, because a BE aimed at a poorly defined cognition will rarely be effective. For example, your client may fear approaching a particular situation without safety behaviours, and his initial prediction may well be something vague, like 'It will be awful'. You are unlikely to be able to test this prediction, because it is not precisely defined. How can you or the client tell whether it is 'awful' or not? What exactly constitutes 'awful'? Furthermore, this kind of BE may indeed turn out to be 'awful', at least in the sense that the client feels anxious. It will usually be much better to work out a clear prediction such as, 'I will collapse' or 'People will laugh at me': something that (a) distinguishes between the belief to be tested and possible alternatives; and (b) can be developed into reasonably clear criteria that will enable both client and therapist to determine unambiguously whether it has happened.

- Having identified a clear cognition, have the client rate how strongly he believes it on a scale from 0–100% (0% Not at all, to 100% Absolutely certain it's true) to provide a baseline against which any change can be measured.

- Choose the best type of experiment to test the cognition, e.g. an active experiment or an observational experiment. Partly this decision will depend on what point the client has reached in shifting his thinking and how threatening the experiment appears to him. Observational BEs are often less threatening and therefore may be a useful first step before moving on to active BEs.

- Design BEs so that as far as possible they are 'no lose', i.e. whatever happens, the client will have gained something. If the experiment 'works' in the sense that negative predictions are not borne out, then that is useful; but equally if some part of the negative prediction is confirmed, that can still be useful if we have learned something and now need to think about what made that happen, which in turn can lead to further productive exploration and new BEs.

- For the same reason, try to be genuinely open-minded about the outcome of BEs. Do not approach them in a way that suggests to the client that you already know for sure what will happen. If the BE does not work out the way you predict, then the client may lose confidence in you and may also feel that he must have failed. It is much better to be genuinely curious: 'I really don't know for sure what will happen here, but maybe it won't be as bad as you fear – how about finding out?'

- Similarly, try to anticipate with the client what might be difficult or go wrong and then develop and rehearse strategies for coping with such setbacks. If you are doing a BE involving other's reactions, what will the client do if indeed he does get a negative response? If the BE involves a client with agoraphobia going into a supermarket alone, how will he cope if he does have a panic attack? BEs are much more likely to be helpful if you have considered such problems beforehand.
- Notwithstanding all of the above, do not ignore the potential for doing spontaneous BEs, prompted by something that has happened within a session. For example, when discussing with someone who fears cardiac problems the effects of a safety behaviour like avoiding exertion, it may be possible to suggest doing a BE right now – for example, running up and down the stairs a couple of times to see what happens. Sometimes your client may be more willing to try something on the spur of the moment than he would be if he has a week to worry about it. This obviously needs to be carefully done, and the client must be clear that he can refuse if he wants to, but it can be very productive.

The experiment itself

Experiments may be carried out by your client independently, for example as part of homework, or your client may carry them out with you – in session or outside in the real world. The latter in-vivo experiments can be very useful, both because you can support and encourage your client and because they offer invaluable opportunities for you to learn more about the problems: in-vivo BEs frequently generate previously unknown thoughts and beliefs, safety behaviours and so on. If you are accompanying your client, there are several things you can be aware of in order to increase the chances of a successful outcome; if your client is trying a BE alone, then you can make him aware of these factors:

- Encourage your client to be fully engaged in the situation rather than just 'going through the motions'. He needs to understand that usually if a BE does not result in any anxiety (for example, because he is distracting himself or not really pushing against his limits) then the BE is less likely to be useful.
- You and/or your client need to be continually monitoring his thoughts and emotions, both in order to be aware of any changes, whether positive or negative, and to be sure that the BE is going along the right lines. For example, it is unusual for a client to go through a BE without feeling at least some discomfort during it; if he remains completely unaffected, it would be wise to investigate whether he is subtly avoiding, or performing safety behaviours. On the other hand, if there is no positive change at all in the client's thoughts or emotional state during a BE, it may indicate that the cognitions have not really been touched, and it may be useful to think about taking it further, or doing something different.
- As noted above, BEs by their very nature are to some degree unpredictable, and the unexpected can and does happen. You and/or your client need to be flexible and ready to respond to unexpected events.

After the experiment

In order to make the most of a BE, it is important to take time to 'de-brief' and help the client reflect on what happened:

- First, you need to go through with the client what actually happened. What were his thoughts? How did he feel? Did events go as predicted or were there significant differences to his predictions? If so, what were they? Did he still use any safety behaviours to prevent some disaster (if so, it may be important to try again with reduced or eliminated safety behaviours)?
- Second, it is important to help the client reflect on the meaning of the BE. What does this tell him that he didn't know before (about himself, or others, or the world in general)? How can he make sense of what happened? Does it have any implications for how he might tackle similar situations in the future? Are there any follow-up BEs that might be useful to extend or generalise his conclusions? Finally, have the client re-rate his belief in the cognitions tested so that both of you can see whether there has been any change.

This post-experiment reflection can help the client gain the maximum possible value from the experiment and may also help reduce the risk of his devaluing the results of the experiment as old habits reassert themselves.

At the end of this chapter is a record sheet that you may find helpful for you and your client to record the planning and carrying out of BEs (Figure 9.1).

Common problems in behavioural experiments

BEs can be an extremely powerful way of changing cognitions and emotions, but, as noted above, their complexity and unpredictability also mean that there is plenty of scope for things to go in unexpected directions. Many of these risks can be avoided by careful planning and preparation, but this section gives some further ideas about how to cope with some common problems.

Therapist worries

It is important to recognise that therapists, as well as clients, may have worries about BEs. If these become too intense, you may communicate your doubts to your client and thus reinforce his fears. It is acceptable – maybe even desirable – for you sometimes to be pushing your own limits, for example, by doing things in public that trigger your own social anxieties. But it is also important that you approach BEs in a positive and encouraging way: 'This may be a bit scary, but it's not going to be a catastrophe.'

Finding a graceful retreat

Even with the best planning in the world, sometimes things go wrong: the test turns out to be harder than you or the client thought; other people react in precisely the 'wrong' way; or the client's nerve fails him. It is at these times that therapeutic skill and creativity are most needed, to find a way to retreat with grace in such a way that the client does not feel he has completely 'failed'. A good general rule is to try always to finish with a success, no matter how small. If the original aim is clearly too ambitious, try to find a smaller goal that the client can accomplish before finishing the exercise.

Experiments that 'fail'

If negative predictions do come true, then we can still learn something useful by examining carefully what happened. Was it just an unlucky chance outcome, or did the client do something that produced that result? Is there some other aspect of cognition or behaviour whose effect we have not fully taken into account? Are there subtle forms of avoidance or other safety behaviours that are reducing the impact of the experiment? It is important to use such 'failures' constructively – even negative information can tell us something we can use to make therapy ultimately more effective.

Therapist–client relationship

There are different demands on the therapeutic relationship between a typical office-based therapy and BEs in CBT where, for example, you may be going to a supermarket with your client and falling over in the shop so that he can observe how others react. What professional issues does this raise? What kind of conversation is acceptable when you are outside the office and not 'on task'? It is important to reflect on these issues and discuss them in clinical supervision so that you can arrive at a way of relating that feels reasonably comfortable to both you and the client whilst respecting essential professional and ethical boundaries (see Chapter 3).

Date	Target cognition(s)	Experiment	Prediction(s)	Outcome	What I learned
	What thought, assumption or belief are you testing? Is there an alternative perspective? Rate belief in cognitions (0–100%).	Design an experiment to test the cognition (e.g., facing a situation you would otherwise avoid, dropping precautions, behaving in a new way).	What do you predict will happen?	What actually happened? What did you observe? How does the outcome fit with your predictions? modified? How?	What does this mean for your original assumption/belief? How far do you now believe it (0–100%). Does it need to be modified? How?

© OCTC 2006

Figure 9.1   Behavioural experiment record sheet

10 Physical Techniques

This chapter reviews some of the physical approaches that supplement the cognitive and behavioural repertoire: specifically, relaxation, controlled breathing, exercise and applied tension. The management of sleep problems is also considered.

Physiological responsiveness is one of the four interacting systems central to the CBT model. CBT may therefore include interventions focused on physiological symptoms. However, the use of such techniques should always follow from the formulation. They are not mechanistically applied as part of an 'anxiety management' package but are only used if the formulation indicates that it would be a good place to break into a vicious circle.

Consider a young man who was experiencing anxiety symptoms across a range of situations and who was finding some imminent exams highly stressful. A possible maintaining cycle for his anxiety, involving physiological changes, is sketched in Figure 10.1.

An alternative view for this man would be, 'If I relax, I shall concentrate better, and may not need to work for so long.' This could interrupt the cycle and help to reduce his anxiety.

We will now look at a number of possible physical interventions.

Relaxation

Physical tension can be part of a maintaining cycle for many problems – anxiety disorders, depression and sleep problems, among others. It may be part of a more general increase in arousal which includes other physical symptoms, such as increased heart rate, light-headedness, heavy legs and trembling. Such elevated arousal can be reduced by using relaxation, either via specific relaxation exercises or by building pleasurable, relaxing activities into the day – for example, by having a soothing bath or a massage.

The benefits of relaxation should not be discounted, but it should be clear to both your client and yourself how the relaxing activity fits into the formulation. We emphasise this point because in some other treatment approaches, relaxation training was a line of first attack, as, for example, in Wolpe's (1958) systematic desensitisation programmes. As a result, relaxation became part of many anxiety-management programmes, with little attention paid to the interactions with beliefs and behaviour that typify a CBT approach. Nevertheless, relaxation has relevance within a CBT approach and can be a powerful tool in testing out beliefs, as well as reducing symptoms directly.

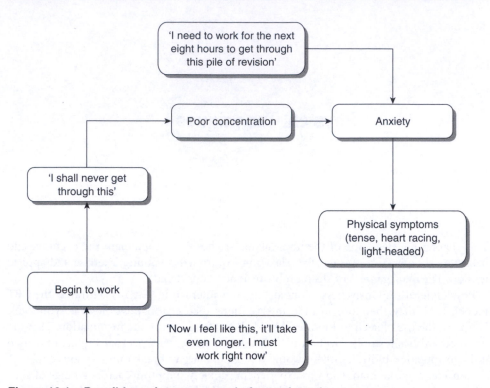

Figure 10.1   Possible maintenance cycle for anxiety about exams

There are a number of approaches to teaching relaxation, most of which rely either on the progressive muscular relaxation described by Jacobson (1970) or the use of relaxing imagery or meditation (or all three). There is some evidence that matching relaxation method to the individual's pattern of symptoms (for example, applied relaxation with clients with predominantly physiological symptoms) may improve outcome, but the evidence is by no means unequivocal (Michelson, 1986), and it is probably better to find out which approach suits your client by trying it out. Many forms of relaxation instruction are available on tape or CD (e.g. Norris & Küchemann, undated), and we would suggest that you find one you like for your own clients. Rather than describe a specific method, here are some general guidelines for teaching relaxation skills:

- Explain to your client that learning to relax is like acquiring any other skill, and that regular practice is required.
- It is important to begin to practise when feeling calm or only mildly anxious or tense – it is difficult to learn any new skill while tense, and this is particularly true of relaxation.
- It is better to begin to practise in a situation relatively close to ordinary life – for example, sitting in a comfortable chair, rather than lying down.
- Nevertheless, it is easier to begin practising with closed eyes, in order to reduce distractions.
- It is helpful to monitor minor or moderate signs of anxiety or tension, so that relaxation can be used to combat symptoms before they have built up to stronger levels.

- Choose a quiet place, with no phone or other distractions.
- It is better not to practise when feeling hungry, as this causes tension; or after a meal, which can promote sleep.

Although a tape has been mentioned as a useful adjunct to learning to relax, the evidence suggests that it is better to go through the relaxation exercises with your client, rather than simply ask them to learn from a tape (Borkovec & Sides, 1979). This is partly because you can then observe the client as he begins to practise and pick up on errors from the start – for example, sitting with tightly crossed legs or tightening up arms and shoulders once another area is focused on. It is also helpful if he can ask questions or express reservations. For example, many clients are concerned that they cannot focus continually on their muscle groups but find their minds wandering; you can encourage them to simply note whatever thoughts come into their mind and to gently encourage themselves to return to thinking about relaxation.

It is probably most useful to spend ten or 15 minutes per session focusing on relaxation training, over perhaps five or six sessions if an approach like applied relaxation (Öst, 1987) is being used as a major component of treatment. However, the remainder of these sessions can then be used for other agenda items. In other cases, relaxation may play a more minor role, and you may only need to go over the relaxation procedure a couple of times. This can be checked out by asking the client to monitor how relaxed he feels following his regular practice sessions and how he feels in whatever situations he then tackles using relaxation.

Applications of relaxation in CBT

Where the client is too scared to carry out a behavioural experiment.

Behavioural experiments often demand a great deal of courage, particularly if the prediction being tested includes elements such as, 'If I do such-and-such, I will probably feel anxious, but I will not collapse/suffocate/jump over the edge ...' (or whatever other catastrophes the client fears). Relaxation can then be used as an aid to facing the feared situation – but it has to be a temporary solution because of the risk of relaxation becoming established as a safety behaviour (see below).

> A client with a height phobia was planning to test out his prediction that he would be likely to jump off the cliff if he were to go onto a cliff path. He thought that he would be too anxious to do it 'cold turkey', so planned to use relaxation in the first instance as a way of getting himself onto the cliff path.

To test out a belief about whether symptoms have an organic basis or are anxiety-related:

If a client's unhelpful beliefs are focused on the aetiology of his symptoms, it may be possible to test out competing hypotheses by using relaxation.

> A woman was fearful that her severe headaches were a symptom of a brain tumour. She practised relaxation on a daily basis and found that as she became more skilled at progressive relaxation, and used it in stressful situations, the intensity and frequency of her headaches decreased. She recognised that this was more consistent with an anxiety explanation rather than a tumour explanation.

To interrupt vicious cycles where increasedarousal interferes with performance:

There are a number of problems where physical anxiety symptoms have a direct effect on performance of a task or function (see Chapter 4, Figure 4.8), and applying relaxation techniques may therefore be useful. For example, anxiety whilst speaking in public, and erectile problems, can both be affected by this process. Similarly, people can have difficulty eating if anxiety is interfering with their swallowing response. In each of these areas, relaxation may make a contribution because it reduces arousal and allows the task to be performed without interference.

To give a break from tension/arousal:

An obvious use of relaxation is where increased arousal is experienced as an unpleasant symptom in its own right. This can be the case with those who are chronically anxious and find the physical symptoms themselves unpleasant. However, it is always necessary to carefully check whether the symptoms have a meaning which should be evaluated. For example, does your client believe that the presence of chronic tension means that he is harming his immune system, or is it a sign that he is constitutionally deficient and ought not to have children, or that he can never hope to change? If the meaning of the symptoms seems to be distorted, then this should be tackled as described in Chapter 9. Having said this, it may be that for your client the unpleasantness of the symptoms itself is stoking the problem and that having a way to reduce this may increase a sense of mastery, which in turn boosts self-esteem, and onwards in a positive cycle. As ever, check it out via the formulation.

To end a stressful treatment session:

It may be helpful to prepare your client to re-enter the real world if the session has been very stressful, for example, restructuring traumatic images.

To provide an opportunity for pleasure:

Your client may have insufficient opportunities for pleasant and rewarding activities. Many people thoroughly enjoy muscular or other relaxation, and fitting it into a schedule may result in improved mood and increased energy for other activities.

To improve sleep:

Relaxation can be a useful part of a programme to improve sleep hygiene, particularly if the client is in the habit of being active right up until bedtime (see the section below on sleep).

Common problems associated with using relaxation in CBT

Safety behaviours

The most common problem is that relaxation, in common with many other strategies described as 'coping techniques', becomes established as a safety behaviour. This is only an issue where the client becomes trapped by the belief that, for example, 'If I had not relaxed, I would have panicked and then I would have lost control/passed out/gone mad, etc.' In essence, the client is left with the fear that he could have been overwhelmed by the problem if the relaxation had not allowed him to scrape through. This means that ultimately he has to face the problem without using relaxation, in order to demonstrate that even in those circumstances he might feel bad, but there is no catastrophic outcome.

Inability to relax if highly aroused

This can be an issue if the client is panicky or is highly aroused for some other reason – as in PTSD, for example. Past a certain level of arousal, it is very difficult to counter high arousal with relaxation, and it is more helpful to use a different strategy, for example a mindfulness approach (see Chapter 17).

Relaxation experienced as losing control

Some clients experience relaxation as anxiety-provoking rather than anxiety-reducing, often because it feels like they are losing control. If this is the case, it may be worth exploring the meaning of losing control and then use relaxation to test your client's predictions about what might happen if he did let go.

Hypersensitivity to small bodily changes

When they first begin to practise relaxation, many clients pick up on small bodily changes of which they were previously unaware. This may occasionally create or increase an attentional bias towards bodily changes, which can be interpreted as indicating a threat of some kind. If this happens, it should be explored and tested in the same way as other distorted thinking and, hence, may provide a useful opportunity to evaluate an unhelpful belief in the session.

Despite these possible drawbacks, there are many imaginative ways that relaxation can be used within CBT to disrupt maintenance cycles causing distress to clients.

Controlled breathing

The catastrophic misinterpretation of benign physical symptoms is the central process of one well-established model of panic (Clark, 1986). One of the benign symptoms often involved is hyperventilation, i.e. breathing at a high rate and volume. This can result in symptoms that mimic the person's panic attacks (for example, shortness of breath, light-headedness, feeling hot, unsteadiness) and which are liable to be interpreted catastrophically as indicating danger of imminent death, collapse, madness and so on. Salkovskis et al. (1986) developed a strategy of controlled breathing to allow the client to reattribute their symptoms to a more benign cause (i.e. that it is a symptom of anxiety) and, hence, break into the vicious circle of misinterpretation that was maintaining the panic attacks. This strategy can be used in order to develop a shared formulation with the client and also as a coping strategy as part of a graded approach to dealing with panic attacks.

Applications of controlled breathing in CBT

Developing a shared formulation using controlled breathing: the following steps can be used in developing a formulation with the client about the role of over-breathing in panic attacks:

- Without explaining why, ask the client to over-breathe.
- Ask him to reflect on his physical state and to describe the similarities to, and differences from, what he experiences in a panic attack.
- Ask him what he makes of that: what could explain it? How he would respond if he felt like that by himself?
- Agree that panic feelings may be related to hyperventilation.

Managing panic symptoms through controlled breathing: having derived a formulation involving the role of breathing, the client can then be taught to manage the symptoms in the following steps:

- Teach controlled breathing – initially by following an instruction tape at a moderate breathing rate, subsequently at a slower rate.
- Ask the client to choose the most comfortable rate.
- Get him to over-breathe and then to reduce the symptoms via controlled breathing.
- Review the role of breathing in panic symptoms.
- Ask how he can use this.
- Ask him to practise controlled breathing twice daily at home.
- Then ask him to practise reversing the effects of hyperventilation through controlled breathing.

This approach is described in more detail in Clark (1989).

Using controlled breathing in behavioural experiments when the client is too scared to continue: As with relaxation, controlled breathing can be used as a short-term coping strategy to allow a client to carry out an experiment which he would otherwise be too scared to do. He could then move on in a graded way to do the experiment without controlled breathing.

Problems associated with using controlled breathing in CBT

Safety behaviours: As with relaxation, it is very important that the client does not use the controlled breathing as a safety behaviour but instead employs it only as a short-term strategy. He may continue to believe that 'If I had not done my breathing, I would have collapsed/gone mad . . . etc.', unless at some point he experiences the panicky feelings and accepts that they are tolerable.

Using controlled breathing when feeling panicky: Some clients are unable to use controlled breathing when feeling very panicky but may learn to do so if they practise repeatedly.

Presence of physical disorder: Hyperventilation is not recommended in a number of physical conditions, unless medical supervision is available. These include atrial fibrillation, asthma and chronic obstructive pulmonary disease, epilepsy and pregnancy.

Hypersensitivity to small bodily changes: The client may develop heightened awareness of minor changes in his breathing, and so care must be taken to interpret these benignly and not as signs of dysfunction or precursors of panic.

Too tense to breathe evenly: It is easier to start the cycle if you suggest that the client focus initially on the out-breath, as the lungs are relatively empty and the body pushes for an in-breath.

Physical exercise

Extensive research over the past 20 years has established the efficacy of exercise in the treatment of depression (Craft & Landers, 1998), and the NICE guideline on the treatment of depression (NICE, 2004a) recommends that all patients with mild depression should be advised of the benefits of a structured exercise programme. The effect of exercise on depression may be mediated by an increase in endorphins, but it may be associated with other effects of increased exercise, many of which may also be important in the formulations of clients with anxiety problems (Taylor, 2000). For example, exercise can provide distraction, as when engaging in a competitive sport. The question is whether intervening with exercise would disrupt a maintenance cycle for your client, and it is worth looking out for symptoms which could be addressed in this way, particularly as exercise can become self-maintaining once the basic skills are learned.

Applications of exercise in CBT

Low mood: the best-established application of exercise is with depression, where apart from the direct effect of increased endorphins, exercise may also provide opportunities for pleasurable and satisfying activity, promoting improved mood.

Low self-esteem: the sense of competence derived from exercise may be relevant for someone low with self-esteem (Fox, 2000).

Chronic fatigue syndrome (CFS): exercise can be central to a graded programme in CFS where the client can test out predictions about tiredness.

Tension release: for clients with chronic anxiety, or in chronically stressful situations, it can be helpful to test out the benefits of exercise on tension levels. This can be especially helpful with younger clients who may not take to relaxation.

Sleep disorders: there is good evidence of the effects of exercise on sleep, as long as it is regular and is not used close to bedtime, when it tends to be arousing.

Health anxiety or panic disorder: many clients with health anxiety or panic disorder have beliefs about the risks which exercise holds for their health. It can be very important to invalidate these beliefs via experiments focused on exercise.

Anger management: it can be helpful for clients with anger problems to test out the effects of exercise on tension levels, particularly if this is followed by a soothing activity such as a relaxing bath.

Problems associated with using exercise in CBT

Becoming overvalued: in some disorders, such as eating disorders and body dysmorphic disorder, exercise is overvalued because of its perceived effect on body shape and weight control. In these cases, the therapist should be circumspect about using it to tackle associated problems such as tension or low self-esteem.

Presence of physical disorder: exercise is not recommended in a number of physical conditions. Medical advice should be sought if the client has cardiovascular problems, for example.

Applied tension

Although many anxious clients feel as though they are about to pass out, sufferers of phobic anxiety about blood or injury are the only group who *actually* faint in response to their anxiety (Öst et al., 1984). This is the result of the typical initial increase in blood pressure being followed in this group by a sudden decrease, leading to fainting. In applied tension, developed by Öst and Sterner (1987), the client is taught to tighten the muscles in his arms, legs and torso for a few seconds and then to return the muscles to normal. He is then taught to identify the signs of a drop in blood pressure (provoked, for example, by exposing him to photographs of blood or other injuries) and to reverse the decrease by using applied tension. This technique is specific to blood/injury phobia.

Problems associated with using applied tension in CBT

Safety behaviour: again, the major risk of using applied tension is that it functions as a safety behaviour. It is important to help the client to view applied tension as a helpful thing to do when his blood pressure drops, just as it is helpful to look both ways before crossing the road – i.e. based on a reasonable caution about the consequences of not doing so.

Presence of physical disorders: before using applied tension, therapists should seek medical advice about any client who is pregnant or has a known physical disorder, particularly hypertension or cardiovascular conditions.

CBT and sleep

We will now turn to problems with sleep, implicated in many mental-health problems as well as being common in the general population.

Insomnia is a problem experienced by up to 40% of adults at any one time (Espie, 1991) and can include delayed onset of sleep; difficulty staying asleep, with multiple awakenings; and waking too early. It can be secondary to a range of physical and psychiatric conditions, although most evaluations of psychological interventions have focused on insomnia as the primary condition.

Many of the early CBT treatments focused on relaxation as a way of reducing physical arousal levels, even though client reports about insomnia often emphasise *mental* arousal – for example, 'I lie calmly in bed, but my thoughts are racing', or 'All the worries of the day come into my mind'. Accordingly, there has been an increasing emphasis on cognitive approaches to sleep problems, as well as attention to other physiological and behavioural aspects. We shall therefore look at the processes which are currently thought to be involved in poor sleeping, taking as an example Cara, who was highly successful in business as well as being committed to her teenage children and was chronically unable to fall asleep. She also woke repeatedly in the night and so had relatively few hours sleep.

Processes implicated in poor sleeping

Unhelpful automatic thoughts and beliefs in bed or by day:

> Cara believed that if she did not have six hours sleep then she would be unable to think productively or relate effectively to her family or colleagues; that she ought to be able to control her sleep, as she controlled other aspects of her life; and that any tiredness she experienced in the daytime was attributable to her insomnia (rather than a busy day with no planned breaks and no time for relaxation).

Safety behaviours, including monitoring internally and externally:

> When in bed, Cara repeatedly checked the clock; she wore earplugs and used a special cushion which she believed increased her control over falling asleep; she monitored her body for signs of wakefulness.

> In the daytime, she tried to avoid complex work following a bad night; she monitored her body for signs of tiredness and for signs of poor concentration.

Poor stimulus and temporal control of sleep behaviour:

> When she went to bed, Cara took a book and an iPod in case she could not sleep; she spent long periods of time wakeful in bed, reading and listening to music (poor stimulus control).

> If she had a disturbed night, she would lie in, if possible, and go to bed early the next night, often when not sleepy (poor temporal control).

Increased mental arousal and possibly physical arousal:

> As she lay in bed, Cara had many worrying thoughts and tried to work out solutions to them (mental arousal).

Poor sleep hygiene:

> In order to tire herself out, Cara went to the gym after her evening meal had settled; she had a glass of whiskey in order to settle herself but then busied herself with household tasks before going to bed.

Interventions for sleep problems

As with other problems, interventions are planned on the basis of a detailed assessment and formulation, taking account of whatever maintaining cycles seem most relevant for the particular client. The most common interventions include:

Re-evaluation of unhelpful or distorted thoughts and beliefs, tackled through verbal challenging and behavioural experiments. Examples specific to insomnia can be found in Harvey (2002).

Reduction in safety behaviours: these are approached in the same way as in other problems. A number of creative examples are given in Ree and Harvey (2004).

Improved stimulus and temporal control: this intervention has been extensively evaluated since Bootzin's 1972 paper. The approach was based on the notion that consistent cues are necessary to allow the client to clearly differentiate environmental and behavioural sleep cues from non-sleep cues and to allow the body to acquire a consistent sleep rhythm. There are debates about whether this hypothesis is correct, but the approach has been shown to be effective in rapidly reducing sleep-onset latency, although it can be difficult for clients to follow. A good description of the procedure can be found in Espie (1991), and the main elements include the following:

1. Lie down to go to sleep only when you feel sleepy.
2. Do not use your bedroom for anything other than sleep. The only exception to this is sex.
3. If you do not fall asleep rapidly (about 20 minutes), get up and go into another room. Do something relaxing until you feel sleepy and then return to bed.
4. If you do not fall rapidly asleep, repeat Step 3. This may initially be required repeatedly during the night.
5. Set your alarm at the same time each morning and get up at that time regardless of how much sleep you have had.
6. Do not nap during the daytime or evening, even for short periods.

Decrease mental arousal: insomnia may be maintained by a failure to 'tie up loose ends' before going to bed so that unresolved issues from the day rush into the mind. It may be helpful for your client to set aside time before going to bed and to experiment with writing down/thinking through issues from the day, including their emotional impact. If this is not sufficient, and there are themes that recur, then it may be helpful to rehearse cognitive re-evaluations of these thoughts (as outlined in Chapter 9) so that the client is prepared in advance.

Decrease physical arousal: although the evidence for increased physical arousal in insomnia is unclear, many studies have shown that progressive muscular relaxation has some impact on sleep-onset latency, on total time slept and, importantly, on the quality of sleep perceived by the client. Furthermore, many clients enjoy muscular relaxation. As in other problems, it seems to make no difference which relaxation approach is used.

Poor sleep hygiene: for most clients, general information and advice would include:

- information about sleep patterns, stages and variability; the functions and effects of sleep; and facts and figures about insomnia (see Espie, 2001);
- advice about exercise (i.e. helpful as part of a regular programme aimed at fitness, but not near to bedtime), diet (i.e. avoidance of caffeine, unhelpfulness of chronic or heavy alcohol intake, benefit of warm, milky drinks);
- advice about quiet comfortable bed and surroundings, with minimal distractions.

Although none of these elements would be sufficient to maintain chronic insomnia, they could each exacerbate sleeping problems.

Problems in sleep management

Safety behaviours: strategies which are initially useful for sleep hygiene can develop into safety behaviours. Encourage your client to experiment with using the strategies flexibly, to challenge the belief that they are essential for his well-being.

Undisclosed drug use: your client may not respond to psychological interventions if he is using drugs that promote wakefulness.

Sleep problem secondary to another problem: a sleep problem may not respond to psychological interventions if it is secondary to another psychiatric or physical condition or to a sleep disorder not classified as insomnia (e.g. sleep apnoea, nocturnal myoclonus and restless legs). In such cases, the primary disorder should be treated.

Summary

It can be rewarding to pay attention to the role that physical interventions can have in problems, even those where cognitive factors such as distorted thinking are clearly important. If interventions are carefully planned with an eye on the formulation, physical techniques may make a useful contribution in a range of disorders.

The Course of Therapy

This chapter will present an overview of the course of therapy and the tasks and problems likely to arise at different stages.

Overall pattern of sessions

For most straightforward problems of the kind described in this book, a course of therapy typically takes from six to 15 one-hour sessions. However, there are no hard-and-fast rules, either about the length of each session or about the number of sessions. For example, sessions may be shorter towards the end of treatment, when the client has become responsible for much of the treatment; on the other hand, if treatment demands lengthy in-session behavioural experiments, then those sessions may last considerably longer than 60 minutes. Similarly, the number of sessions may be extended if the problems are more complex or shortened if the problem is highly amenable to treatment. Sessions are usually weekly to begin with and become gradually more spaced as treatment progresses, with a couple of follow-up sessions after the end of formal treatment.

In the first two or three sessions, you will usually be focused on assessing the client's problems, with the aim of deriving a formulation to share with him. Running parallel with this, you will be attempting to educate him about CBT and his expected role as an active, skilled collaborator in the therapeutic endeavour. Most of the active work on the target problems will be within Sessions 2 to 12, and the final couple of sessions will be concerned with drawing up a blueprint for your client to take forward after discharge.

There are some features that appear throughout the course of treatment, and these include:

- Agenda-setting
- Self-monitoring
- Learning from setbacks
- Updating the formulation.

Agenda-setting

The setting of a mutually agreed agenda at the beginning of each session is a key feature of CBT. As it is a relatively brief therapy, it is important to ensure that time is used effectively, and agenda-setting aids this goal by:

- allowing you and the client to prioritise the issues to be addressed in any given session;
- promoting the structure that is characteristic of CBT;
- helping you both to maintain a focus on relevant problems;
- helping to engage the client as an active participant in the therapeutic process.

As part of the effort to engage your client in a collaborative relationship, it is helpful to address agenda-setting in the first session or two, by saying something like:

It is important that the treatment sessions seem relevant and helpful to you, and given that we only have a limited time in each session, we usually find it helpful to decide at the beginning of the session what we will aim to cover. I usually have ideas about what I would like to include, but you will often want to discuss things that have happened in the week, or thoughts that have occurred to you, and so on. It is really important that we make time for those, and so it would be helpful if you would take a few minutes before each session just thinking over what you would like to include. We can then agree an agenda between us. Does that sound sensible? Would you be willing to have a go at that?

Follow this up by asking at the beginning of each session what the client wants to include on the agenda, and then, *following that*, suggest items which you want to include yourself (if you start with your own items, the client may be less likely to come up with his). This process may take five minutes at the start of each session – this is time well spent, but you need to take account of it when working out how much time is available for other items.

The items you will usually include on the agenda are:

- Brief review of the events of the past week. This does not need to be extensive and should only briefly identify matters which are identified as major agenda items. Clients may be unfamiliar with such a brief review and go into too much detail. In that case, you can model what is helpful by gently interrupting and summarising the main points, for example:

  So what you seem to be saying is that for most of the week, your anxiety level was rather higher than it has been, and the major factor seems to have been your father's wedding plans. However, you have managed to go to work every day and that has felt positive. You only need to give me an overall outline at this point, but have I got the general picture correct? Would it be helpful to put the wedding on our agenda?

- Review of the last session. This may include any problems with what was discussed, any expansion on points made, etc. Many therapists give clients a tape of the session to listen to as part of their homework, and new perspectives may have been gained as a result of that. If you have asked the client to keep notes about the session in a therapy notebook, he can also review that over the subsequent week.

  Issues for the agenda may arise from such reviews and may need to be put on the agenda. For example, look out for whether it seems that the client is giving honest feedback or saying what he thinks you would like to hear. If the latter, you need to decide whether drawing attention to it at this point would weaken or strengthen the therapeutic relationship. If your client cannot remember what went on in the previous session, this should also be tackled as a problem, and ways of overcoming it need to be identified.

- Assessment of current mood. This can be formally assessed using a standardised measure such as a BDI (Beck *et al.*, 1961) or BAI (Beck *et al.*, 1988) or more informally via questioning: Has the client's mood changed since last session? Does any aspect of it need to be included as an agenda item?

- Review of homework, which may heavily overlap with the major topics for the day. (While this is often referred to as homework, some clients have bad associations with that word, for example from school experiences. Alternative terms include assignment, behavioural experiment, tasks for next week, project or a description of the specific task, like 'survey'.)

- The session's main topics for discussion. These may include symptoms (such as low mood, anxiety, sleeplessness) or current external problems (such as issues at work or relationship difficulties). You probably have plans to work on particular CBT skills, such as learning how to identify NATs or the role of safety behaviours in the maintenance of a problem, and it is often possible to cover these at the same time as the client's symptoms or problems are being addressed.

- Homework assignment. This should arise from the main topics discussed and may already have been negotiated as part of that. However, it is worth bearing in mind that setting up homework can take ten minutes.

- Feedback on the how the client has experienced the session. For example, you could say:

  It would be very helpful if you would give me some feedback on how things have gone today. It may be difficult at first to tell me if things have been disappointing, or if I have said something which has upset you, but as we try and work together on dealing with your problems, it is really important that you feel able to say whether things are helpful or not. What would you say are the take-home messages from today? ... Is there anything else that has been helpful? ... Is there anything I have said that is going to play on your mind, or has been unhelpful? ... Any other comments on today?

It will be apparent that, allowing for agenda-setting, agreeing homework and getting feedback, there is not much more than 35–40 minutes for the major topics for the day. This means that usually no more than two topics can be included, unless it is planned to allocate five minutes or so to an additional one.

In order to decide which issues to prioritise during agenda-setting, the following factors can be considered:

- Issues of risk to the client or others, including children.
- Urgent problems, e.g. possible job loss, imminent exams.
- Level of distress.
- Centrality to the formulation.
- Potential for change.
- Relevance to a skill that needs to be learned.
- Whether the problem could be tackled with someone else outside therapy.

In the early stages, it is not usually helpful to tackle highly distressing and complex problems, as it is unlikely that the client yet has the skills to deal with them effectively. Similarly, issues directly related to rigidly held or core beliefs should be avoided.

Once the agenda is set, you should aim to follow it and be explicit about any deviations from it. For example, if the client moves to a different topic and perhaps becomes upset about it, you should not assume that the client would chose to prioritise the new topic. Instead, discuss the dilemma, by saying for example:

This seems to be very upsetting for you, which makes me think it might be an important issue. Would you like us to spend some of our time thinking about this, or would you rather that we focus instead on….., as we agreed at the beginning of the session?

This allows the client to make a choice, sometimes with surprising results. Similarly, if discussion brings up a topic related to risk, then you probably need to prioritise it over other items on the agenda, but, again, discuss it with your client.

The handling of the agenda needs to be managed sensitively, with respect and understanding of the client's position. The client may sometimes wish simply to ventilate feelings about a difficult situation, possibly without any expectation of problem resolution. This could be an entirely reasonable target for one or even two sessions, although it would probably need further exploration if he wanted to take up a good proportion of each session in this manner.

In order to remain with the agenda, it is helpful if you either make, or request from the client, frequent summaries of the major points related to a topic or problem. A summary should cover the main points of a discussion in one or two sentences and include, for example, important NATs, in the client's own words. This helps therapist and client to remain on the same wavelength, and it also serves as a useful break between topics on the agenda. In the first five or six sessions, it is helpful to summarise about every ten minutes and to ask the client whether you have understood accurately. For example:

You seem to be saying … and … Have I got that right? Have I missed anything?

or

Could you put in your own words the main points of what we were discussing?

Common difficulties in agenda-setting

- Setting a vague agenda, where the topic is only described in broad outline rather than being operationalised in detail. For example, if the client says that he wants to talk about his relationship with his family, you need to ask him to identify what aspects of the relationship he wants to discuss.
- Putting too many items on the agenda: you will not usually manage more than two major items.
- Not prioritising which items to consider: tackle the major ones first.
- Beginning to deal with issues as soon as they are mentioned rather than attempting to complete the agenda-setting: many clients need practice in setting agendas and may launch immediately into a detailed discussion of the first item mentioned. Gently interrupt and remind them that it is important to agree explicitly about which issues to address.
- Not having genuine input from the client: this runs the risk that he will introduce his preferred items 'off-agenda' later in the session, or not at all.
- Misunderstanding the meaning of an issue for a client: continue to ask questions and use summaries to clarify meaning and make sure you have got it right.
- Tackling issues not on the agenda without discussion.
- Skipping from one topic to another from session to session, without achieving closure on any of them: make sure that there is a broad strategy that will make progress across sessions.

It is helpful if you regularly review agenda-settings so that difficulties like these can be identified and dealt with. Although it may initially feel uncomfortable if you are used to a less structured approach, it is worth experimenting to test out whether the feared consequences actually occur.

We will now go on to look at the stages in a course of therapy, beginning with the features of the early stages.

The early stages

Goal-setting

Another aspect of CBT which serves to maintain its efficiency as a time-limited therapy is the agreement to work towards mutually agreed goals. This helps to structure therapy sessions and to maintain their focus. Goals are established in a joint effort, and so it is another process that emphasises the collaborative nature of CBT: the goals for therapy are those which are relevant for the client, with input from the therapist.

The emphasis of goal-setting is on the possibility of change, which engenders hope and reduces the client's helplessness in the face of what may seem insurmountable problems. It also implies the possibility of an end to treatment and so helps you negotiate in an open and explicit way when discharge may be approaching.

How to set goals?
Goals should be 'SMART', i.e. be:

- **S**pecific
- **M**easurable
- **A**chievable
- **R**ealistic
- and have a **T**ime frame (i.e. a date for completion).

Setting goals out in specific detail can help clients feel more in control, because a global problem reduced to its component parts may feel more manageable. Questioning can begin with general questions like:

How would you like things to be at the end of treatment?
How would you know if treatment had been successful?
At the end of treatment, what would you like to be different?

For example, the first discussion with a woman who was feeling that her life was controlled by her health worries went as follows:

Therapist:	'How would you know if treatment had been successful? What would be different?'
Client:	'I would stop checking myself for lumps; I wouldn't be thinking about cancer all the time, and boring the family with it. And I would be able to visit people in hospital. I suppose the main thing is I wouldn't get panicky every time cancer was mentioned.'

This client's response demonstrates a common problem: she described how she would like *not* to be, rather than how she would like to *be*. This has been called the 'dead man's solution', i.e. the goals could be achieved by a dead man – no more panicky feelings, no more checking lumps, no more talking to relatives about cancer . . . Ask your client to describe how he wants to be or what he wants to do, rather than where he wants to move *from*.

The so-called 'miracle question' is sometimes a good way of getting at this:

Suppose, whilst you are asleep tonight, a miracle happens, and all your problems disappear, just like that. But you don't know that it's happened, because you are asleep. When you get up the next morning and go through your day, how will you come to realise that the miracle has happened? What would you notice was different about you or about other people? What would others see that would tell them that the miracle had happened?

For the woman above, the goals eventually agreed were that she would carry out a breast check on a monthly basis; that she would discuss topics other than symptoms with her husband 95% of the time; that she would visit relatives in hospital if they were admitted; and that she would respond calmly if she developed symptoms. In order to measure her progress towards these goals, she was asked questions like, 'Can we break this down into smaller steps?' or 'What would be the first sign that you were making progress?'

Part of your role is to make sure that goals are realistic. Clients may have unrealistically extreme goals, such as a socially anxious person who wants to find a life partner by the end of therapy; or the goals may be too limited, such as a client with obsessional disorder who wants to reduce his hand-washing to four hours a day. Occasionally, it may be difficult for a client and therapist to agree on goals. For example, a client with anorexia nervosa may want help to lose weight; one partner in couple therapy may wish the therapist to agree that the other partner is entirely responsible for the problem; or a client with OCD may want therapist reassurance. In these cases, delicate negotiation is required, but the process allows you and the client to be explicit about what he can and cannot hope to achieve through therapy.

It is also important that the goals are achievable and involve change in things which are within the client's control: in particular, he should focus on changing things about himself, rather than other people. For example, it may be reasonable to have job-seeking as a goal, but obtaining a particular job is not ultimately determined by the client, and is therefore not an achievable goal. It is also worth considering whether the person has the resources – finance, skills, persistence, time – to achieve the goals.

The issue of which goals to tackle first can be approached by considering similar factors to those relevant for prioritising topics in a session. It is helpful to tackle initially a goal where change is likely to occur quite rapidly, in order to increase the client's hope. Other factors to take into account include risk or urgency, importance or level of distress in the client and whether any particular goal logically needs to be approached before other ones can be tackled. For the therapist, other considerations are the centrality of a goal in the formulation and the ethical acceptability of the goal.

Homework

There is clear evidence (Niemeyer & Feixas, 1990; Persons et al., 1988) that clients who complete homework tasks show greater improvement than those who do not, and this is presumably because they have more opportunity to generalise what they have learned from sessions into everyday life. Most problems are based outside the clinic rather than in it, and the client can use homework to collect information, test out new patterns of thinking and behaving and learn through direct experience. As the general style of CBT involves handing skills over to clients, it is also important that they have opportunities to practise the skills in real life, whether this involves identifying NATs working out how to reduce safety behaviours or how to increase assertiveness in particular situations.

Because between-session assignments are so central to CBT, it follows that time must be allocated to setting them up, which may need five or ten minutes at the end of a treatment session. However, homework will often follow on directly from the major topics on the agenda and will have been devised earlier in the session as part of that discussion. For example, if the agenda has been concerned with the role of negative thoughts in triggering anxious feelings, an obvious homework task might be for the client to begin monitoring triggers and thoughts associated with anxiety in the following week.

The range of possible homework is boundless and relies on the ingenuity of you and your client in setting up suitable assignments. It can include reading relevant material; listening to treatment tapes; self-monitoring of feelings, thoughts or behaviours; carrying out behavioural experiments; practising new skills, such as the use of thought records or assertive responses; doing a historical review of past experience; or activity scheduling. It is important that it makes sense to the client and that it will be useful either for the subsequent treatment session or for the achievement of a particular goal. For example, the elimination of a safety behaviour may feed directly into the next session, where the results of trying it out may flesh out the formulation, and then lead on to the next manoeuvre. On the other hand, a client may be keeping a positive data log as a long-term assignment aimed at low self-esteem, and discussion of it from session to session may be minimal, unless it were identified as a major topic for the agenda.

Clients often do not do their homework, and this can be for a number of reasons. The principles below will help to ensure that homework is carried out and is useful:

- The homework should *follow logically* from what happened during the session.
- The assignment should be *relevant*, and be seen to be relevant, by the client. Check this out with questions such as, 'Does this make sense? Can you summarise for me how you think this would be helpful?' This is less of an issue later in treatment as the client takes an increasing role in setting up between-session assignments, but may be more problematic earlier on, when the therapist is likely to take the lead in suggesting suitable homework tasks.
- It is also worth bearing in mind that your *client has a life outside therapy*. Although it is important that they prioritise treatment, there are limits to what they can be expected to do, and they will be less likely to complete the homework if they feel overburdened. Check this out with them.
- Homework should be *planned in detail*, spelling out what is to be done, when, where, with whom, etc. Pitfalls and difficulties must be identified and discussed.

> *A woman was very concerned about being what she described as 'a doormat' in relation to her mother and sister. However, after a role play in the session, when an assertiveness task was being set up for a subsequent interaction, she mentioned that she was not likely to see either of the relatives in the next month or so!*

Difficulties may range from embarrassment at using a self-monitoring form at work, through to not having any money to carry out a behavioural experiment in a social situation. Be mindful of any underlying beliefs that may interfere with completing homework assignments. For example, a client with perfectionist beliefs may find an activity schedule difficult to complete because he might think that none of his activities were good enough to include; a client with low self-esteem may find it difficult to do any task where the outcome could be construed as falling short of the therapist's 'wishes'. In the early stages of treatment, anticipated problems should be dealt with in the here-and-now, rather than attempting to modify such underlying beliefs.

- *Make sure that homework cannot be 'failed'*, but rather seen as a source of helpful information, whatever the outcome. For example, if a client is attempting to reduce avoidance of particular situations, set up homework so that he can collect useful information about anxious thoughts and feelings even if he cannot reduce the avoidance.
- *Provide relevant resources*, such as diary forms and reading material, at least early in therapy.
- The agreed assignments should be *written down*, by both you and the client. Although it may be quicker for you to write it down *for* the client, it is helpful to establish his active role in therapy and this kind of recording can be an early step in that direction.
- *Homework review should always be included in the agenda of the subsequent session*. Partly, this is because it should have been designed to be relevant for the session, but, at a more general level, a client is highly unlikely to persist with homework assignments that you never follow up.

  If the homework has been completed or nearly completed, then it should be reviewed in detail. For example, if the client has read a chapter of a book, what was helpful? What rang bells for him? Were there any sections which were difficult to understand? If he has completed an activity schedule, what was the pattern of pleasure and achievements? What did he learn? How can this be taken forward?

  On the other hand, if the homework was not completed, it is important that this is explored and the reasons determined. There may have been practical reasons (someone sick at work, so workload unexpectedly increased); the client may have forgotten; it may not have been discussed in sufficient detail, or not written down; it may be that that the task was too difficult in some way. In all these cases, the task can be modified for a subsequent assignment or, perhaps, carried out with assistance from you or someone else.
- If underlying beliefs have interfered with the completion of the task, then, as described above, this should be tackled pragmatically, at least early in treatment, rather than attempting premature belief change. For example, if it seems that the client has beliefs about control or autonomy which have been activated by a particular assignment, then the task could be modified so as to give him more control. This may not necessarily be spelled out unless the beliefs have been discussed in detail in the formulation, or unless the treatment has progressed to the point where such beliefs are the current focus.

The general point is that it is important to establish from the outset that homework is an integral part of therapy and that it is difficult to proceed without the information and feedback that it provides. This is particularly true when the amount of treatment available is limited by resource constraints. Well-devised homework can mean that very limited treatment can result in enormous changes for the client, as the majority of the work is done outside sessions.

Problems in the early stages

'Low motivation for change'

At the beginning of treatment, it may appear that the client has poor motivation, but it is helpful to understand the client's apparent reluctance to engage with treatment rather than use a trait description like 'poor motivation'. This means that attempts should be made to analyse the problem in terms of thoughts, feelings and behaviours, so that ideas about management can follow on. The following possibilities should be considered:

- *Ambivalence about change.* Prochaska and DiClemente (1986) defined a spectrum of stages in a person's preparedness to change: pre-contemplation (no intention of changing, possibly no awareness of a problem), contemplation (aware of a problem and considering change), preparation (beginning to make changes), action (successful cognitive and behavioural change) and maintenance (working to prevent relapse). It is worth considering which of these stages best describes your client. This needs to be kept under review, as motivation can shift as therapy proceeds: it can increase as your client accrues more successful experiences or it can diminish as he finds that he has to work harder for results, for example.
- *Inaccurate expectations about the nature of the treatment approach.* This is particularly likely to be a problem with clients who have had experience of different psychological treatment approaches.
- *Lack of understanding or acceptance of the formulation.* If a client has not agreed on a formulation with the therapist by around Session 4 it is less likely that treatment will be effective. It is therefore worth spending time on clarifying the formulation, asking for feedback, listening effectively to the client's concerns and trying to take account of them. If the client and therapist cannot come to a shared understanding via a formulation, it is probably not worth pursuing treatment.
- *Hopelessness.* Apart from the hopelessness which is common in depressed clients, hopelessness may also occur in clients who have had a history of unsuccessful psychological treatments. This can be approached using standard CBT techniques, including identifying and evaluating NATs and behavioural experiments focused on hopelessness.

'I don't have any thoughts'

It is difficult for clients to make sense of a formulation that focuses on cognitions if they are unaware of thoughts. It can be helpful for them to practise looking for thoughts, to look for images or to try and identify what situations mean to them, even if they cannot easily identify automatic thoughts. Chapter 8 discusses ways of dealing with this problem, but as cognitions are central to this approach, it is important to deal with the issue rather than try and circumvent it.

Role of health beliefs

Clients may have an explanation of their problems which is different from a cognitive behavioural view, and it is helpful to find a way of working with this as an experiment, without attacking the alternative explanation. For example, clients with somatic symptoms often construe them in terms of physical illness. It may be useful to negotiate with such a client to try for a specified time an alternative approach based on a CBT formulation, as an experiment to see whether it works any better than the physical-illness formulation (the so-called 'Theory A/Theory B' approach). Similarly, some clients with obsessional worries may explain their intrusions in terms of a religious framework, and a similar approach may be helpful. On the other hand, some clients may have differing beliefs about the roles and responsibilities of therapists and clients (for example, 'It is your job to cure me'). An awareness of this can help the therapist devise assignments which could, for example, draw attention to the important contribution that the client can make to the process of change.

Balance of pros and cons

We need to remember that therapy has costs as well as benefits for clients: costs of emotional strain, investing time and possibly money and implications for other changes in the client's life. Sometimes it is necessary to help clients think through the balance of costs and benefits. For example, reluctance to do a particular homework task should not be taken immediately as evidence of an unwillingness to change but rather as indicating that the case for the task has not been made. We are often asking clients to make changes that require a great deal of bravery, and they are only likely to do that if, on balance, they see that the possible benefits outweigh the probable costs.

> *A client with a severe vomit phobia was finding it very difficult to give up safety behaviours such as carrying mints in her bag, driving with her car window open, carrying a moist flannel in her bag and sleeping with the light on (so that she could find her way to the bathroom if necessary), even though she understood the rationale for doing so. Her cost–benefit analysis for dropping the safety behaviours differentiated short-term from long-term effects as set out Figure 11.1. This analysis, set out in this way, allowed her to put her short-term fears in context, and to begin to drop her safety behaviours.*

Although this will often allow clients to move forward, you should also remember that occasionally clients may decide that, on balance, the costs of therapy outweigh the benefits for them right now, and therefore not continue in treatment.

Review points

Because CBT is time-limited, focused and structured, you need to carry out regular reviews throughout treatment. This helps to retain the focus of treatment and to establish whether progress is sufficient to warrant continuing with treatment or whether changes in the approach are required. The review should be related to the goals agreed at the beginning of treatment, and it is helpful if intermediate targets have been identified, as well as end-point goals. Any other measures that are being used, such as questionnaires or other self-monitoring, are also helpful for reviews.

It is helpful to agree at the outset that you will review progress after four or five sessions, in order to assess whether or not CBT is likely to be helpful. Although a decision not to continue with CBT may be dispiriting for someone who had high hopes of its efficacy, it is easier to deal with this at an early stage than after 20 sessions which have resulted in little change. After this initial review, further reviews should be carried out at five- or ten- session intervals.

The formulation developed in the first one or two sessions is tentative, so it is important to review it regularly to take account of any new information which becomes available as

Short-term costs	Short-term benefits
Would feel panicky at the time *Would feel anxious all day* *Would feel nauseous* *Might be sick* *Would worry about the mess*	*Would feel I was doing something for the problem* *Would feel less weak and out of control*
Long-term costs	**Long-term benefits**
Might feel I had to do harder and harder things *Would have no excuse to avoid the places I don't want to visit!*	*I would gain confidence in my ability to cope with problems* *I would have a better chance of overcoming my vomit phobia, and then I could: go out freely; travel more widely; eat more foods; not be anxious all the time; not be embarrassed at formal events; go abroad on holiday; eat in restaurants; feel more adult; relax about cleanliness in the home.*

Figure 11.1   Client's costs and benefits for giving up SBs

therapy progresses. This may be derived from homework assignments, behavioural experiments carried out in sessions and so on. Although the basic outline of the formulation may not change, the details of maintaining cycles are likely to be fleshed out during treatment, with implications for what interventions are likely to be helpful.

> *A man with agoraphobia was unclear about the content of his catastrophic thinking because he had for so long avoided situations that would trigger such thoughts. Once it was established that he had thoughts about not being helped by other people, this could be built into the formulation and experiments set up to test them out.*

It is especially important to review progress if little change is being made or if an impasse has been reached. This may mean that the formulation is not helpful or has significant omissions. It is also worth looking at the therapeutic relationship to see whether problems there are interfering with the application of the formulation to the client's problems. Such problems may include your own blind spots so should be discussed with your supervisor. If no solution can be found, it may be decided that treatment should be discontinued at this point.

Later stages

As treatment progresses, the focus moves increasingly onto intervention rather than assessment; the results of any intervention should always be related to the initial formulation to see whether it needs modifying. The client becomes increasingly independent in determining what items go on the agenda, how long is spent on each item and what home-work is taken away; and as more CBT skills are learned, the client takes the lead in, for example, evaluating negative thoughts and in devising behavioural experiments to test out new perspectives.

You will probably spend most of the time in treatment sessions on the details of thoughts, feelings and behaviour in current situations, but as the end of treatment approaches, you may spend some time on identifying and evaluating unhelpful care beliefs, particularly if you think that the client may be at risk of relapse if the beliefs are not modified.

The emphasis on the portability of skills means that it is important for the client to reflect on what is taking place in therapy, so it is helpful to ask questions such as 'What were we doing there?' 'Can you identify the kind of crooked thinking you were making there?' 'How could you use that in other situations?'. It is important that you attribute progress to the client's efforts, particularly if he is dependent and hence likely to attribute change to your attention and skill rather than his own efforts.

As treatment progresses, the frequency of sessions may be reduced, perhaps moving to two-week gaps between two or three sessions, followed by perhaps a three- or four-week break before treatment ends (see below).

Ending therapy

It is relatively easy to work towards ending therapy if the treatment goals were well defined and if there has been good progress towards them. Similarly, you can keep in mind the idea that treatment will be coming to an end through regular reviews of goals and progress, as this emphasises the short-term nature of the treatment process. The client should gradually have acquired confidence in his ability to apply a CBT approach to his problems, using the skills learned during therapy.

As the end of treatment approaches, it is helpful to develop with your client a *blueprint* for dealing with any problems that may emerge in the future, based on the relapse man-agement work you have done together. This could include:

- what has been learned during therapy;
- what strategies have been most helpful;
- what situations in the future may be difficult or possibly lead to a recurrence of the problem;
- ways of responding to this, given what has been learned in treatment;
- how to handle a significant problem, including if necessary a telephone review with the therapist.

The emphasis should be on the idea that the client is equipped to deal with most problems that are likely to arise, even if, in some circumstances, it would be reasonable for him to ask for your help.

Rather than having an abrupt end to treatment, it may make sense to plan a booster ses-sion or two over the subsequent year. You can then review progress, reinforce the client's success at dealing with problems, check out how he dealt with problems that had been anticipated at a previous session, check on the re-emergence of unhelpful patterns of thinking or behaviour (for example, safety behaviours) and trouble-shoot if necessary.

Despite the gradual withdrawal from therapy, and the emphasis on skills acquisition, some clients continue to worry that they will not cope by themselves after the end of treatment. This can be approached in a standard cognitive behavioural way, by identifying worrying thoughts and helping the client to deal with them. This could include re-evaluating them and setting up behavioural experiments to test out alternative perspectives. If a client is generally dependent, the booster sessions over the year following the end of formal treatment can be used to test out beliefs about coping alone, perhaps via a positive data log.

> *A 59-year-old client who had been depressed as a result of a number of events, including his increasing difficulty with a rapidly changing job, had responded well to treatment and had maintained his progress over a number of months. He nevertheless had thoughts like: 'If I am faced with a real problem, I shall not be able to deal with it, and everything will collapse round my ears.' As a homework task, he thought about what he would say to a friend in a similar position. He reminded himself of a number of situations over the preceding months when he had successfully tackled difficult situations, including getting a new job, coping with his wife's unexpected illness and developing bad dreams as his medication was reduced. He discussed with his therapist the risk that he might focus excessively on times when he was struggling, and, to counteract this, they agreed that he would, for a couple of months, keep a log of any examples of successful coping.*

Some clients will not have benefited from treatment or will have only partially benefited, and this can be especially difficult for them if they came to cognitive therapy having had little success with other treatment approaches. If the absence of progress was identified at an early review stage, it may be less dispiriting for the client to finish at that point, where the lack of progress could be attributed to a failure in cognitive therapy, rather than the client. For example, the therapist could say:

> *It seems that we have not managed to make much difference to your distress. Cognitive therapy has been found to be useful with a lot of people, but there are cases when it does not seem to relieve the feelings, however committed the client is to working in this way. Research is still needed into how to find new ways of changing beliefs or behaviour, so that more people can benefit from it, but I think at this point we have to say that cognitive therapy is not going to be helpful for you. Perhaps we should look at what has been helpful, so that you can take away some strategies for helping you feel better. For example, we found that you were good at breaking problems down into different elements and that then you could tackle difficult situations more easily. Is that something you can take away and use in the future?*

While it may be difficult to end treatment with little in the way of gain, it is unfair to maintain false hopes for a client who is unlikely to benefit, and continuing with treatment can further dispirit the client. If it seems that a different approach would be more useful, then this should be discussed with the client: for example, if there are significant marital problems, then couple therapy, or possibly systemic therapy, could be suggested; or it may be worth considering medication if this has not been exhausted previously. However, happily, the outcome of CBT with the majority of Axis I disorders is good, and, for most clients, a plan based on the blueprint will be a more positive note on which to end treatment.

Depression

Cognitive therapy's early success arose largely from the impact of Beck et al.'s (1979) book on depression, coupled with research trials showing the effectiveness of this new approach. In this chapter, we will describe some of the classic CBT strategies for depression. See also Chapter 17 for a brief description of some of the more recent innovations in working with depression, including mindfulness-based cognitive therapy and behavioural activation.

Characteristics of depression

As well as depressed mood, depressive disorders are marked by many others symptoms. In the American Psychiatric Association's *Diagnostic & Statistical Manual* (APA, 2000) these other symptoms include: loss of interest or enjoyment in activities; changes in weight and appetite; changes to sleep patterns; being either agitated or slowed up; loss of energy; feeling worthless or guilty; poor concentration; and suicidal thoughts.

The classic Beck model of depression centres on the 'depressive cognitive triad', i.e. a pattern of negative thoughts about:

- oneself (guilt, blame, self-criticism) – 'I'm useless, inadequate, lazy ...';
- the world, and current and past experience (selective attention to the negative, anhedonia, etc.) – 'Nothing is worthwhile, everything works out badly, no one cares about me ...';
- the future (pessimism, hopelessness) – 'It will always be like this, I'll never get better, there's nothing I can do ...'.

Perception, interpretation and recall of events may all be negatively biased so that depressed people are more likely to *notice* information which is consistent with their negative view, more likely to *interpret* any information negatively and more likely to *remember* negative events. Negative events are typically attributed to stable, global and internal factors and seen as having lasting consequences and implications for self-worth (Abramson et al., 2002) – e.g. 'This is my fault', 'I always mess up like this', 'It just shows how useless I am'. Positive events, on the other hand, are attributed to temporary, specific and external factors, with no lasting consequences – 'That was just a lucky break', 'It's the exception that proves the rule', 'It only worked out because my wife helped me'.

The primary symptoms of depression are often exacerbated by secondary negative or self-defeating thoughts *about* the symptoms of depression, thus giving rise to vicious circles. For example:

- Loss of energy and interest lead to thoughts such as 'It's not worth it, I'll wait until I feel better'.
- Poor memory, concentration, etc., may lead the client to think 'I'm stupid' or 'I must be going senile'.
- Loss of sexual interest and irritability may be interpreted as indicating 'My marriage has major problems'.

Common maintenance processes

Figure 12.1 shows some of the common maintenance cycles in depressed people (as always, these are possibilities to explore, not rules to force your clients to obey!). First, there is a possible vicious circle linking depressed mood with negative biases and negative interpretations of symptoms, which leads to a negative view of the self, thus maintaining the depressed mood. Second, those negative biases and symptoms of depression may lead to reductions of activity ('I'm too tired, there's no point . . .'), which maintains the low mood because activities that previously gave pleasure or a sense of achievement are lost. Finally, the depressive biases and symptoms may lead to reduced attempts to cope and deal with problems, which leads to increased hopelessness and, thus, reinforces the depression.

It follows from the above account that the goals of CBT for depression will usually include:

- helping the client to counteract any negative cognitive biases and develop a more balanced view of himself, the world and the future;
- restoring activity levels, especially activities that bring a sense of pleasure or achievement;
- increasing active engagement and problem-solving.

As always, your task as therapist is to construct a formulation that makes sense for you and your client and then to devise cognitive behavioural strategies that will help to break maintaining cycles. The main approaches to cognitive strategies and behavioural experiments in depression are broadly similar to the standard approaches outlined in Chapters 8 and 9, and, therefore, this chapter, after an outline of the broad approach to therapy, will focus on the interventions aimed at activity and problem-solving which are particularly characteristic of treatment for depression.

Course of treatment

CBT for depression usually contains the following elements, although, of course, this list needs adapting to your individual client. For instance, severely depressed clients may need more behavioural strategies, especially early in the course of therapy.

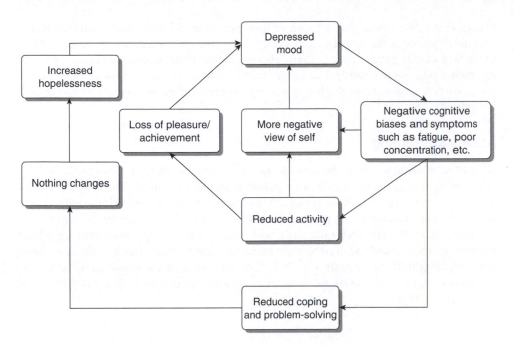

Figure 12.1   Common maintenance processes in depression

1. Identify the initial target problem list (i.e. a list of *specific* problems, not a general description such as 'depression'; a problem list might contain items such as 'Poor sleep', 'Difficulties in marital relationship', 'Lack of enjoyable activity' and so on).
2. Introduce the cognitive model and how it may apply to this client, through building a formulation (as in Chapter 4).
3. Begin work on reducing the symptoms, through behavioural or simple cognitive strategies.
4. Focus in the central part of therapy on the main work of identifying and challenging NATs through thought records, discussion and behavioural experiments.
5. Towards the end of therapy, identify and modify dysfunctional assumptions and/or core beliefs as necessary, with a view to reducing the risk of relapse.

Components of CBT for depression

CBT for depression usually contains the following components:

- behavioural strategies, including activity scheduling and graded task assignments;
- early cognitive strategies, including distraction and counting thoughts;
- main cognitive behavioural work of monitoring and testing NATs;
- relapse prevention, including working with dysfunctional assumptions and/or core beliefs, and revising earlier strategies.

Beck et al. (1979) prescribed a course of therapy lasting 15–20 sessions, with the first few sessions delivered at the rate of twice a week. Many ordinary clinical settings modify this to a standard weekly pattern and, perhaps, also reduce the total number of sessions. Clinical experience suggests that the protocol is sufficiently robust to withstand such modifications, but it is worth considering whether more frequent sessions are both desirable and feasible in particular cases.

Activity scheduling

Activity scheduling is one of the core therapeutic techniques in CBT for depression (Beck et al., 1979). It is based on the ideas embodied in the 'Reduction of activity' vicious circle in Figure 12.1, i.e. the notion that one maintaining factor for low mood is the reduction of activity that commonly accompanies it, which in turn leads to a loss of enjoyment and achievement, thus maintaining the low mood. Activity scheduling was derived from basic behavioural ideas about the need to build up reinforcing activities but has since developed into a sophisticated cognitive strategy. In fact, current conceptions would construe activity scheduling partly as a specialised form of behavioural experiment (see Chapter 9, and Fennell et al., 2004).

The weekly activity schedule (WAS)

The WAS is the essential tool for activity scheduling and is illustrated in Figure 12.2. It is basically a simple timetable grid with hours of the day down one side and days of the week across the top, so that there is a slot for every hour of the day. The version shown here has sufficient hourly slots to accommodate most clients but can be adapted if, for instance, you have a client who has severe early morning waking, so that the grid might need to start at 4 a.m. instead of 6 a.m. Note also that if you are making a template WAS, it is best to (a) make it much bigger than this, so that there is more space for the client to write – one A4 or letter page is usually sufficient; and (b) leave the days of the week blank so that a client you are seeing, for example, on a Wednesday can start his WAS on that or the following day, filling in the 'days' column headings appropriately.

Using the WAS as a record

The first stage of activity scheduling is to use the WAS as a self-monitoring tool, to gather information about the client's activities. This information may be used in two ways, as in the two approaches to behavioural experiments described in Chapter 9:

- The WAS may be used in the sense of *discovery*, simply to find out what is happening, how the client is spending his time and what activities are giving any pleasure or achievement (see below).
- The WAS may also be used in a spirit of *hypothesis-testing*. For example, for a client whose negative thoughts lead him to dismiss his efforts at coping as 'useless' or 'pathetic', the WAS can be used to get a more accurate record of what he is actually doing, in order to test the client's belief that he is 'useless'.

	Days of the week						
Time of day	Wed	Thu	Fri	Sat	Sun	Mon	Tue
6–7							
7–8							
8–9							
9–10							
10–11							
11–12							
12–1							
1–2							
2–3							
3–4							
4–5							
5–6							
6–7							
7–8							
8–9							
9–10							
10–11							
11–12							
12–1							

Figure 12.2   The weekly activity schedule

In either case, typical guidance for clients using a WAS should contain the following points:

- Complete the record *at the end of each hour,* or as close as possible to it (to avoid the effects of negative memory bias if you do it later).
- Each hour slot should contain:
    (a) a brief description of how you spent the time during that hour;
    (b) two numbers, labelled P (for Pleasure) and A (for Achievement).
Use these numbers to say how much you *enjoyed* what you did during that hour (Pleasure) and how much you felt you'd managed something it was *hard* for you to do (Achievement). These numbers can be anywhere from 0 (none at all) to 10 (the most

possible). So P1 would mean it was only slightly enjoyable. P8 would mean it was very enjoyable. In rating your Pleasure and Achievement, remember to use your current activity level as the standard. When you are well, it might not be much of an achievement to get up and dressed (it might rate only A0 or A1), but it might well be a considerable achievement when you are depressed (maybe even A8 or A9 on some days).

- Note that 'P' and 'A' don't necessarily go together. Some activities are pleasurable but don't give much sense of achievement (e.g. eating a bar of chocolate); some are achievements but not necessarily pleasurable (e.g. doing a chore); some activities may give you both (e.g. going to a social occasion when you didn't feel like it but ending up enjoying it).

Figure 12.3 shows part of a completed WAS.

Time of day	Monday	Tuesday	....
7–8	Got up, dressed P 0 A 5		
8–9	Breakfast for children, to school P 1 A 6		
9–10	Walked the dog P 3 A4		

Figure 12.3   A sample WAS

Using WAS records

There are three main things for you and your client to look for when the completed WAS is returned.

1. You can get a better picture of how active the client really is. Sometimes it shows that the client is actually doing more than he initially indicated – maybe even overworking. On the other hand, the record may show that indeed he is doing very little (in which case, increasing activity will be useful later).
2. Second, the record can help you see which activities, if any, give the client at least *some* sense of achievement and pleasure. When you start to think about changes, these are the activities it may be worth increasing.
3. Finally, you can use the information to plan changes. What does it suggest needs to change? Is the client spending long periods doing very little except feeling low? Does it look as if there are lots of chores which must be done, but very little enjoyable activity? Are there any activities which he enjoys at least a bit, or which improve his mood even a little and which he might do more of?

In addition to these activity-specific observations, the WAS provides an excellent laboratory in which you and the client can begin to observe NATs, noticing how thoughts and behaviour affect each other and using this to encourage the client to start spotting NATs in action (e.g. NATs that block activity). You can watch out for this kind of thought and work with them via discussion or behavioural experiments. For example, if your client's attempts to do a particular task are blocked by NATs along the lines of 'I won't enjoy it' or 'I'll only make a mess of it', then you could set up a behavioural experiment to see how true that is.

Using the WAS as a planning tool

The next step is for you and the client to use what you have learned to plan future activity. There are three common ways to improve mood through activity:

1. To increase the overall level of activity if it is low.
2. To focus specifically on doing more of the things that give the client some sense of pleasure and achievement. If nothing is giving much pleasure at the moment, then it is worth thinking about things the client *used* to enjoy and plan to restart some of those.
3. Activity scheduling can be used as a way of doing behavioural experiments to test out negative cognitions about activity. For example, using a WAS to monitor and rate Pleasure and Achievement may enable your client to combat 'all or nothing' thinking that tends to see Achievement as being either complete success or complete failure.

During this phase, instead of simply monitoring what he does, the client uses the WAS as a timetable to plan increases in activity and, specifically, activities identified as providing some pleasure or achievement. How much detail is needed, and how much activity should be aimed for, will depend on the individual client: in general, the more depressed the client is, the more detailed planning he may need and the lower the initial goals for activity may need to be. Early on, you may need to be closely involved in planning, but later on the client can take on more of this task for himself.

Graded task assignment

The best general principle in planning activity is 'graded tasks'. In other words, aim to build up activity step by step, rather than attempting to go in one jump from no activity at all to being busy all day. Because of the depressed client's extreme sensitivity to any possibility of failure, it will usually be counterproductive to agree tasks which are too far forward from where the client is now. If he does not manage to complete the task, it will be likely to be counted as a failure and taken as further reason to lose hope. It is usually better to agree a smaller but manageable task. For example, if your client wants to take up reading again after giving up because of concentration difficulties, then it is unlikely that he will be able to read a whole novel by next week. It will usually be better to negotiate a target he believes he can achieve, even if this is only to read one page by next week (but make sure that the target does not get so small that the client sees it as trivial).

Exercise

There is some evidence that reasonably high levels of physical exercise – perhaps of the order of three sessions per week, each of 45 minutes to one hour – may have a significant effect on depression, with some studies finding effects comparable to anti-depressants (Greist & Klein, 1985; Martinsen et al., 1985). It is therefore worth encouraging clients to make exercise sessions a part of their activity planning (see also Chapter 10).

Common problems in activity scheduling

Lack of pleasure

It is important to realise that in the early stages of fighting depression, clients are not likely to enjoy anything as much as they did before the depression. It is important to prepare clients for the fact that initially they will probably have to force themselves to do things even though there is not much pleasure. Persevering should at least give the client some sense of achievement, and, eventually, the enjoyment should return as well. It is also important to convey the idea of pleasure as a continuum, not all or nothing. We are looking for *some* increase in enjoyment, not an instant return to full enjoyment.

Excessive standards

It is also important that the client recognises that achievements do not have to be at the level of winning the Nobel Prize to be worthwhile. Spending ten minutes tidying up a messy kitchen drawer can help the client feel he has done something useful today and may be a considerable achievement. It is important to help your client apply realistic standards in evaluating tasks and activities. What was easy when he was well may be difficult (and therefore warrant a higher achievement score) when he is depressed.

Vague planning

When planning activities, it is better to be specific. In other words, try to help the client move from vague goals like 'I must do more' to specific activities at specific times, e.g. 'Go and buy that birthday card on Wednesday morning'.

Jacobson's dismantling study and the behavioural activation approach

Lest anyone doubt the value of activity scheduling and behavioural methods in treating depression, Jacobson et al.'s (1996) study makes fascinating reading. In this study, Jacobson et al. compared outcomes between three versions of CBT for depression, based on 'dismantling' the classic Beckian therapy. One treatment was normal Beckian therapy, and this was compared with two 'stripped down' versions: one in which therapists used only the behavioural components of CBT (including activity scheduling) and one in which they used both behavioural and cognitive methods but only at the level of automatic thoughts, with no direct targeting of assumptions or core beliefs. What they found was that all three treatments produced similar outcomes and *also similar changes on measures of negative cognitions*. One possible conclusion is that different methods may achieve the same end result of cognitive and emotional change by different pathways. Following on from this study, colleagues of Jacobson's elaborated their behavioural treatment into a new therapy for depression known as 'behavioural activation' (see Chapter 17).

Cognitive strategies in depression

There are two phases of cognitive work in classic CBT for depression. In the first phase, the aim is to help the client get some symptom relief by using simple strategies to reduce the impact of NATs on mood (with the useful secondary aim of providing evidence about how thoughts can influence mood). In the second phase, the NATs are confronted more directly, with the aim of helping the client consider them more carefully and, if appropriate, find alternative thoughts through all the methods discussed earlier in this book: finding alternatives, looking for evidence, devising behavioural experiments and so on.

Early cognitive strategies

The goals of these strategies are to distract the client from his NATs, and/or to change his attitude towards them. Other exercises are designed to promote a change of attitude towards NATs. Instead of getting 'swallowed up' by them, the aim is to get some distance from them, for the client to see them as 'just thoughts' rather than obvious truths about themselves or the world. Counting the thoughts can help – not paying any other attention to them, just counting them, with the same attitude one might have in spotting how many pigeons there are in one's neighbourhood: 'There's one … and another … oh, and there's another'! One metaphor to describe this approach is to imagine one's stream of thoughts as a rather dirty and polluted river, with all kinds of sewage and garbage in it. Initially, your client may be like someone who has fallen into the river and is being swept along by it, surrounded by all the garbage. The new attitude is like climbing out of the river and standing on the bank, watching it all go by; the garbage is all still there, but he is likely to be less affected by it. This is similar to the mindfulness approaches outlined in Chapter 17.

Main cognitive strategies

The bulk of a course of CBT for depression will be taken up with NATs, using the approach outlined in Chapters 8 and 9. That is, sessions will include, in varying proportions according to the stage of therapy and the client's reaction to therapy:

- identifying NATs, using self-monitoring, thought records, in-session mood changes, etc.;
- verbal discussion of the NATs, to examine their accuracy and helpfulness;
- identifying realistic alternative thoughts;
- using behavioural experiments to gather evidence that will help the client to test out NATs and the new alternative thoughts.

Medication

CBT is, of course, not the only effective treatment for depression, and, in particular, anti-depressant medication is helpful for many depressed clients. There is currently less concern about dependence and withdrawal for anti-depressants, compared to anxiolytics, and there is no conflict between pharmaceutical treatment and psychological therapy. In fact, there is some evidence that for people with more severe depression, the combination of both forms of treatment is better than either alone (e.g. Thase et al., 1997).

Dealing with suicidal thoughts

The risk of suicide in depressed clients should not be overestimated – the vast majority of depressed clients do not commit suicide – but it clearly needs to be taken seriously, and you should respond to any sign of suicidal ideation, sometimes even if it means breaking confidentiality. Professional consensus is that amongst the risk factors for suicide are the following (Peruzzi & Bongar, 1999):

- Acute suicidal ideation
- A history of suicide attempts, or family history of suicide
- The medical seriousness of any previous attempts
- Severe hopelessness
- Attraction to death
- Recent losses or separations
- Misuse of alcohol.

Management of suicidal clients

You need to have a basic management plan in place so that you can safely continue cognitive therapy. The elements of such a plan might include:

- making sure that the client is either supervised or has immediate access to support whenever he needs it;
- taking steps to help the client or others to remove any easily accessible means of suicide (e.g. potentially toxic medication, poisons, ropes, guns, car keys, etc.).
- establishing ways of managing suicidal crises, should they occur: for example, arranging for the client to contact a friend or family member, or contact a crisis team if one is available. Ensure that plans are specific and clear and, perhaps, have a written copy for your client to carry around.
- working on building up the therapeutic relationship so that the client will see you as someone who is trustworthy and understanding and who can offer some credible hope.
- consider seeing if the client will agree at least to postpone suicide and not carry it out until a certain time has passed (e.g. not before your next meeting).
- use aspects of therapy to 'play for time' until the crisis has passed: e.g. encourage engagement in therapy and curiosity about where it is going; 'build bridges' from the end of one sessions to the next session ('That's interesting – shall we explore that next time?').

Exploring and working with reasons for suicide

It is important to give clients a space in which to talk about suicidal thoughts and to approach the topic in a matter-of-fact way that gives the clear message that the topic is not off limits. You will not make someone more likely to commit suicide by asking about their suicidal thoughts, and you may have a chance to prevent suicide if the topic is in the open. Important aspects of this discussion will include:

- exploring the client's reason for suicide – there are two common main categories of reason:

    (a) to escape from an unbearable life, depression etc, ('It's the only way out'). This is probably the most common reason for suicide, and the most dangerous;
    (b) to solve an external problem (e.g. to hold onto a relationship, take revenge, or elicit care);

- building up with the client reasons for living versus reasons for dying, including past reasons for living which might become valid again in future;
- exploring the beliefs leading to hopelessness and using guided discovery to help elicit information which might be inconsistent with those beliefs;
- working on a problem area that has a high probability of being resolved fairly quickly, so as to decrease hopelessness;
- using problem-solving for 'real-life' problems that are leading to hopelessness (see below).

Structured problem-solving

There is evidence both that depressed people have deficits in social problem-solving and that teaching structured problem-solving can be an effective therapy for people with depression (see, for example, Nezu et al., 1989; Mynors-Wallis et al., 1997; Mynors-Wallis et al., 2000). This may be especially useful with clients whose formulation includes something like the poor coping/hopelessness maintenance cycle outlined in Figure 12.1; it may also be helpful in dealing with suicidal ideas as outlined above.

The main steps for your client to follow in doing problem-solving are as follows:

- *Identify the problem he wishes to work on.*
  It is important to be clear about what exactly the nature of the problem is. For example, not just 'Problems in my marriage' but something more precise about the nature of those problems, such as 'My wife and I don't talk together enough' or 'We never have any time to go out together.'
- *Think of as many possible ways of solving this problem as he can.*
  This stage can be difficult, particularly with problems which have been around for a long time. Clients may have an immediate negative response to every solution they think of: 'That wouldn't work', or 'I've tried that'. To overcome this, it can be helpful to start with 'brainstorming', in other words trying to come up with as many ideas as he can, *without any judgement* at this stage as to whether they are useful, sensible or even possible. The aim is to generate lots of approaches, no matter how wild or impractical they may seem.

The rule is to write down *anything* which comes into his mind as a possible solution, no matter how daft. The reason for this is that even wild solutions may generate other thoughts which might be useful. With more severely depressed clients, it may also be helpful for the therapist to begin with some suggestsions if the client is completely stuck.

- *After generating the list of possible solutions, work out which solution, or combination of solutions, seems to be the best.*
  Again, it is best to structure this process so that your client thinks carefully about each possible solution, without dismissing any of them too early. Only solutions which are clearly unacceptable should be disposed of immediately.

  A good way to weigh up solutions is to think systematically about the pros and cons of each one, making sure you consider both long- and short-term ones. Take the first possible solution and make a list of what the advantages and disadvantages of that solution would be. Then do the same for the next possible solution, then the next, and so on. Use this list of pros and cons to pick out and rank-order the best few solutions.

- *Pick the solution that seems to offer the most favourable balance.*
  Two problems can arise here. First, it can sometimes be true that no solution emerges as positive overall: they all have more negatives than positives. If that is the case, and you really have gone through every possible solution, then the client needs to accept that he has no choice but to pick the *least bad* one – it may not be good, but it is still better than the others.

  Second, you may find that when you go through the list, they all come out pretty much the same, with your client feeling that there is no clear winner. If that is so, and again if you really have gone through *all* possible solutions, then just pick one solution randomly and try that. Sometimes, the process of doing this will help the client realise that actually he does have a preference for one solution, because he finds himself wishing he had picked that one.

- *When a solution is identified, use the principle of 'small steps'.*
  As always, small steps are usually better than giant leaps, because they are more likely to be successful and thus generate hope. Ask your client to think about what would be the *first step* towards carrying out his preferred solution. For instance, if he has decided a solution to a problem would be to find a new job, the first step might be to buy the local paper and look at what kind of job is available at the moment. It is probably much easier to do that first step than to imagine the whole process of ending up with a new job. Take it one step at a time.

- *Put into action whatever is the first step to a solution, and then review how it went.*
  Does this solution seem to be along the right lines? If not, why not? Do you need to modify the initial plan in the light of what has happened? Even solutions that look good on paper may turn out not to work in practice. Don't worry if this happens. By trying it out, your client will probably have learned something useful which may help him work out a better solution. If some major problem arises when he tries to put his solution into practice, you may need to identify that as a new problem. Then start the whole process again so that you can first find a solution to *that* problem.

- *Continue this process until the problem is solved or it is clear that there are no possible solutions.*
  You can go round and round the cycle of identifying problems, solutions and steps towards solutions until the problem improves. Of course, some problems may not have any practical solution – but beware of jumping to that conclusion too quickly. If there really is no solution, then you probably need to go back to cognitive strategies to help the client find a different way of reacting to the situation.

Potential problems in treating depressed clients

The nature of depression

It is obvious – but nevertheless important to remember – that the depressed client is often negative in his thinking, lacking in drive and energy and hopeless about the possibility of change. Depression can also result in a 'depressing environment': e.g. your client's depression leads to his losing his job, or to marital difficulties, which then tend to maintain his low mood. It is therefore hardly surprising that you may find yourself struggling to engage clients: they may find it difficult to take any action, greet every suggestion with 'That will never work' and be tempted to give up at every real or imagined 'failure'.

Therapists too may have difficulties in working with depression. You may find yourself 'infected' by the client's pessimism, silently thinking that he is right and things are indeed as bad as he thinks they are. Of course, that could be an accurate view, but you should be careful about buying into it too easily without a great deal of evidence. Although it may be the case that your client is facing genuine difficulties and at least some of his negative thoughts are accurate, there is usually still room for questioning and looking for alternatives. It may be bad, but it is usually not *so* bad that 100% of people would feel as the client does, so there must be some room for alternative views. On the other hand, it is also important not to get so bound up with being sceptical and positive that you come across as unempathic or impatient. Clients need to know that you understand where they're coming from before you start trying to help them see where they might go to.

These problems may be particularly difficult when working with chronic and severe depression: see Moore & Garland (2003) for a useful guide to such work.

Hopelessness and 'Yes, buts'

As we have just noted, most depressed clients will inevitably bring to therapy some of the same negative thinking as pervades the rest of their lives. They will be hopeless about the possibilities of change and tend to have negative thoughts about therapy, with 'Yes, but . . .' being a common reaction to attempts to broaden their thinking. For you, as a therapist, it is important not to be too influenced by this way of thinking but to remain (realistically) optimistic and to understand that your client's reactions to therapy are part of the depressive syndrome. Graded task assignments, as discussed earlier in this chapter, are a good way to get small successes that will help to build the client's confidence. Behavioural experiments are also a good way to drive home verbal discussions so that new ways of thinking are not just vague theoretical possibilities but are tested out in action. Sometimes such 'Yes buts' reflect extremely fixed fundamental beliefs, so it may be helpful to consider some of the schema-focused strategies in Chapter 17.

Slow pace

Depressed clients may be slowed up in their thinking and behaviour and, even if they are not, the pace of sessions and the speed of change early in treatment is likely to be slow. It is helpful if you are prepared for this, and adapt to it, but do not become discouraged by it.

Monitoring progress using some measure such as the BDI (Chapter 4) may also be useful in picking up small but steady changes.

Feedback in sessions

As noted in Chapter 11, asking the client to give you feedback on a session is a standard part of CBT. However, it may be particularly important to encourage the depressed client to do this openly, because his negative bias makes it particularly likely that some words or behaviour on your part may be misinterpreted as being critical or rejecting of him. For the same reason, it is always worth noting and enquiring about any apparent decline in mood during a session: what went through your client's mind when that happened?

Anxiety Disorders

Introduction

The first treatment manual for cognitive therapy for *anxiety* disorders was published by Beck and his colleagues in 1985, and was an exciting development in the world of CBT. It heralded the beginning of the revolution that has gradually applied CBT to an ever wider range of problems.

The application of CBT to anxiety disorders was understandable given their prevalence (13.3% of the US population [NIMH, 2001]), and evidence of its efficacy in treating anxiety disorders has been compelling (see, for example, Clark & Beck, 1988; Heimberg, 2002).

The anxiety response

It is important to remember that the anxiety *response* is a normal, vital reaction to threat. When we perceive danger, our bodies rapidly produce adrenaline that primes us to respond to dangerous situations. The classic responses are 'fight' (challenging the fear directly) or 'flight' (escaping from or avoiding the fear), although 'freeze' (being physically or mentally immobile) is a third possible reaction. When faced with perceived threat, we feel fear and the mind and the body get ready to deal with it. The mind considers the worst-case scenario, and the body prepares to tackle it – breathing increases to provide more oxygen; the heart beats faster to get the oxygen-rich blood to key muscles; sweat glands become active to cool the body during activity; and blood is diverted away from the skin, which can result in uncomfortable sensations and paleness.

The response reflects the four systems referred to in Chapter 4: emotional, cognitive, physiological and behavioural. This quite complex response happens swiftly and efficiently every day, for example:

> *A mother is standing at the side of the road close to her small son. A bus is heading towards them. The mother has a fleeting image of her son stepping into the road in front of the bus. She feels fear. Her adrenaline rises, she becomes tense, focused and primed for action. Swiftly, she takes her son's arm, despite his protestations, and holds him close to her as the bus passes them safely.*

Thus, the anxiety response is a normal and largely unconscious process that regularly occurs in each of us. Anxiety only becomes a problem when the normal response is exaggerated or occurs in the absence of real threat. For example,

> Sally frequently had intrusive images and thoughts about her children being hurt on the street. Several times a day, she would feel very nervous about this. She never let them go out alone and she tried to take them everywhere in her car.

> Geoff had suffered a panic attack and now lived in fear of having another. In order to minimise the likelihood, he tried not to vary his breathing for fear of hyperventilating; he moved slowly in order not to get light-headed; and he avoided situations which, he predicted, would be stressful. As a result, his life was very restricted.

In these examples, fears are exaggerated or dangers overestimated such that the individuals feel compelled to take quite dramatic actions to alleviate their fears. They have each developed an anxiety disorder.

A person's interpretation of events determines his responses, so throughout this chapter you will note the use of the term '*perceived* danger' or '*perceived* threat'. This means that two individuals can be in precisely the same situation but anticipate different consequences and, therefore, react in different ways. Imagine two musicians both waiting for the concert to begin:

> The first musician is filled with dread: she fears that she will make a mistake, or that the audience will be hostile. She feels tense, her heart races and she concludes that these are bad signs. This undermines her confidence further. The other musician is looking forward to the opportunity of performing, anticipating an enjoyable experience. He feels tense, his heart races and he concludes that this is what will give him the energy necessary to perform. Thus, in the identical situation, the first musician is worried and interprets her reaction as a bad thing; the second is excited and assumes that his physical responses are helpful.

Characteristics of anxiety and anxiety disorders

Typically, dealing with anxiety is a linear process:

Trigger → perceived threat → anxiety response → successful coping reaction → resolution of anxiety.

For example:

- A driver sees a child run out in front of a car → production of adrenaline → this promotes quick and focused thinking which enables the driver to brake and swerve in time → resolution of anxiety.
- A student learns of an impending assessment → production of adrenaline → the resulting focused thinking and raised energy levels enable the student to study efficiently → resolution of anxiety.

However, anxiety disorders are represented by a circular process (Figure 13.1) in which cognitive and behavioural responses serve to maintain or worsen anxiety.

For example:

- An anxious driver sees a child who he thinks is about to run out in front of his car → he is highly anxious and becomes physically tense and cannot think straight → he swerves to avoid a child who is not actually in the road and is reprimanded by another motorist for driving dangerously → this confirms that driving is hazardous and he remains a highly anxious driver.
- An anxious student learns of an impending oral assessment → she finds this threatening and experiences high levels of anxiety → her thinking becomes overly focused on the exam and she becomes tense that she cannot study effectively → she does not perform well in the assessment; this promotes her belief that she is incapable, and she remains a highly anxious student.

The 'ultimate' fear cycle is probably 'fear of fear', where the experience of anxiety itself becomes aversive and is therefore avoided long after the original trigger for the anxiety has receded.

Roger thought that he had had a heart attack, but at the hospital he was reassured that he had experienced a panic attack. Roger was not totally relieved by this, as he had found the panic attack so unpleasant that he now lived in dread of it happening again.

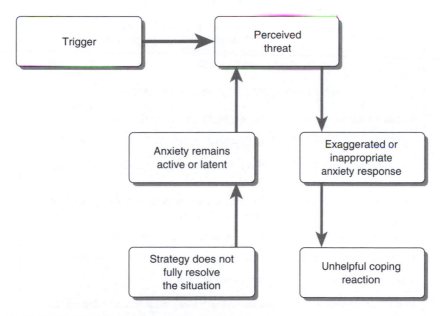

Figure 13.1   The cycle of problem anxiety

As we have seen, anxiety prepares the mind and body for dealing with danger: the mind is focused on the bad things that could happen, and the body is primed for action. Thus, anxiety comprises both psychological and physical symptoms, symptoms which become exaggerated and unhelpful in anxiety disorders. This is summarised in Figure 13.2.

As we have seen, anxiety disorders are characterised by distorted beliefs about the dangerousness of certain experiences. This can be triggered by particular situations (for example, being on a high building) or internal stimuli (such as a chest pains or an alarming thought).

There are many types of anxiety disorder, not always easily distinguished from each other. Below is list of the anxiety-related problems that you might encounter in your clinical practice (DSM-IV-TR; APA, 2000).

FROM ANXIETY	TO ANXIETY DISORDER
A sense of threat	Overestimation of threat and/or overestimation of consequence; also underestimation of ability to cope, or available resources. Focus on threat Rumination, excessive worry, inability to think flexibly, persistent and threatening thoughts and images
Apprehension	Fear of losing control, of going 'crazy' or of suffering health problems.Constant checking.
Temporarily exaggerated thinking	Habitual exaggerated thinking such as repeated catastrophisation, highly selective attention, pervasive 'all or nothing' thinking.
THE CONTINUUM OF PHYSICAL SYMPTOMS	
FROM ANXIETY	TO ANXIETY DISORDER
Increased heart rate	Palpitations
Muscular tension	Fatigue, trembling, muscular pain; e.g., chest, head
Increased breathing rate	Dizziness, light-headedness, derealisation or depersonalisation
Changes in digestive system	Nausea, urge to go to the lavatory
Changes in blood circulation	Blushing or paleness, unpleasant skin sensations
Increased sweating	Excessive sweating
In addition, chronic anxiety is associated with sleep disorders and depression.	

Figure 13.2   Symptoms of anxiety

- **Acute Stress Disorder (ASD)**: diagnosed when a person who has been exposed to a traumatic event develops anxiety symptoms, re-experiencing of the event and marked avoidance of stimuli that trigger recollections of the trauma. The disturbance occurs within four weeks of the traumatic event and lasts for a maximum of four weeks. After this time, the condition would be diagnosed as PTSD (see below).
- **Generalised Anxiety Disorder (GAD)**: manifest as persistent and excessive worries, fears and negative thoughts that lead to distress and/or impairment of performance. Typically, sufferers are beset with 'What if …' worries, pervading many aspects of their lives.
- **Health Anxiety or hypochondriasis**: characterised by a preoccupation with, and fears of, having a serious illness, now or in the future. Sufferers tend to misinterpret benign bodily symptoms, and to seek reassurance.
- **Obsessive-Compulsive Disorder (OCD)**: characterised by recurrent obsessions (persistent and intrusive thoughts, images or impulses) and/or compulsions (compelling repetitive behaviours or mental acts intended to put right or neutralise the obsession). Sufferers believe that they are responsible for the safety of self or others, and fears centre on contamination (e.g. passing on germs by not washing hands sufficiently); disaster due to neglect to do something properly (e.g. switching off switches); behaving inappropriately as a consequence of having improper thoughts (e.g. thinking about swearing in church resulting in swearing).
- **Panic Disorder**: defined by the experience of recurrent panic attacks which are sudden increases in anxiety accompanied by symptoms such as palpitations, breathlessness and dizziness. Such symptoms are typically misinterpreted as signs of impending or current ill health, like a heart attack or a stroke (Clark, 1986). Panic disorder can occur with or without agoraphobia, i.e. a fear of being in places or situations from which escape might be difficult, or in which help may not be available in the event of a panic attack or panic-like symptoms.
- **Post-Traumatic Stress Disorder (PTSD)**: occurs following an event deemed seriously threatening to oneself or others. Symptoms include intrusive memories of the traumatic events (nightmares, flashbacks), avoidance, numbing and hyperarousal. Concerns focus on an *enduring* sense of danger, although shame, disgust and anger are also reported. Typically, clients with PTSD can recall fragments of the event in detail, but the entire picture is jumbled or incomplete (Foa & Riggs, 1993).
- **Social Anxiety**: characterised by a marked and persistent fear of social or performance situations in which a person feels scrutinised by others and fears embarrassment or humiliation.
- **Specific Phobia**: defined as a persistent fear of an object or situation and, often, a fear of one's reaction to it. The fear is often recognised as exaggerated, but the sufferer tends to avoid the phobic stimulus (overtly or covertly), and functioning is disrupted. Phobias can focus on a range of things: animals, the natural environment, blood, specific situations and so on.

There are also anxiety disorders that fall outside a formal diagnostic category, and 'Anxiety Disorder Not Otherwise Specified (Anxiety Disorder NOS)' is used (DSM-IV-TR; APA, 2000). This reminds us that we should not assume that our clients will slip neatly into a category, and we should certainly not try to 'ease' them into one.

Maintaining processes

Why do anxiety disorders persist? The key to this (and to managing problems) is identifying the maintaining cycles that explain their persistence.

There is a common pattern to the maintenance of anxiety problems (see Figure 13.3). In response to an internal or external trigger, the anxious client assumes threat or danger and either draws a catastrophic conclusion (something bad has happened and this has frightening implications for the future) or makes a catastrophic prediction (something bad will happen). Understandably, the client then tries to protect himself from the perceived threat. For example, the person with agoraphobia retreats to a 'safe' base or the client with health anxiety seeks reassurance. Such responses give immediate relief but do not challenge the validity of the belief. Thus, the person with agoraphobia fails to learn that it is possible to be in a public place without something terrible happening; the client with health anxiety does not learn to assure herself of her good health. In short, the original fears remain intact, ready to be triggered sometime later.

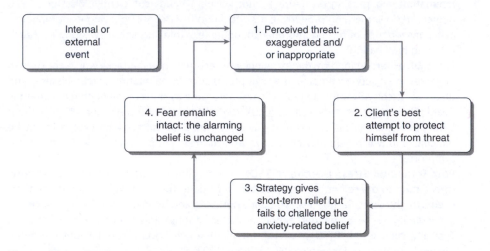

Figure 13.3   Anxiety maintenance

Essentially, anxiety disorders are perpetuated by how we feel, what we think and what we do. Clark (1999) has proposed that six processes maintain distorted beliefs about the (irrational) dangerousness of certain situations, even in the face of evidence that the world is a safe place. These are summarised below and might give you some hypotheses about the nature of your client's problems(s).

1. **Safety behaviours** (Salkovskis, 1988): these are behaviours or mental activities which are carried out in an attempt to minimise or prevent something bad from happening (see also Chapter 4). Of course, behaving in a safe way is not dysfunctional: looking both ways before we cross the road is a highly functional safety-seeking behaviour. However, standing at the kerb side repeatedly checking for cars, unable to take the risk of crossing, is an exaggerated and unhelpful safety-seeking behaviour – it is the latter that Salkovskis

describes. In Figure 13.3, they fall into Box 2. These responses can prevent a person from learning that they overestimate danger, because each 'safe' experience is attributed to the success of a safety behaviour. For example, a young woman with vomit phobia might get through the day without feeling nauseous and certainly without being sick. This should provide assurance that she is not at risk of vomiting. However, if she has been sucking mints as a safety strategy, she will attribute her well-being to the sweets. Alternatively, a man with panic disorder who fears having a heart attack may move around slowly in order to remain safe; he may attribute his good health to slow movement rather than realise that he has a healthy heart.

The distinction between 'helpful coping behaviour' and 'unhelpful safety behaviour' reflects the intention behind the behaviour. For example, a man might relax his shoulders and slow his breathing in response to feeling tense and, subsequently, feel calmer. If he interpreted this as, 'I'm only feeling better because I did my relaxation routine and if I had not done it something terrible would have happened', it is unlikely that he would develop confidence that he could manage tension and, need not be afraid of it: the 'relaxation routine' would be a safety behaviour. However, if he concluded, 'If I'm tense, I relax', then relaxing is simply a functional coping behaviour, and he is likely to grow confident that he can cope.

2. **Focus of attention**: this falls into two categories, (1) attention directed *towards* threat cues and (2) attention directed *away* from them. Examples of the former would include the person with a spider phobia who scans the room for signs of webs or spider droppings, or the person with social anxiety who ruminates on his behaviour at a party, concentrating on all the dissatisfying aspects of it. This serves to emphasise the fear, as it is constantly in mind and because the person who scans for threat is vulnerable to making false positive judgements. Thus, a hairline crack in the wall 'is' a spider web, a piece of dark fluff on the carpet 'is' a spider. In this way, this person experiences an inappropriately increased amount of fear.

Examples of attention being directed away from threat cues include the person with social phobia who avoids eye contact, or the road-traffic-accident victim who averts his gaze when nearing the site of the accident. In doing this, the fundamental fears are not faced, not even named in some instances, and it becomes impossible to challenge the perceived threat.

3. **Spontaneous imagery**: several studies indicate that mental images can enhance the sense of threat (Ottavani & Beck, 1987, Clark & Wells, 1995). For example, the person with social phobia might hold a vivid mental picture of himself looking incompetent, or the client with panic disorder might have a catastrophic image of herself losing control. Such images appear to heighten anxiety. Imagery is particularly relevant in the maintenance of PTSD, where vivid intrusions are thought to maintain a sense of *current* threat to the individual and thus prevent anxieties from remitting.

4. **Emotional reasoning**: this refers to the process of believing that 'If I feel it, then it must be so' (see also Chapter 8). Arntz et al. (1995) showed that anxious patients rate situations as being more dangerous than control subjects do – even when given information that assured them of safety. Anxious clients conclude that there must be a threat because they feel anxious. Thus, based on her feelings, a highly nervous woman might not be able to identify danger but would *assume* it existed; or she might feel unstable and light-headed and *presume* that others would observe her wobbling or swaying. Often, such assumptions serve to further heighten anxiety.

5. **Memory processes**: Clark (1999) suggests that there are distortions of memory that account for the perpetuation of problem anxiety: selective recall of threat and poor recall

of anxiety-provoking situations. Selective recall means that anxious individuals tend to have the capacity for more negative and traumatic recall of their own experiences than do non-anxious individuals (Mansell & Clark, 1999). This, of course, helps maintain a view of the world as personally threatening. Selective recall also prevents the individual from being able to appraise the bigger picture. Without this, fears cannot be put into perspective. The most striking example of this process is PTSD, where sufferers have intense recollections or flashbacks which maintain a sense of current threat whilst having an imprecise recall of the entire event – which would otherwise help to put the intense recollection into context and combat the impression of danger being current.

6. **Interpretation of reactions to a threat event**: the conclusions that a person draws when experiencing anxiety symptoms can exacerbate the problem. For example, if someone with a perfectly normal response to threat jumps to the catastrophic conclusion 'I am going crazy!' or, 'I'm going to pass out!' this can heighten the anxiety, provoke anticipatory anxieties and result in clients using avoidant strategies which are likely to prolong their fears.

Another process that has been associated with protracted or exaggerated anxiety is worry (Borkovec, 1994). Although a brief period of worrying is helpful as it guides our attention to potential threats (Davey & Tallis, 1994), prolonged worrying becomes unproductive and can even be actively undermining. For example, whilst on holiday, I might worry about losing my passport. This focuses my thinking: I check that I have my passport and I consider where I might put it for safety. A more anxiety-prone person might worry about losing his passport but continue this cycle of worry even though he had checked that he was carrying it. He might keep thinking, '. . . but what if . . .' and increase his anxiety levels with each repetition of this (usually unanswered) question. This further exacerbates the problem because the sufferer, locked into repetitive worrying, often avoids addressing more central concern(s), hence preventing problem-solving. For example, Tom came to therapy for help with his concern about contracting genital herpes back in his village in Africa. Exploration and challenging of his fear always ended in: '. . . but what if I have caught it and it will show itself later?' Over several sessions, he began to talk about the shame that he would experience *if* he had herpes and later spoke of his shame for having run from his village when he saw military-police vehicles. He later discovered that several members of his family had been shot by the military police that day.

Clearly, the groups of thinking biases described in Chapter 8 (selective attention, extreme thinking, relying on intuition, self-reproach) can also play a part in the maintenance of problem anxiety.

In summary, then, understanding the maintaining cycles that drive problem anxiety is fundamental to managing it. What implication has this for therapy? The beauty of maintaining cycles is that we can plan interventions to break unhelpful patterns, and in the next section we will look at this.

Treatment approaches

As we indicated earlier in this chapter, it is essential that you carry out a thorough assessment before attempting to classify your client's problem. In those cases where it becomes clear that that the difficulty does indeed fall into a recognisable DSM category, you are urged to use the established cognitive model and treatment protocols for that disorder. These are elaborated in the next chapter.

Earlier we outlined the generic anxiety cycle: a trigger taps into a fear, the client responds in a self-protective way (usually a form of avoidance), the fear is unchallenged and remains intact, ready to be triggered in the future.

John has a specific phobia. He is so scared of confined spaces that he can no longer travel by air or public transport, he cannot use lifts and he will not ride in another person's car. His alarming prediction is that, in a confined space, he will not be able to get sufficient air and will suffocate. John protects himself as best he can: for example, if he has to travel, he will use his own car; he will choose a route which allows him to stop as he feels necessary; he will have the windows open to ensure that he gets enough air. The consequence of his use of safety behaviours is that he avoids the lack of air that he fears and, so his belief that something dreadful will happen remains intact.

Pamela has OCD. She fears contamination of herself and loved ones and has a catastrophic prediction that someone might die as a result of contamination. Like John, she does her best to deal with her fear and engages in quite elaborate cleaning rituals and uses plastic covers on her furniture to repel dirt. She also asks her family to remove their shoes outside the house, immediately go into the cloakroom by the door and to 'scrub up' before entering the main living areas. Each of these strategies ensures that Pamela avoids facing her fear and, as a result, she never gains confidence that she can relax her standards for cleanliness. Her problem is further enhanced by her family members colluding with the avoidance.

Essentially, if John and Pamela are to overcome their problems, they need to break the cycle by challenging their fears (Figure 13.4).

John, with the help of his therapist, agreed to let go of some of his safety behaviours (giving up all of them was too threatening to begin with), and he began driving with his window closed. He found that he had ample air and the only times that he felt short of breath were when his anxiety increased because of a driving challenge and not because he would run out of air in his car. This began to undermine his fear-related beliefs and he dared to relinquish more of his unhelpful behaviours. He and his therapist worked out a programme of BEs, and he began to drive on motorways where he might have to stay on a stretch of road for miles before being free to take a break. He gradually took on increasingly challenging tasks and soon became comfortable driving on any stretch of motorway. By now his fearful predictions of catastrophe were significantly undermined and the maintenance cycle for his fear broken. As a result, he was able to begin to use public transport with relative ease. In John's case, the results of behavioural changes facilitated cognitive change: his behavioural achievements challenged his earlier beliefs with very little input from the therapist.

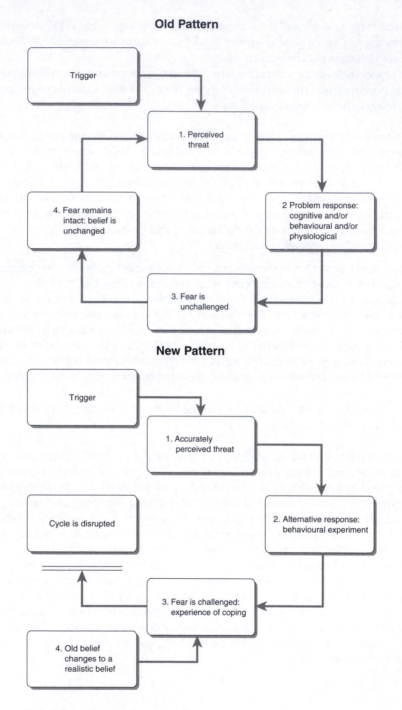

Figure 13.4   Breaking maintaining cycles

Pamela's excessive cleaning and her demands on her family members eventually became intolerable, and her husband and children persuaded her to seek therapy. At first, Pamela was both sceptical of therapy and very frightened of making changes. It seemed improbable that she would begin to change her behaviours without some compelling assurance that it would be worth the risk. Thus, her therapy began with a cognitive emphasis (see Chapter 8) and data-gathering, using a survey method of BE (see Chapter 9). Using this approach, she began to see the advantages of change and was then able to engage in a series of behavioural experiments that systematically helped her to relinquish her safety behaviours.

When aiming to break unproductive cycles, you are always faced with the question of what interventions to use. As cognitive therapists, we have a collection of cognitive, behavioural and physical strategies at our disposal (see Chapters 8, 9 and 10). The key is in identifying relevant components of the maintaining cycle and 'matching' the techniques accordingly.

The physical strategies are particularly useful when the physical consequences of being anxious impair performance or when physical activity becomes aversive and is avoided. The behavioural techniques are invaluable in tackling avoidance head on and can also be used in self-monitoring and planning, as with activity scheduling. The cognitive approaches are relevant for helping clients 'stand back' from their problems and identify the components of a maintenance cycle, for helping them evaluate the usefulness of certain ways of processing information and in helping them re-evaluate unhelpful perspectives.

An additional adaptable technique is the 'Theory A vs. Theory B' or 'Hypothesis A vs. Hypothesis B' strategy. This collaborative intervention, developed by Salkovskis and Bass (1997), promotes therapy as a behavioural experiment offering the opportunity for testing two opposing theories. You do not propose that the client is incorrect in holding a particular belief:, instead, you suggest that *perhaps* the client is right and *perhaps* there is another possibility. These alternatives are then explored in therapy: Theory A reflects the client's predicted fear (for example, 'I am seriously ill'), while Theory B states an alternative explanation (for example, 'these symptoms are due to anxiety') . You and your client can test the theories both retrospectively (by reviewing past beliefs, behaviours and outcomes) and prospectively (by setting up behavioural tests). This both brings the benign theory into the client's awareness and potentially collects data to support it.

Figure 13.5 shows several examples of techniques and problems for which they would be relevant.

In summary, anxiety disorders reflect a normal reaction to stress or threat which has become exaggerated by heightened physical reactions, skewed thinking and/or problem behaviours. This sets up unhelpful cycles which can be broken by introducing techniques to counter problem sensations, cognitions and behaviours.

Problems when working with anxious clients

Self-fulfilling prophesies: cognitive

It is not unusual for the mental effects of heightened anxiety to undermine thinking. We have all probably encountered the client who describes his mind 'going blank' or who

EXAMPLES OF TECHNIQUES	EXAMPLES OF PROBLEMS
Physical Relaxation Exercise	Muscular tension impairing sleep or public speaking. Avoidance of exertion because of a prediction of threat to health.
Behavioural Graded practice Activity scheduling Behavioural experiment (Theory A vs. Theory B)	Avoidance of perceived threat. Unawareness of relevant patterns or fluctuations in anxiety. Focusing on the worst prediction.
Cognitive Decentring Distraction Cognitive challenging Problem-solving	Poor insight into the processes of maintenance. Chronic and unproductive worry cycles. Skewed beliefs or images which perpetuate anxiety. Inability to make decisions and to plan ahead.

Figure 13.5 Problems and techniques

complains that so many concerns race through his mind that he cannot think straight. A graded approach to facing difficult situations, backed up by strategies to lower stress levels (such as constructive self-talk) can help your clients systematically face their fears.

Self-fulfilling prophesies: physical or behavioural

Similarly, we often encounter clients who report that the physical effects of anxiety impair their performance: public speaking, writing in public and so on. Again, a series of graded and systematic behavioural experiments can help your clients build a body of positive data that will help to consolidate their confidence.

The power of avoidance

Avoidance is the most compelling safety behaviour. It often represents the path of least resistance, providing tremendous short-term reward. Avoidance can be passive, as with clients who simply do not engage with their fears (not leaving the house, not using public transport, not attending social events, for example), or it can be active, when a client puts much active effort into avoiding facing their fears (for example, the person with OCD who carries out elaborate or time-consuming rituals in order to avoid facing a fear of contamination or a fear of causing harm). Avoidance can also be subtle: for example, a person carrying out a frightening task but drinking a unit or two of alcohol first; or a socially anxious person helping with 'hostess duties' to avoid having to engage in proper conversations; or someone with agoraphobia using a mobile phone as a constant link to his safe base. A thorough assessment is needed to clarify the complexities of avoidance – remember to ask questions such as: 'And is there anything else that helps / that you use to get you through such times?', 'What do you do that you wouldn't do if you did not have this problem?', 'What do you not do as a result of having this problem?'

In order to help clients reappraise the usefulness of avoidance, we can:

- encourage self-monitoring – including the longer-term consequences of avoidance;
- share a formulation – clearly illustrating the disadvantages of this choice of coping;
- negotiate a graded reduction in the use of avoidance for the particularly reluctant client (using a series of behavioural experiments). The positive feedback of success will then support further reductions.

'I'm anxious all of the time'

This common statement rarely stands up to self-monitoring. Although a client's retrospective appraisal might be, 'I have the headache all of the time' or 'The images are with me all of the time', both daily thought records (see Chapter 8) and activity grids (Chapter 9) can reveal a variation in levels of physical tension and visual intrusions. Once these variations are clear, patterns and correlates can be established and cycles understood and ultimately managed.

'I do all the things that we agree, and my anxiety does not decrease'

If this is the case, look for subtle forms of avoidance and safety-seeking behaviours, including superstitious behaviours such as doing or saying things so as 'not to tempt fate'. This can include the misuse of distraction, which results in the client concluding, 'I only got through this because I distracted myself', rather than concluding, 'I took my mind off my worries and calmed myself.' In addition, you might find it helpful to consider the rate at which the client is facing the feared situation: although graded practice can be helpful, if it is too gentle and cautious, the client will gain little sense of achievement.

Not being bold enough to face the fear

This can apply to both you or your client. When your client is reluctant to tackle a demanding challenge, you need to ask, 'is this an appropriate task for this person at present?' Although it is important to encourage clients to engage in challenging tasks, they should not be *over-stretched*, as this can cause demoralisation and drop-out. However, it is possible that the task is appropriate yet the client cannot overcome reluctance to take it on. This might be because they have inhibiting beliefs about feeling anxious, such as: 'feeling anxiety is bad or dangerous and I must avoid it.' Ensure that your client appreciates that feeling anxious is not synonymous with failing and that it is to be expected during a behavioural assignment geared to facing fears. Also, make sure that you have shared a rationale that makes clear the advantages of tolerating the discomfort of the task. Similarly, you may need to address unhelpful assumptions concerning behavioural assignments, perhaps including behavioural experiments to test such assumptions.

The client relies on medication to manage anxiety

This is only a problem if your client really invests his confidence in medication so that CBT intervention holds little credibility for him and his motivation to engage is low. Even so, it is worth looking at assumptions about drugs and CBT to see if it is possible to engage him in behavioural experiments that might help him develop more confidence in a psychological approach. It is not unusual for even well-motivated clients to be taking anxiolytic medication when they begin therapy. They often readily learn cognitive-behavioural techniques and then systematically reduce their medication – but this should always be done with medical supervision.

Anxiety Disorders: Specific Models and Treatment Protocols

Introduction

Many of the anxiety symptoms that our clients experience will fall into diagnostic categories, for which there are specific cognitive models and treatment protocols evolved from clinical trials. Major references for key models and protocols are summarised in Table 14.1.

In this chapter, we will introduce the cognitive model for each of these disorders along with the associated treatment guidelines. You will probably notice similarities across models, but it is important to note the sometimes subtle differences between them. Empirically, the subtle differences matter.

Table 14.1   Key models and protocols for anxiety disorders

Anxiety disorder	References
Generalised anxiety disorder (GAD)	Wells (1997, 2000), Borkovec and Newman (1999); Borkovec et al. (2002)
Health anxiety	Salkovskis and Warwick (1986); Warwick and Salkovskis (1989)
Obsessive-compulsive disorder (OCD)	Salkovskis (1985, 1999); Wells (1997)
Panic disorder and agoraphobia	Clark (1986, 1999); Wells (1997)
Post-traumatic stress disorder (PTSD)	Ehlers and Clark (2000)
Social anxiety	Clark and Wells (1995); Wells (1997); Clark (2002)
Specific phobia	Kirk and Rouf (2004)

Generalised anxiety disorder (GAD)

As described in the previous chapter, GAD is defined as chronic, excessive anxiety and worry pertaining to a number of events or activities (DSM-IV-TR; APA, 2000).

> *Sam was 64 years old and felt he should be looking forward to his retirement – his wife certainly was. However, as usual, he was beset with worries about it: What if he and his wife did not get on? What if their financial planning had been insufficient? He found his worrying shameful but familiar, and he could not remember a time when he had been free of it, just times when it was slightly better or worse.*

Cognitive models of GAD give prominence to worry as a key cognitive factor. There are several possible mechanisms for persistent worry:

- Focusing attention towards the perceived threat can be an attempt to avoid addressing a more distressing fear, as 'What if?' statements are superficial to the real concern. The real concern would be revealed by answering the 'what if' question (Borkovec & Newman, 1999).
- It can also reflect an attempt to avoid facing uncertainty (Dugas et al., 1998; Ladouceur et al., 2000).
- The meaning of the worry itself can be alarming (e.g. 'I am going crazy'), which can trigger more worry (Wells, 1997, 2000). It also can constitute a superstitious response ('If I worry, bad things won't happen') or a misconception about worry ('If I am worrying, I am doing something useful'), so that continuing to worry becomes a safety behaviour (Wells, 1997, 2000).
- Worry can be a habit (Butler & Hope, 1995)
- Worry undermines ability to problem-solve, so that a person loses confidence in their problem-solving ability, which supports further worry.

Treatment for GAD focuses on breaking this cycle by understanding and then eliminating unhelpful worry and helping your client address the underlying fears.

The required steps include:

- *Overcoming avoidance* by encouraging articulation of the fear (e.g. personal harm or harm to loved ones) beneath the 'What if?' question.
- *Accepting uncertainty.* Behavioural experiments can be effective in helping your client achieve this. Butler and Rouf (2004) recommend that experiments focus on challenging thoughts that reflect intolerance of uncertainty rather than trying to review the likelihood of the feared events actually happening we aim to help the client simply accept uncertainty. This means that, as a therapist, you focus on clarifying the alarming answer to 'What if?' rather than debating the probability of the worst-case scenario.
- *Identifying and testing unhelpful cognitions* concerning worry, such as 'This is an indication of my weakness', or 'I must worry so that I am never caught unprepared', followed where apppropriate by behavioural testing.
- *Teaching alternative strategies* to worry, such as distraction or limiting time permitted for worry. For example, a person who spent five hours in the evening worrying about the next day might develop a plan to worry during the 30 minutes between getting home and

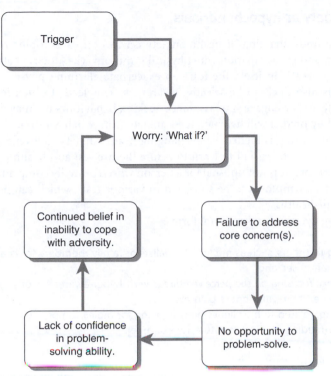

Figure 14.1   A cognitive model of GAD

supper, with other worrying thoughts 'held over' until the next day. Distraction can be a useful strategy, or writing worries on a paper which is then destroyed can help the client learn to 'put worries aside' (Butler & Rouf, 2004).

Sam was encouraged to articulate his fears: he said that he was terrified that his wife would realise he had nothing to offer her and would leave him; that they would run out of money and be unable to afford decent health care; that his wrong decision in taking retirement would cost him his marriage, his security and, worst of all, would prove that he was useless. By using cognitive strategies, he was able to both de-catastrophise specific negative thoughts, but also to appreciate his resilience (he had managed many personal and business crises in the past) and that enabled him to tolerate the uncertainty of his future. Throughout, there was a theme of shame, worthlessness and responsibility, and these general negative themes were also reappraised.

Sam carried out a behavioural experiment comparing his ability to problem-solve when he focused on his worries with his ability to do so when he distracted himself from them. He learned that worrying was counterproductive and recognised that it had become both a habit and a source of comfort, as he believed that he could ward off bad luck by worrying. Once he understood this, he readily distracted himself from worrying, thus breaking an unhelpful pattern.

Health anxiety or hypochondriasis

The cognitive understanding of health anxiety centres on catastrophic predictions concerning health and preoccupation with physical symptoms (i.e., focus of attention towards the perceived threat). In itself, the fear can exacerbate alarming physical symptoms, for which there is also likely to be selective awareness. This leads to high levels of anxiety. Clients tend to either engage in reassurance-seeking behaviours or in avoidance of situations which they predict will heighten their anxiety (safety behaviours).

*Re*assurance-seeking is ineffective in changing health anxiety as it reflects a reliance on external support: sufferers fail to learn to *assure* themselves, and health concerns remain intact. Furthermore, it is not unusual for a person who repeatedly complains of potentially harmful physical symptoms to be subjected to various tests, which can be interpreted as proof of real ill-health.

Maintaining cycles can take several forms:

- Turning to others, such as medical specialists or family members, for comforting reassurances (safety-seeking).
- Scanning: *focusing on the perceived threat* with hyper-awareness of physical sensations such as heart rate, numbness, pain, etc.
- Checking: related to the client's body (looking for moles, lumps, etc.) or to external information (reading medical literature, for example).

Tina woke each morning with thoughts that she might have breast cancer. She tried unsuccessfully to avoid the media and, instead, noticed every article about cancer. Each day she felt compelled to check her breasts, armpits and neck for signs of lumps or enlarged glands. She believed that it would be dangerous not to check, as a missed tumour could become malignant. She always found something that gave her concern, so she persuaded her partner to 'double-check' for her. The relief each time she was reassured was exhilarating, although short-lived.

As with GAD, the *interpretation* of the preoccupation needs to be explored, as some clients hold beliefs about their continued concern such as: ' . . . if I am vigilant for signs of illness I will be OK', or ' . . . if I think about my illness I will bring it on.'

Figure 14.2 illustrates how health anxiety can be maintained through:

1. Avoidance
2. Reassurance-seeking
3. Scanning.

The treatment approaches for health anxiety reflect these models and incorporate:

- *Defining and challenging the content of the catastrophic prediction:* as therapist, you will need to ascertain the worst outcome for the client: for example, abandonment or protracted physical or mental torment. For some clients, the worst scenario is death, or the nature of death or its consequences. For example, a client may not be worried about dying

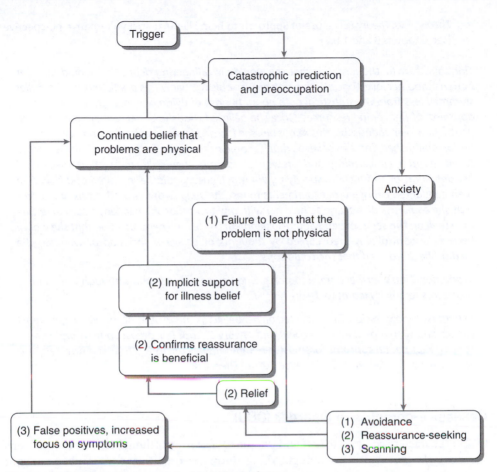

Figure 14.2   Cognitive model of health anxiety

from a heart attack (perceived as rapid and dignified) but may be preoccupied with the fear of dying slowly from a neurological disorder, needy and incontinent. It is also wise to explore possible superstitious thinking such as, 'If I don't think/do think about the illness, I will be protected from it.'

- *Testing unhelpful health-related beliefs*, such as: 'Chest pain means my heart is weak' or 'Every worrying symptom has to be checked by my doctor.' This can be achieved through cognitive interventions and behavioural experiments.
- *Reducing safety behaviours* (reassurance-seeking and avoidance), including scanning. Sometimes, an explanation of the role of these behaviours allows the client to reduce them; in other instances, it is necessary to challenge beliefs concerning safety behaviours, possibly via behavioural experiments. This can also be relevant to carers who collude with unhelpful behaviours.

- *Theory A vs. Theory B*, is a useful approach to help clients gain an alternative perspective (see Chapters 9 and 13).

Tina's most awful thought was that she would die a lingering death that would torment both her and her loved ones. With help, she was able to review this prediction, but her relief stemmed less from the statistical data about her risk of dying of cancer than from her re-appraisal of her coping resources. Once she believed that she could tolerate a protracted death (however undesirable this might be), she focused less on her health and her preoccupation diminished. She also believed that if she did not reassure herself, she would be unable to withstand the uncertainty, and this would undermine her ability to function. She refined her definition of 'to function', specifying what activities would be impaired and how. She then conducted behavioural experiments to test the validity of her predictions and learnt that she could use distraction to help her with any tasks that she needed to complete. She then built on this series of behavioural experiments by testing her prediction that she would become uncontrollably preoccupied by thoughts of cancer if she read or watched the media. She discovered that she could cope.

In addition, Tina's partner agreed to stop giving her reassurance and, although Tina initially objected, she quickly learnt to assure herself.

At her first review session, Tina reflected on her beliefs in Theory A (that she would get breast cancer and would be unable to cope) and Theory B (that her preoccupation and safety-seeking kept health concerns foremost in her mind). She concluded that she now felt that Theory A was unlikely and she believed 80% in Theory B.

Obsessive-compulsive disorder (OCD)

OCD is characterised by recurrent and unwanted obsessions (thoughts) and compulsions (actions). Unwanted intrusive thoughts, in the form of words, images or impulses, are not in themselves pathological, but the response to them can be (Rachman & de Silva, 1978). Cognitive models of OCD share the basic premise that intrusive thoughts are in themselves normal but become problematic when they are interpreted as indicating that something bad might happen and that the sufferer is responsible for preventing it. To manage this fear, the sufferer engages in safety behaviours (avoidance, reassurance-seeking and cognitive or motor rituals), which prevent him from learning that his worries are not accurate. The aim of CBT is for the client to learn that such intrusive thoughts do not indicate a need for any action and can safely be ignored.

The most common obsessional worries relate to:

- fears of contamination, such as infection from touching a dirty cloth or surface, leading to washing or cleaning rituals;
- fears of missing something potentially dangerous, such as electric switches, or an unlocked front door, leading to checking and/or repeating rituals;

- over-concern with orderliness and perfection, leading to repeating actions until things feel 'right';
- fears of uncontrollable and inappropriate actions such as swearing in public, or sexual or aggressive behaviour, leading to unhelpful attempts to control thoughts.

The most common safety behaviours are:

- motor rituals: e.g. cleaning, checking and repeating actions;
- cognitive rituals: neutralising 'bad' thoughts by thinking other thoughts (e.g. prayers or 'safe' incantations, or other 'good' thoughts);
- avoidance of situations, people or objects that trigger the obsessional worries;
- seeking reassurance about the worries from family, doctors or others.

Most OCD sufferers have motor rituals, but some have predominantly cognitive rituals with few if any motor rituals (so-called 'pure obsessions' – a presentation which may be harder to treat).

Vince had always been very cautious and was proud of his high standards for safety. However, since a promotion (with responsibility for ensuring departmental security), his safety checks had become exaggerated and he was now struggling to leave the building at night. He often returned five or six times to recheck – occasionally driving in from his home. He tried unsuccessfully to put the worrying thoughts out of his mind. His fear was that insufficient caution would result in a catastrophe for which he would shoulder the blame. He thought that the shame of this would destroy him.

It has been suggested by the Obsessive-Compulsive Cognitions Working Group (1997), that the key cognitions in OCD are:

- **thought–action fusion**: the idea that having a 'bad' thought can result in 'bad' consequences (e.g. if I think about harm coming to someone, that may make that harm happen in reality); or that having a thought about something 'bad' is morally just as bad as carrying out a bad action;
- **inflated responsibility**: an assumption that one has the power and the obligation to prevent bad things from happening;
- **beliefs about the controllability of thoughts**: e.g. the belief that one ought to be able to control 'bad' thoughts;
- **perfection**: the dichotomous assumption that only the best is effective or acceptable;
- **overestimation of threat**, which is often related to;
- **intolerance of uncertainty**: a belief that things can and must be certain, e.g. I ought to be able to be *sure* that an action is safe.

As with other anxiety disorders, thoughts about negative thoughts (e.g. 'There must be something fundamentally wrong with me for having such thoughts') can heighten anxiety (Wells, 2000). Emotional reasoning (the assumption that feelings are a reliable source of information about a situation – for example, 'I feel anxious, therefore this must be a dangerous situation') is also common amongst sufferers of OCD (Emmelkamp & Aardema, 1999). (See Figure 14.3.)

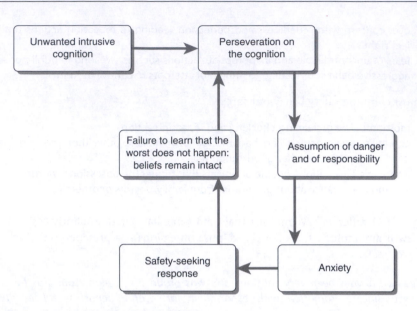

Figure 14.3   A cognitive model of OCD

Interventions for OCD incorporate:

- *Exposure and response prevention (ERP)* is the best-established intervention for OCD. The aim is for the sufferer to expose himself to the feared situation (e.g. something 'contaminated') without engaging in his usual safety behaviour (e.g. washing). Although originally conceived as a behavioural intervention, ERP is readily adapted to a cognitive model in which it is seen as a BE through which the client learns that his obsessional predictions of disaster are not justified.
- *Challenging unhelpful beliefs* such as 'If I think it, it will happen', or 'I am responsible for the welfare of others', by using the cognitive and behavioural strategies described in earlier chapters. The continuum method, or scaling, can be particularly helpful in addressing the extreme perspective of the perfectionist (see Chapter 17). As with the other anxiety-related problems, it is often necessary to challenge unhelpful beliefs about beliefs.
- *Reducing safety behaviours* by generating a rationale via formulation and testing this out in BEs. It is possible that family, friends or professionals collude or assist with the safety behaviours, and it may therefore be necessary to involve them in this aspect of therapy.
- *Theory A vs. Theory B:* as with health anxiety, this intervention can be useful in highlighting a benign perspective. The aim is to learn that OCD is not really about the need to prevent a real threat but rather about being excessively *worried* about such a threat.

Vince's most unhelpful belief was: 'I am wholly responsible for any crisis that arises at work'. He challenged this by recognising the cognitive biases in his thinking and by constructing a 'responsibility pie' (see Chapter 17), which helped him to apportion responsibility more realistically. However, he also had to work on the dichotomous thinking that underpinned his unrealistically high standards: continuum work (see Chapter 17) helped him to become more flexible. He addressed other key beliefs such as 'I will be destroyed if I am to blame' using standard cognitive interventions.

Feeling more confident that he could tolerate the worst-case scenario, he agreed to a pro- gramme to reduce his safety behaviours. This incorporated an agreement that his wife would not reassure him when he was at home feeling uneasy about his department's secu- rity. He struggled initially at refocusing his thoughts away from catastrophic possibilities. He kept (meticulous) diaries of his experiences, and these showed clearly that he felt less anx- ious and more content on the days that he reduced safety behaviours and catastrophic thinking. He also recognised that catastrophes never ensued at these times, giving him evi- dence that his safety behaviours were not necessary.

Panic disorder

Panic attacks are defined as sudden increases in anxiety, while panic disorder describes recurrent panic attacks. (See Figure 14.4.) A prominent cognitive model of panic disorder is that of Clark (1986), which identifies the maintaining factors as:

- Catastrophic misinterpretation of bodily sensations (particularly those associated with anxiety) as indicative of impending mental or physical harm, such as an imminent stroke or heart attack.
- Safety behaviours employed in order to reduce the likelihood of catastrophe. These include frank avoidance, such as not going to certain places or events, and subtle avoidance, such as holding on to someone to avoid collapse or sucking ginger to avoid vomiting.
- Selective attention as sufferers become highly sensitised to 'dangerous' sensations or situ- ations, and their attention becomes biased towards them.

When Wendy had a panic attack, her chest tightened, she fought for breath and she trem- bled. She felt pain in her chest and arms and experienced tunnel vision. She thought she was having a heart attack and could die. She avoided any situation where she feared she might exert herself as she feared provoking a heart attack. For example, she no longer did the weekly supermarket shop, nor took her children to the park. She knew that she was becom- ing physically unfit, and this heightened her fears.

The management of panic disorder typically involves:

- *Generating less catastrophic explanations* for the origin of feared symptoms and less cata- strophic predictions of the consequences – for example, attributing chest pains or a racing heart to anxiety, which is not harmful.
- *Setting up behavioural experiments* (i) to discover the benign origin of an unpleasant sen- sation: for example, asking a client to exert himself to trigger feared sensations such as muscular pains or palpitations; and (ii) to test the validity of the new perceptions which have been generated through cognitive challenging – such as 'I'm feeling the symptoms of anxiety and this will pass'.

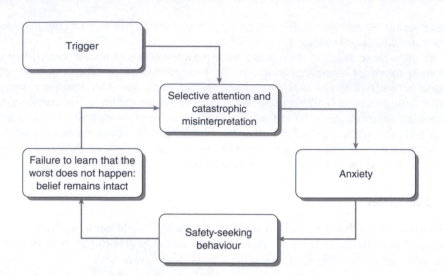

Figure 14.4   A cognitive model of panic disorder

- *Reducing safety behaviours*, by cognitive and behavioural work, to generate new explanations which, in turn, can be reinforced through behavioural testing. For example, through preliminary cognitive-behavioural work, a client began to consider it possible that she could walk around the supermarket without leaning on a trolley for safety. However, shopping without the trolley actually consolidated her confidence.

Wendy's therapist raised the question of whether her muscular pain and difficulty breathing could result from the muscular tension associated with her state of heightened anxiety. Wendy was eventually convinced of this when she agreed to exercise in the session – even though the prospect had frightened her and had initially provoked the predicted symptoms. Her belief changed to, 'I am not having a heart attack but I am highly anxious and it will pass.' Once she had gained this new perspective, she engaged in increasingly physically demanding activity. She began by exercising in the session and then between sessions, and grew confident that a racing heart or muscular tension was not harmful to her. Ultimately, she attended a gym regularly and ceased avoiding situations which she feared would over-exert her.

PTSD

Cognitive models for PTSD have been only relatively recently elaborated by researchers such as Ehlers and Clark (2000). Cognitive models tend to put an emphasis on:

- the emotion of fear, although it is recognised that emotions such as guilt and shame can be prominent too;
- memories being experienced visually, although recollections of a traumatic event can also be experienced as sounds, physical sensations and smells for example;

- vivid memories experienced as if the danger is current;
- memories disconnected from an intellectual understanding of the trauma;
- memories also experienced as nightmares or as flashbacks.

The memories are emotionally highly provocative and remain so for several reasons:

- *Safety behaviours:* in an attempt to manage high anxiety, PTSD sufferers often use behavioural and mental avoidance to inhibit the memories.
- This *prevents processing of the memory* (i.e. reviewing the content so that it can be linked with information about time, place and outcome), and the memory remains a disconnected, emotionally charged recollection which, in itself, triggers high levels of distress.
- *Misinterpretations:* unhelpful appraisals of the traumatic experience (e.g. 'This proves that no man can be trusted';'I brought this on myself through carelessness') or the PTSD symptoms (e.g. 'I am weak', 'I am going crazy') can further worsen the distress associated with the intrusions and can therefore lead to more safety behaviours.

In addition, the cycle of PTSD can be maintained:

- Spontaneous imagery is peculiarly significant in the maintenance of PTSD. Although the memories related to PTSD can relate to any sensory modality, visual intrusions are common and can be powerfully aversive.
- Selective memory processes can also distort recollections such that they are biased towards negative aspects of the trauma – thus heightening distress.
- Over-estimation of danger: it is not unusual for trauma victims to overestimate threats to their safety. This, in turn, further promotes safety behaviours.

See Figure 14.5.

Alistair had been involved in a road-traffic accident when his car tyre exploded at high speed. He had had a lucky escape. Eight months later, he still experienced vivid memories of his car flipping over, memories of the sights, sounds and smells as if it were happening again. He was particularly likely to have flashbacks when he smelled petrol or when he returned to the area where the accident took place. Therefore, although he still drove his car, his partner would always refuel, and he never drove near the site of the crash.

The proposed treatment for PTSD involves addressing:

- *Spontaneous imagery.* Strategies are introduced to diminish the very high levels of arousal associated with the images, so that they can be processed and contextualised. This means that they form memories which are subject to rational appraisal. The sense of *present* threat is then eliminated, by placing the image in context of time, place and longer-term outcome. This is often achieved by using cognitive restructuring while 'reliving' the trauma (Grey et al., 2002) or cognitive processing therapy (Resick & Schnicke, 1993, Ehlers et al., 2003) where the client writes a detailed account of the traumatic experience for cognitive review. Along with constructing more helpful interpretations of the traumatic memory,

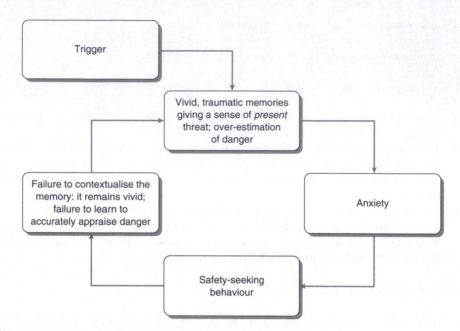

Figure 14.5   A cognitive model of PTSD

clients are encouraged to expose themselves to real-life situations linked to the trauma so that they might challenge their anxiety-provoking cognitions *in vivo*.

- *Safety behaviours* can be reduced by reviewing unhelpful beliefs and field-testing new possibilities, as with other anxiety disorders.
- *Misinterpretations* can be reappraised by reviewing these conclusions and generating plausible alternatives, again using 'standard' CBT interventions.
- *Selective memory processes* can be usefully addressed, as can all of the cognitive biases by teaching the client the technique of decentring.

Alistair's intrusive memories responded well to cognitive restructuring. Ultimately, his therapist helped him to talk through his experience as if it were currently happening, pausing at the emotional 'hot spots' to review his cognitions in the light of what he now knew. By doing this, Alistair was able to challenge his most salient thought: 'I am about to die.' He was able to remind himself that he got out of the crashed car with few injuries and, in doing so, he reduced the intensity of the flashbacks. He was also able to revise a shameful belief which had developed after the accident, namely that he was responsible for the incident. This further reduced the anxiety that the memories evoked.

He was gradually able to revisit the site of the crash – first with his partner and later alone – and to talk and read about accidents. His predictions that he would have flashbacks were not borne out, and his confidence returned. His avoidance of smelling petrol was more difficult to tackle, as fears associated with smells are particularly resilient.

The precipitants of PTSD may be impersonal, such as a natural disaster, or perceived as highly personal, for example when a person has been assaulted in some way. In cases of personal attack, there is likely to be a need for greater sensitivity to interpersonal relationships and, perhaps, to sexual relationships where the assault has been sexual.

Social anxiety

Sufferers of social anxiety fear humiliation or embarrassment. This might be in the more severe form of social phobia or the milder 'shyness'. Cognitive models for social phobia have been developed, (see Figure 14.6) most notably by Clark and Wells (1995), which, suggest Butler and Hackmann (2004), are readily applicable to 'shyness' and incorporate the following:

- Perceived social danger: typical assumptions and predictions of the socially anxious person are: 'If I talk to them they will find me boring and reject me'; 'If I don't get this just right, I will be humiliated.' Essentially, these are fears centring on being negatively judged and on not coping.
- Focus of attention: the social-anxiety cycle is propelled by intense self-awareness which can also manifest as self-referent *imagery* (Hackmann, 1998). This heightened self-consciousness is distracting and, thus, disabling. It also prevents the sufferer from reviewing situations objectively, so that he tends to misinterpret the reactions of others.
- Emotional reasoning: intense introspection about the sensations of anxiety render the sufferer acutely aware of symptoms (such as shaking and blushing), which he assumes others can see and judge negatively.
- Safety behaviour: the socially anxious person will attempt to avoid predicted humiliation or embarrassment by avoiding social contact – for example, focusing on a task or avoiding eye contact. In doing so, the social fear is not addressed and remains intact, ready for the next social challenge.

Bette anticipated rejection. Her prediction in social situations was that others would realise that she had nothing to offer and would not want to know her. If someone did show interest, she discounted it: 'They don't know the real me', or 'They were just being polite'. As far as possible, she avoided social gatherings, and when she attended them, avoided eye contact but could 'feel' the critical gaze of others. She tended to busy herself attending to the practical needs of guests. If she became involved in conversation, the intensity of her negative intrusive thoughts rendered her unable to chat.

Interventions for social phobia involve:

- *Re-focusing attention away from introspection*. This strategy was particularly elaborated and evaluated by Wells and Mathews (1994).
- Developing an *assertive or compassionate inner voice* to combat the harsh criticism predicted from others (Padesky, 1997 and Gilbert, 2000).
- Cognitive re-evaluation of the cognitions relating to perceived social danger and emotional reasoning, including behavioural experiments. Particularly useful are (i) the use of

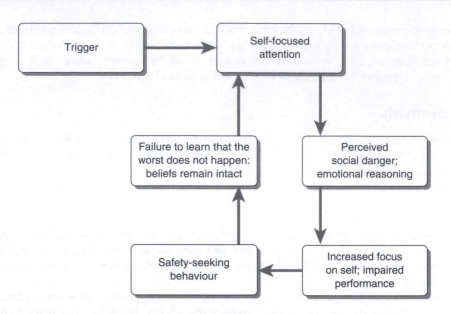

Figure 14.6   A cognitive model of social anxiety

videoed sessions which allow clients to evaluate the severity of their overt anxiety symptoms and (ii) modelling of feared consequences by the therapist. The latter means that you might have to appear to have blushed, sweated or wet yourself in a public place – but be comforted that this seems to go unjudged by the general public.

Betty learnt several strategies to combat her social anxiety. First, she described her worst-case scenario and challenged her predictions that (i) she would almost certainly be criticised and ostracised and (ii) that she would not cope with criticism but would accept it and become deeply depressed. Cognitive restructuring, developing a strong but caring inner voice and role play with her therapist helped her to conclude that she was unlikely to be openly criticised, but even if she were, she could stand up for herself and not spiral into despair. She also learnt strategies to refocus attention from her negative, self-referent thoughts. In addition, she carried out behavioural tests: she allowed her therapist to log the number of people who looked at her critically when they attended a social gathering – to her surprise, the therapist noted no one. Finally, she engaged in a series of assignments focused on not tending to guests' practical needs (i.e. dropping her major safety behaviour). As she progressed through the hierarchy of assignments, she built her confidence that she could mix socially.

Specific phobia

This refers to an exaggerated and persistent fear of an object or situation. There is, as yet, no evaluated 'cognitive model' of specific phobias, although a preliminary model has been proposed by Kirk and Rouf (2004). In brief, they suggest that clients with specific phobias (for example, of a particular animal or situation or of blood) are hyper-vigilant for threat cues. Thus, the cycle begins with:

- focusing on the perceived threat and selective attention for fear cues; then
- perceiving a threat, whether this is actually what they fear (e.g. a spider or blood) or a mis-interpretation (e.g. a piece of fluff on the carpet or tomato ketchup), which triggers the phobic response, which has both psychological and physiological elements.
- over-estimating the probability of harm and under-estimating ability to cope (Beck, et al.,1985).

These primary cognitions exacerbate

- physiological arousal, which can be further interpreted as threatening.
- safety behaviours, such as overtly avoiding certain places (e.g. shops, zoos) or situations (e.g. writing in public) or covertly avoiding feared situations (e.g. carrying smelling salts to ward off fainting). These then prevent anxious predictions from being disconfirmed, the fear remains unchallenged and the sufferer remains hyper-vigilant.

Beliefs about the meaning of the phobia (secondary cognitions) can also heighten anxiety, with beliefs such as: 'I am foolish', 'I am going mad'. (See Figure 14.7.)

Karen had always been fearful of wasps. The thought of them made her shudder, and the sight of one triggered a panic attack. If she saw one, she could not think straight and would run away – recently she had left her youngest child outside a shop when she ran for cover. She coped by doing all she could to avoid wasps: never going into the garden during the summer months; not allowing her children to eat sweets outdoors in case this attracted wasps; keeping the doors and windows closed in her home. It was hard for her to verbalise what made her so afraid, but she had an image of being unable to escape angry wasps caught in her hair.

Helping a client overcome a specific phobia involves:

- *decreasing focusing on the perceived threat* by setting up behavioural experiments to evaluate the consequences of reducing the amount of time spent checking or anticipating the worst;
- *reducing safety behaviours* through behavioural experiments (often graded) to test the predictions of harm;
- *addressing misinterpretations* by teaching decentring and cognitive reappraisal of situations. This is relevant to both primary and secondary cognitions.

Karen wanted to tackle her phobia head on and was prepared to try to confront a wasp. She and her therapist made predictions about her probable responses to a hierarchy of

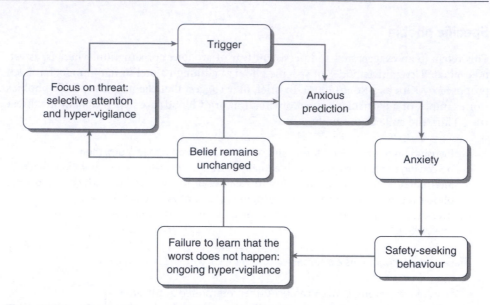

Figure 14.7   A cognitive model of specific phobia

wasp-related tasks, beginning with looking at photographs through to releasing a wasp from a jar into the garden. When she got as far as releasing wasps, she realised that they flew from rather than to her: her images of the wasps caught in her hair then diminished. This success gave her courage to work towards dropping her safety behaviours. Each lent itself to behavioural testing, and, through this, she discovered that her anxiety was heightened by her excessive hyper-vigilance. She also learned that if she left windows open, or let her children eat sweets outdoors, she encountered wasps, but far fewer than she had predicted, and that she coped better than she had anticipated.

Blood and injection phobias are dealt with in Chapter 10.

Co-morbidity

Anxiety disorders can present as discrete problems, in combination with other anxiety disorders or as co-morbid with other problems – for example, the high standards of the person with OCD might predispose her to an eating disorder, the chronicity of an anxiety problem might give rise to depressed mood, while coping strategies such as comfort eating or drinking can develop into difficulties in their own right. Remember to take this into account during assessment and throughout treatment and remain aware that other problems might exist.

Conclusion

The previous chapter reviewed a generic understanding of anxiety disorders, while this chapter has focused on specific models and the treatment approaches linked to them. In your practice, you will need to be aware of both the generic and specific approaches so that you can be flexible and responsive to your client's needs. The models give an elegant and invaluable understanding of particular anxiety disorders, while the generic overview provides you with the 'first principles' that you can fall back on if the models and protocols do not meet your client's needs.

Potential problems when working with specific models and treatment protocols

Assuming the validity of a diagnosis without carrying out a full assessment and then adhering to a treatment protocol

Although many of your clients will fulfil criteria for a particular diagnostic group, do not presume this without carrying out a proper assessment. There will be times when the referrer's diagnosis or your first impressions are wrong.

Trying to force a client's experiences into a specific model

Keep a curious and open mind during your assessments. If your client's presentation does not fit neatly into the model which you anticipate being relevant, perhaps the model is invalid for this person.

Sticking too rigidly to a protocol when the client is not responding well

While it is important to follow a protocol, there will be individual differences amongst your clients and aspects of their presentation which, at some point, may fit with the protocol. In some instances, the deviation will be sufficiently marked for you to have to reassess your client and consider if the protocol is the optimum approach. At other times, staying with the protocol will be in your client's best interest, but you may need to adapt it slightly – for example, introducing a session on specific skills training (assertiveness, time management and so on) or temporarily diverting to tackle an issue which appears to obstruct progress (anger, unresolved grief or flashbacks, for instance).

15

Wider Applications of CBT

Introduction

Over the past 25 years, CBT has been applied to an ever-widening range of psychological problems. This chapter will briefly review its application to some of those which you are likely to encounter in routine clinical practice. Our intention is twofold:

- to highlight salient aspects of the disorders to help you recognise them;
- to outline what might be involved in the management of such problems so that you can decide whether to refer on or to take a client yourself. Remember that additional training and supervision may be required to manage these disorders.

At the end of each section, we will refer you to further reading.
 We will review:

- eating disorders
- trauma
- anger
- psychosis
- relationship difficulties
- substance misuse.

Eating disorders

CBT has been the most exhaustively researched form of treatment for eating disorders, particularly bulimia nervosa. In recent years, cognitive therapists have developed a transdiagnostic understanding of the eating disorders (Fairburn et al., 2003). None the less, there remain distinct differences in the presentations of the separate conditions, differences which must be taken into account in their understanding and treatment.

- **Anorexia nervosa (AN)**: the DSM-IV (APA, 2000) criteria for anorexia includes low weight (with cessation of menstruation in women), an over-concern with weight and shape and a disturbance in body image. There is a sub-classification of restricting AN (pure restriction of caloric intake) and of binging/purging AN (episodes of over-eating with extreme compensation for this). Excessive exercise is not uncommon in AN.
- **Bulimia nervosa (BN)**: DSM-IV criteria include an over-concern with weight and shape, but an essential criterion is recurrent episodes of binge eating (rapid consumption of a large amount of food in a discrete period of time, experienced as being uncontrollable). In BN, there is significant compensation for binge eating – for example, self-induced vomiting, purging, fasting or excessive exercise.
- **Binge-eating disorder (BED)**: this is a provisional category in DSM-IV and describes binge eating without extreme compensation. This may or may not be associated with being overweight.
- **EDNOS**: this category of 'Eating Disorders Not Otherwise Specified' has only one positive criterion (that an individual should have an eating disorder of clinical severity) and one negative criterion (the disorder should not fulfil criteria for AN or BN). It is notable that this can be the most common diagnosis in eating-disorder services (Palmer, 2003).
- **Obesity**: although often included in psychiatric conditions, obesity refers only to a medical state of overweight – a state which can result from psychological or non-psychological factors.

Eating disorders commonly occur in young women, but take care not to overlook them in men and older women.

In clinical practice, body mass is estimated by using the body-mass index (BMI= kg/m^2). Classification of under- and overweight can be seen in Table 15.1.

When working with someone with an eating disorder, it is usually necessary to keep track of their BMI, especially when it is low. Some clients weigh themselves excessively, and this should be tackled as a form of reassurance; others are reluctant to do so, a potential obstacle to treatment which needs early intervention. The use of behavioural experiments is limited if a client is unable to weigh herself, the therapeutic alliance can be compromised, and, most importantly, low weight carries health risks and must be monitored. This can be

Table 15.1   Body-mass index

BMI (kg/m2)	WHO classification
<18.5	Underweight
18.5–24.9	
25–29.9	Grade I overweight
30–39.9	Grade II overweight ('obesity')
>= 40	Grade III overweight ('morbid obesity')

done by you as therapist, by a GP, or by another member of a multidisciplinary team. Do not be persuaded that your client can make an accurate estimate of her size – felt sense of fatness is notoriously unreliable.

Features shared by the eating disorders are summarised below.

1. Interplay of cognition, emotion and behaviour

Identifying such patterns is fundamental to helping clients with eating disorders, whatever the diagnosis. This includes the person categorised as EDNOS, when a cognitive behavioural maintenance cycle will be your guide. Three examples are illustrated in Figure 15.1: (1) a cycle of self-starvation, (2) a cycle of over-compensation for eating, (3) a cycle of over-eating.

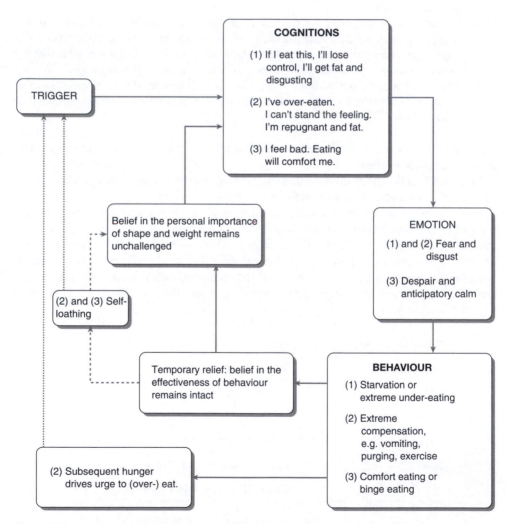

Figure 15.1   Maintaining cycles in eating disorders

2. Common core themes

NATs often beg the question, 'What is so bad about that?' As eating disorders are unlikely to be driven purely by concerns about shape and weight, we have to ask, what's so bad about being normal body weight/being over-weight/being top-heavy/and so on. Themes that emerge from clinical report and research include:

- **Social and interpersonal issues**: these include fears of being abandoned, of social evaluation, shame and low self-esteem (see Waller & Kennerly, 2003, for a review). Thus, systemic (particularly family) factors need consideration at assessment, and partners or parents might be usefully involved in treatment.
- **Control**: This has long been recognised as a powerful factor in the aetiology and maintenance of eating disorders, and its role has recently been elaborated (Fairburn et al., 1999).

3. Cognitive process

Extreme cognitive processes are as pertinent to the development and maintenance of eating disorders as they are to other psychological problems. Specifically, perfectionism and dissociation have been identified as playing a powerful role in their maintenance:

- **Dichotomous thinking**, the 'all or nothing' view, is common and tends to be expressed as perfectionism. This is apparent in extreme goals for thinness and in extreme over- or under-eating, for example. It is often underpinned by negative self-evaluation, which drives a compensatory behaviour of attempting to overachieve. When a client succeeds, this usually fuels the belief that performance equals worth, and the negative self-view is unchallenged; when a client fails, this feeds the low self-esteem (see Figure 15.2).
- **Dissociation**, namely mental processes of 'tuning out' or disassociating from current emotional or cognitive experience, has been linked with eating disorders, as it can be induced by self-starvation or by over-eating (Vanderlinden & Vandereycken, 1997). Repeated dissociation in the face of perceived negative emotions results in a person failing to learn that the emotions can be tolerated; and thus dissociation through misuse of food remains a major coping strategy.

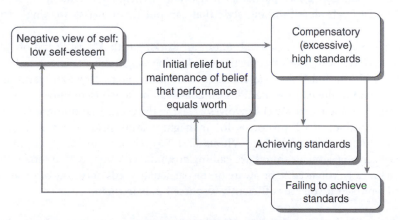

Fi̖̗re 15.2   Perfectionism maintaining an eating disorder

4. Affect

There is now substantial evidence for the role of emotion in driving eating behaviours (e.g. Waters et al., 2001). This is relevant to both over- and under-eating, and research suggests that sensations of hunger or satiation are overridden by emotion.

5. Motivation

Clients with eating disorders often show an ambivalence about, or even overt resistance to, change, with therapists often focusing on enhancing motivation. This costs time, and currently there is little evidence that adding a motivational element to CBT improves outcome (Treasure et al., 1999).

6. Health risks

Severe physical consequences are possible with both acute and chronic eating disorders. Thus, clients should be taken on with caution and managed in consultation with a physician. For most therapists practising in the UK, this will be your client's GP. The main concerns include:

- **Anorexia and bulimia nervosa**: malnourishment and its consequences, cardiovascular complications, gastrointestinal problems, deficiencies in the immune system, biochemical abnormalities, central nervous system changes, amenorrhoea, osteoporosis, renal failure.
- **Obesity**: metabolic complications, cardiovascular complications, respiratory problems, osteoarthritis.

Using CBT with the eating disorders

Whatever the diagnosis, you will need to carry out a thorough assessment. Your resulting formulation will guide you towards appropriate cognitive and behavioural interventions. This is especially important if you discover that your client does not fit one of the established models relating to DSM diagnoses. The characteristic dichotomous thinking style of those with eating disorders can be addressed using continuum work (see Chapter 8), and relapse management is particularly relevant in helping clients manage powerful cravings and the absolute thinking style that can put them at risk of binge eating (see Chapter 6).

There has been a long *behavioural* tradition of working with AN, BED and obesity. These interventions have been relatively effective in achieving weight reinstatement and stability in those with AN and reduced binge eating in those who binge. However, gains are poorly maintained, and in the past two decades, emphasis has switched to modifying cognitions.

As in other problems, treatment involves breaking the cycles that maintain the problem. The most prominent CBT protocols for managing eating disorders are based on very specific 'maintenance models' (see Vitousek, 1996); generic models and models that encompass schema-level meanings are gaining ground (see Waller & Kennerley, 2003, for a review). Clinically, you need to be aware of the particular needs of eating-disordered clients and to ask yourself if you are sufficiently resourced to help them.

Treatments for AN need to take into account:

- the consequences of prolonged low body weight – there is general agreement that those with anorexia should have regular medical screening (Zipfel et al., 2003).
- The effects of starvation – including behavioural and cognitive changes which reduce motivation and impair the ability to engage in cognitive therapy.
- Denial or lack of an appreciation of the medical dangers of anorexia – reducing the client's ability to engage in treatment.

Engagement is further undermined because sufferers feel that their behaviour is appropriate and not dysfunctional.

Treatments for bulimia nervosa need to take into account:

- the medical risks of extreme compensation for perceived over-eating (vomiting, purging, etc.).

Treatments for binge-eating and obesity need to take into account:

- the medical risks of over-eating and being overweight.

Recommended reading

Treasure, J., Schmidt, U. and van Furth, E. (2003). *Handbook of eating disorders* (2nd edn). Chichester: Wiley.

Trauma

Psychological trauma can be evoked by many incidents: for example, witnessing atrocities, being in a natural disaster, sexual assault (in childhood or in adulthood). DSM-IV (APA, 2000) defines traumatic stressors as events involving actual or threatened death or serious injury or a threat to the physical integrity of self and others. Without this, the diagnosis of PTSD cannot be made, regardless of how distressed a person appears. None the less, we see clients who have not experienced trauma as defined above yet who struggle to cope with the psychological consequences of trauma. We also see clients who do not fulfil other DSM criteria, like re-experiencing the trauma and emotional numbing, but who appear to suffer from the psychological legacy of trauma.

Terr (1991) distinguished two types of trauma victim:

- Type I : who have experienced a single traumatic event;
- Type II : who have been repeatedly traumatised.

She originally made this distinction with regard to children, but the division has been applied to adults. Rothschild (2000) has suggested further refinements to the adult Type-II classification, in order to distinguish those with and without stable backgrounds and to distinguish those who can recall discrete traumatic events from those who have a generic recall of trauma. Scott and Stradling (1994) have proposed a further category, that of *prolonged duress* stress disorder (PDSD), which describes the client who has experienced ongoing stress such as chronic illness or emotional cruelty during childhood, rather than specific trauma.

These distinctions remind us that trauma survivors are not a homogenous group. Research cognitive therapists have tended to focus on trauma victims who have PTSD, for whom there are well-developed treatments. If you are working with survivors of trauma who do not fulfil criteria for PTSD, you will have to work from first principles: formulation leading to intervention, rather than assuming that PTSD protocols fit all trauma survivors.

Those who have suffered childhood trauma are more likely to experience psychological difficulties in adulthood (Mullen et al., 1993). Therefore, survivors of childhood trauma can present with any combination of psychological problems, such as eating disorders, depression or interpersonal difficulties. Many of the presenting difficulties of survivors of Type-II trauma are familiar to cognitive therapists, and a cognitive understanding of the problem(s) already exists.

1. Interpersonal aspects

Many survivors of interpersonal trauma have difficulty in developing a trusting relationship with others, including you as therapist. It is not unusual to have to 'invest' sessions in building up your working alliance in preparation for the CBT per se (see Chapter 3). Survivors of accidents, impersonal attack and natural disasters may find it much easier to establish rapport.

Survivors of interpersonal trauma often develop difficulties in their real-life relationships, and a systemic overview of your client's situation can be helpful. This means frequently updating your understanding of their relationship with their children (are the children at risk of neglect or abuse?); or with significant others (is your client at risk of harm? Is their partner at risk?). Repeated early life trauma has often been linked with personality disorders (Beck et al., 1990; Terr, 1991; Layden et al., 1993), and, as a clinician, you need to be prepared for this possibility.

2. Memory of trauma

As we have already said, presentations of non-PTSD trauma are diverse. One manifestation of this is the range of available memories of traumatic experience(s).

- **Lack of memories of trauma**: some clients do not have accessible memories of trauma. Sometimes a victim is so distracted or dissociated that full memories are never laid down. Clients will say things like:'My mind froze, I don't remember what he said/did.' Or,'I can see the knife but I can't recall anything else.' In such cases, there might be no more memory to retrieve. You should not try to force recall because of the danger of creating false memories (see below). It has also been suggested that traumatic memories can be repressed (British Psychological Society, 1995): there will be stored recollections of the trauma, but again, do not force recollection because of the danger of encouraging distortions.

- **Intrusive memories**: Although it is not inevitable, many survivors of trauma have intrusive memories that can involve any, or all, of the senses. For some these memories will have the quality of flashbacks. Some memories will reflect specific incidents reasonably accurately, some will have become inaccurate, while some will be a composite of several events. The empirically-based methods of managing intrusive memories in Type-I PTSD (Ehlers & Clark, 2000, for example) may not be the best option for managing Type-II trauma intrusions – we do not yet know.

- **False memory** has been well-researched, and is recognised to exist (British Psychological Society, 1995). All memories are vulnerable to distortion, as they are not stored in the brain like a video-recording, but more like a collection of jig-saw pieces which are reformed each time a memory is recalled. However, we know that while memory for detail is rather unreliable, general memories are not. Thus, we might accurately recall that we enjoyed or hated a holiday, but our recollection of the detail of it would be considerably less reliable. Clinically, the guideline is not to get too obsessed with detail as it can be inaccurate.

3. Schema-level work

Childhood trauma, especially if chronic, can impact on a person's fundamental sense of self, of others and of the future, which can result in the development of powerful belief systems (or schemata) which, by adulthood can be both rigid and unhelpful. Schemata and schema therapy are described in Chapter 17, so suffice to say that you need to hold in mind the possibility that your client may express a wide range of difficulties underpinned by inflexible belief systems.

4. Complexity of presentations

Sometimes, when working with survivors of complex or chronic trauma, you may find that the client presents with a combination of problems or lives in a dysfunctional environment, which undermines therapy. In short, the picture can be complex, possibly involving co- morbid problems, or multi-impulsive behaviours (including self-injury). You are again reminded to formulate the 'bigger picture' for such clients by asking questions that will elicit more information – 'Is there any thing else that you do that might affect this . . . ?'; 'Are there other occasions when . . . ?; 'And in your work life . . . ?'; 'And in your home life . . . ?'

CBT with survivors of trauma

With the exception of research focused on Type-I PTSD, evaluation of CBT with survivors of trauma has not been systematic, and there is a paucity of RCTs. However, guidelines from highly experienced practitioners exist to help you develop your approaches to working with survivors of trauma who have personality disorders (e.g. Layden et al., 1993; Beck et al., 2004). There is increasing research supporting Gilbert's compassionate mind therapy (CMT) as an effective intervention with those who have been left with fixed self-blaming and self-attacking beliefs (see Gilbert & Irons, 2005, for a review). There is also evidence that supports the use of cognitive techniques for specific aspects of a client's presentation (for example Arntz & Weertman, 1999) and for interventions for particular categories of trauma (for example Resick & Schnicke, 1993).

In summary, with Type-II trauma, there are no well-established protocols to follow, and you will have to call on the generic skills of cognitive therapy. However, we would promote the following guidelines:

- Formulate the *big* picture.
- Remember the qualities of memory.
- Focus on the accessible Axis I problems as far as possible, using treatment protocols where appropriate.
- Bear in mind the possibility of your having to accommodate interpersonal difficulties, schema-driven problems and multi-problem presentations.
- Keep risk assessment on your agenda.

Recommended reading

Beck, A.T., Freeman, A. and associates (2004). *Cognitive therapy of personality disorders (2nd edn)*. New York: Guilford Press.

Layden, M.A., Newman, C.F., Freeman, A. and Byers-Morse, S. (1993). *Cognitive behaviour therapy of borderline personality disorder*. Needham Heights, MA: Allyn & Bacon.

Mcnally, R.J. (2003). *Remembering trauma*. Cambridge, MA: Harvard University Press.

Petrak, J. and Hedge, B. (2002). *The trauma of sexual assault: treatment, prevention and practice*. Chichester: Wiley.

Anger

Anger is an emotion, and, like other emotions, it is not necessarily a problem. However, anger may become a problem when it is excessive in frequency or severity and when it leads to behaviour which is dangerous to self or others or which hinders rather than helps people in achieving their goals. It can be at the heart of a range of interpersonal problems such as domestic violence – physical or emotional – or aggressive outbursts in the workplace, on the road, in social settings and so on.

Although anger has received less attention than other emotions, there is evidence that CBT can be an effective treatment for anger problems (Beck & Fernandez, 1998). The Beckian approach sees anger as arising in situations where people feel that important 'rules' about how others should behave are violated or as a defensive reaction when under perceived threat (Beck, 1999). However, the best-known CBT approach to anger control was developed by Novaco (1979, 2000) and derives more from Meichenbaum's (1975) stress inoculation training than from Beckian cognitive models. In brief, the therapy typically consists of three stages:

- **Preparation**: the client is helped to identify patterns of anger, including triggers and typical thoughts, feelings and behaviours, through the usual assessment and formulation.
- **Skills acquisition**: the client learns techniques to help him lower his arousal when provoked. These may include relaxation, and 'self-instructional techniques' (see below).
- **Application training**: the client rehearses the techniques in progressively more difficult situations, perhaps starting off with practising in imagination and progressing through role play to in-vivo application.

The self-instruction which is central to Novaco's approach teaches the client to manage different stages of a potentially anger-provoking situation. These stages include:

- **preparing for the provocation** (e.g. recognising situations which may be difficult; reducing excessive expectations of other people).
- **coping with physical arousal** (e.g. through relaxation and/or breathing control).
- **coping with cognitive arousal** (using self-instruction statements such as 'Getting angry won't help me').
- **post-confrontation reflection** (evaluating the outcome and working out how to move forward).

Apart from the need for careful risk assessment, the main difficulty in therapy for anger is that clients are often not well engaged. Anger has often been perceived as useful to them in the past, is often rewarding in the short term, and clients may have been referred to therapy because someone *else* thinks their anger is a problem (e.g. their families or the courts). Also, many people are reluctant to look for alternative perspectives when they are angry. Engagement in a collaborative relationship and careful assessment are, therefore, crucial, and as therapist you also need to consider carefully whether you may be at risk.

Recommended reading

Beck, A.T. (1999). *Prisoners of hate*. New York: HarperCollins.

Novaco, R.W. (1979). The cognitive regulation of anger and stress. In P. C. Kendall & S. D. Hollon (Eds), *Cognitive-behavioral interventions: theory, research, and procedures*. New York: Academic Press.

Novaco, R.W. (2000). Anger. In A.E. Kazdin (Ed.), *Encyclopedia of psychology*. Washington, DC: American Psychological Association & Oxford University Press.

Psychosis

Most of the work on CBT for psychosis has focused on medication-resistant symptoms in schizophrenia, although there has also been some interesting work on CBT for bipolar disorder (see, for example, Basco & Rush, 1996; Lam et al., 1999; Scott, 2001). Within schizophrenia, the most common symptoms which may be amenable to CBT interventions are:

- **hallucinations**, particularly auditory hallucinations (i.e. experiencing unusual or distorted sensory perceptions which do not seem to exist outside one's perception);
- **delusions** (false beliefs that persist despite a lack of evidence and which are not explained by cultural norms);
- **problems of mood** such as depression or anxiety;
- **other related problems** such as low self-esteem, relationship problems and social withdrawal.

In addition, there may be an important role for working with families or other carers – Pilling et al. (2002) have reviewed CBT and family therapy for schizophrenia.

In principle, CBT for psychosis is like CBT for any other disorder: your task is to build a formulation and apply CBT therapeutic strategies to the maintaining factors in that formulation. Nevertheless, working with psychosis has sufficient risks and complications that we would urge you to make sure you are familiar with using CBT in more straightforward problems before you try to use it with psychotic symptoms and that you have recourse to suitable supervision. It is also important to note that almost all trials of CBT for psychosis use CBT as part of a care package which also includes anti-psychotic medication and mental-health team support, rather than using CBT as a stand-alone treatment.

CBT theories of psychosis are less well established than in other disorders, and the field is still being actively developed. However, most current models suggest that hallucinations are a product of cognitive processes which include disturbances of attention, perception and judgement, including the misattribution of one's own thoughts to an external source; and, furthermore, that delusions may represent attempts to make sense of the anomalous experiences that can result from these processes, with the delusions then being maintained by biases in reasoning and attention (see, for example, Fowler et al., 1995; Chadwick et al., 1996; Garety et al., 2001; Morrison et al., 2003).

The aims of CBT for psychosis are usually to help the client manage psychotic symptoms better, to reduce the distress and disability caused by those symptoms and to reduce the risk of relapse. Some of the standard features of CBT described earlier in this book are particularly important in psychosis. Building a collaborative relationship and a formulation which can give an alternative, non-threatening and non-stigmatising account of the symptoms is vital. The formulation is then used to identify and test cognitions about the source, meaning and controllability of symptoms. BEs can be a key part of this exploration (see Close & Schuller, 2004) but need to be planned and carried out with particular sensitivity.

Other factors which may need special care include engaging clients who may be suspicious and who sometimes perceive themselves, rightly or wrongly, as having been abused by psychiatric systems; the pleasurable experience of mild mania which can prevent a sufferer from wanting to manage it; idiosyncratic thought processes which may make it difficult for you to keep track of the client's thinking; and the sometime neediness of the client's family or carer.

All these complications mean that CBT for psychosis often needs to be a longer-term treatment, taken at a relatively slow pace; and that you need skilled supervision and support.

Recommended reading

Chadwick, P., Birchwood, M. & Trower, P. (1996). *Cognitive therapy for delusions, voices and paranoia.* Chichester: Wiley.

Lam, D., Jones, S., Bright, J. & Hayward, P. (1999). *Cognitive therapy for bipolar disorder: a therapist's guide to concepts, methods and practice.* Chichester: Wiley.

Morrison, A.P., Renton, J.C., Dunn, H., Williams, S. & Bentall, R.P. (2003). *Cognitive therapy for psychosis: a formulation-based approach.* Hove: Brunner-Routledge.

Relationship difficulties

Difficulties in relationships are common in clients who ask for help. This is true for people with DSM Axis I disorders (APA, 2000), as well as for people with long-standing problems typified as personality disorder. For example, in Axis I disorders, a client with social anxiety may have difficulties in asserting himself, someone with low self-esteem may be overly dependent on others, and a depressed client may have become socially withdrawn. A cognitive behavioural formulation allows issues such as these to be approached in similar ways to other problems, by looking at the interlinkages between cognitions and emotions, behaviours and physical state, where the cognitions will be concerned with relationships.

A woman who had been depressed for a number of months had gradually reduced the amount of time she spent with her friends. If she were invited to see someone, her automatic thought would be, 'I am boring and have nothing to say. If I see my friends in this state, I shall lose them.' She therefore turned down most invitations, with the result that her friends made less contact with her.

With a client like this, where the automatic thoughts were typical of her depressed state but not of her thinking in general, the problem could successfully be approached at the level of automatic thoughts. For people with a personality disorder, the difficulties in relationships are likely to be more pervasive and enduring and a central feature of the disorder. However, the CBT approach still emphasises the central role of cognitions about self, others and relationships and their linkages with behaviour and emotions, though it is likely to be more necessary to also tackle underlying beliefs.

A man with a history of emotional neglect had a powerful and pervasive belief that 'No one is there for me.' In response to this, he had developed a rule that 'If I am honest about my failures, I shall be rejected,' and, as a result, frequently chose lying as a way of protecting himself. In the short term, this allayed his fears, but in the medium term presented him with real difficulties, as he had to weave more and more complicated stories to cover his lies. Treatment partly involved experiments with confessing to small failures and keeping careful notes of the responses that this drew from others, particularly his wife.

One setting where relationship problems can be viewed as they occur is the therapeutic relationship. Safran and Muran (1995) have described how interactions in the therapeutic relationship can be used to invalidate unhelpful beliefs about relationships (see Chapter 3). Safran and Segal (1990) proposed that the ways that others respond can play a role in the maintenance of dysfunctional thinking about relationships. They suggested that a client's interpersonal behaviour towards others may 'pull' a predictable interpersonal response, which then confirms the client's original belief.

A woman who was bullied at school had a belief that she was not easy to be with, and that if she tried to join in, she would be rejected and feel isolated and desolate. As she assumed that she would not be welcome in groups, she acted in an aloof and arrogant manner when she was in group situations (for example, at professional conferences), on the basis that 'If you don't want me, I am not going to demean myself by looking as though I want you.' Her colleagues responded to this by turning to others who were easier to approach, thus confirming her belief that she was not welcome in groups.

If an unhelpful belief has been identified, then in the therapy setting the therapist can experiment with *not* being 'pulled' into responding in the predicted way, and therapist and client can reflect on the impact that this has on the client's beliefs. The client can then experiment with using different interpersonal behaviours based on his modified belief.

A therapist needed to change the regular time for appointments because of a teaching commitment, and as the client interpreted this as indicating that the therapist was trying to find a way not to be with her, she became aloof and rigid about alternative dates. The therapist rejected the 'pull' to respond with 'Well, suit yourself!' and, instead, was warm and concerned about their difficulty with rescheduling, showing non-verbally that she very much wanted to find a solution so that she could see the client. After the practical problem was dealt with, the therapist asked the client to reflect upon how she had construed the situation and what implication the therapist's response had for her original belief (which in this case had been extensively discussed in earlier sessions).

Beck et al. (2004) and Young et al. (2003) have also written creatively about ways of dealing with interpersonal problems (see Chapter 17), and Linehan (1993) has developed a group programme called dialectical behaviour therapy (DBT) for helping clients with borderline personality disorders (see Chapter 17). The programme is lengthy, taking up to a year, but the outcome data so far are encouraging, with significant impacts on interpersonal and social adjustment.

Finally, there are many useful ideas about working with relationship problems incorporated in Dattilio and Padesky's (1990) work with couples, as described in Chapter 16.

Recommended reading

Dattilio, F.M. & Padesky, C.A. (1990). *Cognitive therapy with couples.* Sarasota, FL: Professional Resource Exchange.

(Continued)

Safran, J.D. and Segal, Z.V. (1990). *Interpersonal process in cognitive therapy.* New York: Basic Books.

Safran, J.D. & Muran, J.C. (1995). Resolving therapeutic alliance ruptures: diversity and integration. *Session: Psychotherapy in Practice,* 1, 81–92.

Substance misuse

When we refer to substance misuse, we tend to think about misuse of alcohol, psychoactive drugs and, possibly, smoking. It is worth bearing in mind that other behaviours such as gambling, over-eating, self-injury and compulsive spending have also been viewed as 'addictive' so may be amenable to the management outlined for substance misuse. This section will focus on the substances covered by DSM-IV (APA, 2000), namely alcohol and drugs, where:

- **substance abuse/misuse** refers to a maladaptive pattern of use leading to significant impairment or distress (e.g. failure to fulfil responsibilities, legal or interpersonal problems);
- **substance dependence** is more severe and includes increased tolerance, withdrawal, use of increasing amounts of a substance and a persistent desire for the substance even though the person recognises the negative consequences of its use.

Why misuse substances?

In the face of the negative consequences, why do people misuse? Among the most common reasons are:

- **mood regulation**: to control depression or anxiety or to enhance positive moods like happiness;
- **to cope with adverse circumstances**, e.g. abusive relationships, poverty;
- **to contain severe psychiatric symptoms**.

It is very difficult for to people to stop misusing substances, partly because they often report that nothing competes with the positive effects of the substance (mood enhancement, blanking out problems) or that they experience powerful peer pressure. This is exacerbated by *physical dependence*, where *withdrawal symptoms* are experienced if the individual stops using the substance.

The CBT approach to substance misuse emphasises the additional role of dysfunctional thinking in the maintenance of the behaviour (Beck et al., 1993; Marlatt & Gordon, 1985), and this will now be considered.

The cognitive behavioural approach to substance misuse

Liese and Franz's (1996) developmental model for substance misuse is similar to the general CBT model of development (see Chapter 4), with the specific addition of exposure to, and experimentation with, addictive behaviours (e.g. family members who use drugs, friends who encourage drug use) and consequent development of drug-related beliefs ('If I use drugs I shall feel less anxious', 'I will fit in more easily if I use drugs').

The general CBT approach is similar to that used with other kinds of problems, including socialisation to the model, structured sessions and the range of cognitive, behavioural and physical techniques described throughout this book. However, there is a very strong emphasis on a non-blaming conceptualisation and a collaborative therapeutic alliance. This can be difficult in the face of frequent relapses, anti-social and illegal behaviour, dishonesty and so on, but one of the challenges of working with clients with problems of this kind is to maintain a genuinely compassionate and empathic stance. This is facilitated by framing difficult behaviours in terms of the formulation.

An important concept, highly relevant for this group of clients with marked ambivalence about change, is that of *preparedness for change* (Prochaska and DiClemente, 1984) (see Chapter 11). This readiness to risk changing behaviour can fluctuate, depending on the level of craving that a client experiences. Powerful, physiologically driven urges to engage in misuse can undermine commitment to therapy, and you need to anticipate this and encourage clients to develop substitute behaviours which can help take the edge off the cravings: for example, forms of self-soothing or distraction.

The issue of whether you should encourage your client to aim to control his substance misuse or to become totally abstinent (as advocated by major influences such as Alcoholics Anonymous) has continued to divide people who work in this area. It is possible that controlled misuse is more relevant for the very large group with less severe problems (Sobell & Sobell, 1993). The *harm-reduction approach* is one attempt to circumvent this issue while accepting the need to take account of the stage that the client has reached. The goals of therapy are to limit the impact of substance misuse rather than to aim for total abstinence (Marlatt et al., 1993).

The cognitive behavioural approach emphasises the individual's capacity to exercise control. Another important aspect of this is *relapse prevention* (Marlatt & Gordon, 1985), including the identification and avoidance of high-risk situations, exploration of the decisions that lead to substance use, lifestyle changes and learning from relapses in order to reduce future ones (see Chapter 6).

Some of the problems of working with substance misusers have already been identified – marked ambivalence about change, difficult behaviours such as non-compliance, dishonesty and powerful cravings. Substance misuse may also be difficult to identify because the manifestations may be subtle (e.g. sleep disturbance, panic attacks) and your client might not be aware that he is misusing alcohol, for example. Thus, it is important to bear it in mind as a hypothesis.

Recommended reading

Beck, A.T., Wright, F.D., Newman, C.F. and Liese, B.S. (1993). *Cognitive therapy of substance abuse.* New York: Guilford.

Liese, B.S. and Franz, R.A. (1996). Treating substance use disorders with cognitive therapy: lessons learned and implications for the future. In P.S. Salkovskis (Ed.), *Frontiers of cognitive therapy.* New York: Guilford.

Other applications of CBT

Clearly, the application of CBT extends beyond the few described here. It is used with diverse clinical populations: children and adolescents, older adults, those with learning disabilities, or sexual problems, in settings that are forensic, physical health, occupational – and so on. However, interesting as these applications are, it is beyond the scope of this book to describe them, though we want to alert you to the versatility of CBT. There will be training events, specialist supervision and textbooks to guide you if a client has specialist needs, and we strongly urge you to make use of them. However, remember that the principles described in this book are relevant to *every* CBT intervention, and the methods that we have described will be useful across client groups. The foundation set out in Chapters 1 to 11 will stand you in good stead for carrying out a cognitive assessment, offering a formulation and, where appropriate, beginning work with a range of clients.

Alternative Methods of Delivery

16

Introduction

Traditionally, 'classical' psychotherapy comprises weekly sessions of a 50-minute 'thera-peutic hour' of face-to-face contact between therapist and client. CBT has often followed this style but has also investigated whether other modes of therapy may have advantages over traditional models. These alternative approaches are usually motivated by the desire to achieve one or more of the following:

Making therapy more cost-effective

This goal arises from a perennial problem in most publicly funded health-care systems, namely that the resources available for psychological therapy are insufficient to meet demand, with the inevitable result that long waiting lists for treatment are common.

It is fairly easy to derive a common-sense 'equation' for waiting time, as follows:

$$\text{Waiting time } \alpha \ \frac{\text{Number of referrals} \times \text{Average therapist hours per referral}}{\text{Available therapist hours}}$$

This is not a true mathematical equation, but, nevertheless, it helps us to remember that in principle we can reduce waiting times by:

- reducing the number of people seeking therapy (e.g. by limiting referrals or by improving the general psychological well-being of a population so that fewer referrals arise);
- increasing the amount of therapist time available (e.g. by providing more therapists or by increasing the proportion of their time therapists spend doing therapy);
- decreasing the average number of therapist hours taken by each client (e.g. by seeing clients for shorter times or seeing more clients at one time in groups).

Some of the approaches we shall consider reflect the last of these variables: by reducing the amount of therapist contact per patient, they anticipate increasing the throughput of clients and hence offer more or faster treatment.

Improving the accessibility and/or convenience of therapy

Finding an hour a week during the working day (plus possibly lengthy travel time) is not easy for many clients. They may have jobs that do not easily allow them to take time off or that lead to loss of pay if they do so; they may have children or others to care for; or they may live in places that make getting to therapy difficult and expensive. These difficulties make it hard for many people to access therapy, and we need to think of ways to overcome them. A classic paper summarising the arguments for greater flexibility about modes of delivery was written by Lovell & Richards (2000), where they coined the acronym 'MAPLE', standing for Multiple Access Points and Levels of Entry. In essence, they argued that CBT should offer clients the mode of treatment that best combines effectiveness, accessibility and economy for that individual.

Improving the effectiveness of therapy

Some 'non-standard' ways of delivering therapy have as their main aim the harnessing of extra resources which the clinician believes will increase the effectiveness of therapy. Thus, practitioners of group or pairs therapy (see below) believe that these approaches are not just economical or convenient but also that they allow the clinician to tackle problems in ways which are not available in conventional one-to-one therapy.

Modes of delivery for CBT

We consider five main alternatives to traditional therapy in this chapter: self-help, large groups, conventional groups, couple therapy and pair therapy (see Table 16.1).

Table 16.1   Main goals of different delivery methods

Method	Cost	Accessibility	Effectiveness
Self-help	✓	✓	
Large groups	✓	✓	
Conventional groups	✓		✓
Couple therapy			✓
Pair therapy		✓	✓

Self-help

Here we refer to a range of approaches where clients use media to teach themselves CBT therapeutic strategies, with therapist contact being either entirely absent or much reduced, compared to traditional therapy. Thus we include under 'self-help' the following approaches:

- *Bibliotherapy*, i.e. client use of CBT books to carry out their own therapy. Although CBT books are frequently used by therapists as an *adjunct*, we shall focus here on the use of bibliotherapy as a more or less complete *substitute* for traditional therapy, where an important aim is to reduce the amount of therapist contact time. Bibliotherapy can be used by clients without *any* actual contact with a therapist, in what we might call *pure* self-help (either because some clinician recommends they use a book instead of therapy or because they just pick up a book in a shop); or they may still see a therapist, but for a reduced amount of time (*assisted self-help*). Although we shall concentrate here on books which are specifically about therapy, we recognise that novels or other books that do not directly offer therapeutic advice might nevertheless assist in the process of therapy.
- *Computerised CBT (CCBT)*, i.e. the use of computer programs, delivered either by CD- or DVD-ROM or via the Internet, aimed at teaching clients how to use CBT. Such programs often use a multimedia approach, including, for example, video clips, written text, user-completed questionnaires or diaries and so on.
- Recently developed approaches to self-help include the use of so-called *book prescription* schemes. In this approach, developed by Frude (2005), the public libraries in a locality stock a list of self-help books that people can borrow on extended loan by getting a 'book prescription' from a primary-care health worker. Another recent approach is the assisted self-help clinic in primary care, in which clients have brief appointments with a mental-health worker, who guides and supports their use of CBT bibliotherapy materials (Lovell et al., 2003).

The evidence on these approaches is at least modestly hopeful, suggesting that both bibliotherapy and CCBT can give outcomes in primary-care settings which are superior to treatment as usual; however, the evidence is limited and the quality of studies is often not high, so further evaluation is needed (Bower et al., 2001; Lewis et al., 2003; Richardson & Richards, 2006). For example, although an early uncontrolled pilot study on assisted self-help clinics was very promising (Lovell et al., 2003), more recent controlled trials have not shown the same advantages (Richards et al., 2003). In addition, it should be noted that most research findings to date come from primary care, so there is less evidence to support the use of such approaches with more severe or complex problems in secondary or tertiary care.

Despite these uncertainties, self-help approaches continue to be developed and recommended as one stage in a stepped-care programme (e.g. NICE, 2004a). As well as their benefits in terms of cost-effectiveness and accessibility to a wide range of people who might not come to conventional therapy, self-help approaches may have other advantages. They help clients avoid extensive involvement in psychiatric systems – perhaps minimising stigma and dependence; they promote self-efficacy; and they provide a form of help which is permanently available to the client for future revision. There are, of course, also some potential negative effects. Apart from the possibility that they do not work, some people have suggested that 'failed' self-help attempts may 'inoculate' clients against CBT: they may conclude that CBT is useless and then miss out on what might have been an effective treatment (we know of no evidence about whether this theoretical risk is significant in actual clinical practice).

Our view is that self-help approaches are well worth trying, particularly in primary care, but, whenever possible, their efficacy should be evaluated. Clinical experience suggests that the main guidelines for using such approaches as total or partial substitutes for conventional therapy are:

- Clients need to be literate and comfortable with reading (or using computers for CCBT) and not have physical or mental disabilities that prevent reading.
- Self-help should be used as the first step in a CBT approach (not for clients who have already had CBT, except perhaps as a 'top-up' for a client who merely wants to be reminded of CBT strategies).
- Clients need to be willing to give self-help a try: it is probably wise always to check clients' thoughts about self-help and to help them think through any significant doubts.
- Self-help may be more likely to succeed with relatively mild and circumscribed problems, rather than complex and enduring problems (but may still be of some help in some aspects of the latter).
- At least some therapist contact – i.e. 'assisted' or 'supervised' self-help – seems to increase the chances of success. This can be very limited: for example, Lovell's self-help clinic used 15-minute appointments, and the average total therapist contact time in a course of 'therapy' was just over one hour. Such limited contact is usually focused on suggesting appropriate literature, supporting and encouraging clients' attempts at self-help and helping them to problem-solve when difficulties arise.
- In bibliotherapy, there is insufficient evidence to compare the relative efficacy of different books, but the book prescription schemes described above can guide you towards books with some consensus of support from clinicians (see, for example, the list available on the Internet from the Devon Book Prescription Scheme, 2004). For CCBT, the National Institute for Clinical Excellence is currently reviewing the most recent evidence, and an appraisal is due at the time of writing.

See Williams (2001) for further discussion of some of these points.

Large groups

Another approach to 'economical CBT' is White's stress-control programme for anxiety (White et al., 1992; White, 2000). White's approach is delivered to groups of 20–50 clients, who also receive a written version of the course content which they can work on during and after the course.

Although calling this approach 'large group' conveys one of its distinctive features – the sheer number of people involved – it may in other ways be misleading since it is not group therapy in the usual sense, but is educational, more akin to an evening class. The course consists of six two-hour sessions, usually held in the evenings, in a primary care or non-health-care setting, and clients are encouraged to bring their partners if they wish to. Outcome studies suggest that the programme can result in good outcomes for anxiety disorders, and that improvements are well maintained in follow-up (White et al., 1992; White, 1998). White (2000) gives a comprehensive account of the approach, including practical advice on how to set up and run classes.

Possible advantages of this format include its obvious capacity to provide help to large numbers of people in a way which is very economical of time, both for clinicians and for clients. Its approach to anxiety problems, conceptualised as 'stress' which can be managed using teachable skills, may also appeal to populations who would be less likely to access conventional psychological therapies – White originally developed the approach partly to appeal to such groups. Apart from the size of the large group, which means that no one stands out unless they want to, one of the course's guidelines is that members are discouraged from discussing their particular problems in any detail, a rule which some clients find very reassuring. There may also be non-specific and destigmatising benefits from the sheer size of the class: 'I can't be that weird if 40 other people have the same kind of problem!' On the other side, of course there are clients who will not respond to such a relatively unpersonal approach and who might find it difficult to cope with such a large number of people – although bringing a partner along may counteract this.

Conventional groups

Another way of reducing costs while maintaining a more clinical relationship with one's clients is to develop a CBT group, by generalising the CBT approach used with individuals to a small-group format but without mimicking the principles of psychodynamic groups. The CBT structure of agenda-setting; monitoring of affect, thoughts and behaviour; re-evaluation of dysfunctional beliefs; homework tasks; and BEs has been maintained in group settings (Freeman, 1983). Initially the focus was on groups for depressed clients (e.g. Hollon & Shaw, 1979), but this has gradually been extended to a wide range of other disorders. Apart from economic considerations, there are other advantages of working in this way:

- Economy of therapist time (but see discussion below).
- Normalising group members' experiences, as the symptoms and problems of others are shared.
- Clients can often spot in others what was not obvious in themselves – e.g. increased ability to recognise links between thoughts and feelings or others' cognitive distortions (Rush & Watkins, 1981).
- Group support for doing difficult tasks – e.g. behavioural experiments where courage is demanded.
- Development of a culture of homework completion, etc.
- Potential for group members acting as co-therapists for each other, facilitating skills acquisition (Hope & Heimberg, 1993), for example, in tracking 'hot thoughts'.
- Capacity for doing BEs within the group, particularly (but not exclusively) for social anxiety.

However, the advantages need to be offset against a number of possible disadvantages, including:

- Reduced ability to tailor the sessions to the idiosyncratic beliefs/behaviours of each client.
- Possible reluctance to disclose shameful beliefs.
- Risk of one or a few individuals monopolising the sessions.
- Different improvement rates among the group may be discouraging for some.

- Drop-outs may have a dispiriting impact on the group.
- Potential for unhelpful culture to develop; e.g. of off-target discussion or non-compliance with homework.

Nevertheless, the potential saving in therapist time has proved very tempting, and a number of different kinds of groups have been developed.

Format of CBT groups

Groups have been developed for different purposes (e.g. in-patient vs. out-patient), and Morrison (2001) has differentiated them as follows:

Open-ended: clients can join for a number of sessions at any point. Such groups may have a strongly educational tone. They necessarily focus on broad issues, for example, links between affect and cognition, with less opportunity to consider individual issues.

Open, rotating theme: (e.g. Freeman et al., 1993). There is a prearranged programme so not all sessions may be appropriate for any individual client. They are often at a higher frequency than usual – e.g. three times a week.

Programmed: Highly didactic and the least interactive – similar to the large group format described above.

Closed: Everyone joins the group at the same time and goes through the whole programme, so all are at a similar level of skill with CBT.

Membership of groups

This is largely dependent on the function of the group. If the group is designed to deal with problems like panic disorder or borderline personality disorder, then there would need to be a screening process. If, on the other hand, the group is intended to increase skills in the management of problems across diagnoses, as may be the case with an open-ended in-patient group, then it would be more likely that a wide range of clients would be included, independent of diagnosis. The relevant questions are what the aim of the group is and who would be most likely to benefit.

Therapist input

The general view (e.g. Freeman et al., 1993) is that it is easier to run a group with more than one therapist, partly because of the twin tasks of providing the technical input (e.g. teaching how to use a DTR) at the same time as attending to interactions between group members. Hollon and Shaw (1979) suggest that six group members is about the maximum an individual therapist can handle unless a co-therapist is available.

Frequency

Open groups can continue for an indefinite period, but closed groups tend to run for between 12 and 20 sessions, usually on a weekly basis in out-patient settings, more frequently with in-patients. They generally last for one and a half or two hours, which allows sufficient time for group discussion in addition to the didactic and technical elements.

What outcome can be expected from group CBT?

Morrison (2001) looked at the outcome studies for different kinds of groups, across diagnoses and formats, and these are summarised succinctly in her paper. Overall, it was difficult to demonstrate advantages for group over individual treatment, largely because the studies were inadequate for the purpose: in many studies, the samples were too small (e.g. Rush & Watkins, 1981, for depression; Scholing & Emmelkamp, 1993, for social phobia); or the outcomes for individual treatments were lower than in other published studies concerning the same problem (e.g. Telch et al., 1993, for panic); or the group programme offered was not consistently CBT (e.g. Enright, 1991, with OCD). Nevertheless, Morrison concluded that outcome studies generally support the efficacy of CBT offered in groups, although it seems probable that clients with more serious disorders, those with serious depression, or OCD, do better with individual treatment.

Cost-effectiveness of group CBT

Much of the argument in favour of group CBT lies in its cost-effectiveness, but this may be more apparent than real, for the following reasons:

- group sessions usually last one and a half or two hours rather than the single hour typical of individual therapy;
- the screening process may be very time-consuming, with referrers taking a chance on clients likely to be unsuitable for the group;
- there is often a lot of preparation of materials for groups – hand-outs, questionnaires/ ratings, etc.;
- time is taken for preparation of the group programme, probably with a co-therapist;
- time is required for debriefing with a co-therapist after each session;
- it may be more difficult for clients to take two hours plus travel time off work; Antonuccio et al. (1997) argued that this cost needs to be factored in when looking at comparative costs;
- there may be less treatment gain for each individual in the group, and the gain per unit of therapist time may need to be considered.

By all means, go ahead and develop CBT groups, but it is important to evaluate the progress made by individuals in the group and to compare this with the progress made by similar clients seen individually in your own practice or in published research. As long as your clients make progress, you may consider that it is more equitable to offer more people a group, with less expected gain, than it is to offer a smaller number of clients individual therapy, even if you know the small number are likely to do better if seen individually. Morrison (2001) suggested that it may be useful to offer clients two or three individual sessions before moving them into a group, to identify idiosyncratic features for attention in the group and to socialise them to the CBT approach. You may then get the best of both worlds.

Couples

Working with couples is another way of increasing the effectiveness of therapy when it is apparent that their relationship is central to the problems presented by one or both clients.

The CBT approach to therapy with couples assumes that the beliefs of each client about themselves, their relationship and relationships in general are crucial in understanding how they feel about their own relationship and each other and how they behave towards each other. These beliefs may have been learned early in life and may not be verbally articulated, so a major task is to help the couple identify those beliefs (Beck, 1988). It is important to pay *equal attention* to each partners' expectations about relationships and how those expectations may distort their perceptions of their current relationship.

The general principles and characteristics of cognitive therapy apply to this kind of working, with an emphasis on structured sessions and inter-session assignments. The assessment includes a joint session, plus individual sessions with each of the partners, where ground rules are laid down about, for example, telephone calls outside the session and arguing within the session (see Dattilio & Padesky, 1990). Having developed a problem list and formulation, therapy is likely to focus on three broad areas:

1. Modifying unrealistic expectations

This is done following the principles and techniques described for individuals in earlier chapters.

> *A woman who felt hopeless about her marriage held the belief 'Unless I am the centre of his life, our relationship means nothing' and had automatic thoughts like, 'We never do anything together', whenever her partner engaged independently in an activity. Therapy involved looking at the evidence for each partners' NATs and gradually worked towards jointly defining a belief that took account of their experience of current relationships – for example, 'Our lives can interconnect and overlap in important areas and be separate in other areas; and our relationship can still be meaningful.'*

Beck (1988) gives good examples of typical cognitive distortions and how to tackle them.

2. Modifying faulty attributions of blame

It is common for couples to be locked in a vicious cycle of mutual recrimination and blaming, with neither partner accepting responsibility for the difficulties in the relationship. It is a priority to help them identify and re-evaluate their beliefs about responsibility so that they can collaborate in working on their problems.

3. Communication training and problem-solving

Couples typically need help in developing new skills to help them reduce destructive interactions. Communication training emphasises good listening skills, clearly stating one's needs and taking responsibility for one's feelings and is well described in Burns (1999). It is important that couples learn how to deal with intense anger while they are learning to communicate effectively, and this can usefully be rehearsed in treatment sessions.

Once they can communicate more effectively, many couples need to learn to problem-solve to deal with areas of disagreement. Jacobson and Margolin (1979) set out general principles for problem-solving in couples, including:

- specifically defining the problem;
- focusing on solutions rather than blame; and
- learning to compromise.

Behavioural approaches to couple therapy (for example, Stuart, 1980) emphasise the exchange of positive behaviours, where each partner acted in specific ways to please the other. Within CBT, this strategy can be used to identify dysfunctional beliefs and incorporated into behavioural experiments.

Issues that need special attention within couple therapy include crises, such as recently divulged infidelity or newly developed violence within the relationship. Defusing a crisis would take priority at the early stages of treatment. Other problem areas are where one partner wants the relationship to end; where one partner has a secret (e.g. infidelity) he does not want to disclose; where one partner has another ongoing relationship; and where one partner has a significant psychiatric disorder. Problems such as these are addressed in Dattilio and Padesky (1990) and should be discussed with a supervisor, ideally one experienced in couple work.

Pair therapy

This describes therapy delivered simultaneously to two clients with similar difficulties. To our knowledge, pair therapy in CBT was first presented by Kennerley (1995), who described offering it to trauma clients who wanted to share their difficulties with others in a structured and therapeutic setting but who were unable to join a CBT therapy group. The main reasons for wanting to work with other clients were to destigmatise the experience of childhood abuse and to discover how others coped, objectives which would have been met in a therapy group. The predominant reasons for not joining a group were: being too socially anxious to participate in a group, having personality disorders that precluded them from the group therapy on offer or facing a lengthy wait for the next group.

Pairs were matched according to similarities in their traumatic history and current difficulties, and then a single therapist took them through the same programme used in a group intervention (see Kennerley et al., 1998). Norris (1995) gives a detailed account of two women's experience of pair therapy. Although this approach to managing problems related to childhood trauma has not been used in a controlled trial, the preliminary indications were that clients found it acceptable, gained the social benefits of sharing their problems without having to join a group and did as well in treatment as those in group therapy.

Developments in CBT

Introduction

CBT was originally developed to help those suffering from clinical depression and has gradually been extended to a wide range of psychological disorders. By the 1990s, the model had been elaborated to include the cognitive, emotional and behavioural processes that might underpin the difficulties of clients who experience more complicated problems, including personality disorder.

The most clinically prominent models are those which emphasise the role of schemata (or schemas) in cognitive and behavioural difficulties, and these have given rise to approaches to cognitive therapy which are overtly schema-focused (Beck et al., 1990; Young, 1990) and those that indirectly address problem schemata (Gilbert, 2005; Linehan, 1993). These schema-focused developments will be given prominence in this chapter, as well as other important models and theories which have given rise to exciting possibilities for enhancing or shifting the emphasis of interventions. These include the interacting cognitive subsystem (ICS) model (Teasdale & Barnard, 1993), which underpins mindfulness-based cognitive therapy (MBCT) (Segal et al., 2002); and relational frame theory (Hayes et al., 2001) which provides the theoretical basis for acceptance and commitment therapy (ACT).

The past decade has also seen the emergence of behavioural activation (BA) (Jacobson et al., 2001), a therapy that focuses on a single component of CBT for depression (see also Chapter 12).

Each of these developments can only be briefly reviewed in this chapter; therefore, the reader is advised to refer to the available training manuals or publications for detailed guidance.

Why consider moving outside the framework of traditional CBT?

First, on an ad-hoc basis, traditional CBT might require modification or elaboration to be effective. This may mean extending treatment sessions beyond the number indicated by a treatment protocol or 'adding' an extra intervention to supplement the protocol when the client has, for example, to deal with an unforeseen life event.

Furthermore, CBT is not the optimum therapy for all psychological problems and is not accessible to all clients. In some instances, other forms of psychotherapy are more helpful, for example, family therapy in the treatment of AN (see Eisler et al., 2003, for a review).

Second, some practitioners have elaborated cognitive therapy in a substantial way in order to increase its accessibility to those with chronic and complicated problems. This includes the expansion of interest in interpersonal processes in cognitive therapy (Safran & Segal, 1990), the development of schema-focused cognitive therapy (SFCT) (Beck et al., 1990), schema therapy (Young et al., 2003) and MBCT (Segal et al., 2002), which combines CBT with mindfulness training.

Third, some practitioners have streamlined traditional CBT by focusing on specific aspects of it. For example, BA (Jacobsen et al., 2001) de-emphasises the cognitive components of traditional CBT in the treatment for depression.

A therapist might consider moving outside the traditional framework of CBT when the 'classic' approach seems to be insufficient yet the client seems suited to CBT and the formulation of the client's problem appears to support a cognitive-behavioural intervention. In some instances, there are guidelines to indicate which clients might be helped in this way. For example, MBCT is advocated as a treatment for recurrent depressive disorder, compassionate mind training for those whose progress seems arrested by self-criticism and shame, and SFCT for clients who are 'stuck' because of the resilience of long-standing negative belief systems. These approaches are discussed later in this chapter.

Schemata in therapy

What is a schema?

A description of schema-related work always begs this question. There is agreement that a schema is more than a belief: it is an information-processing structure that enables us to classify incoming information and to anticipate events. Some authors argue that it is a purely cognitive structure, while others argue that it is more complex and multisensory. We all have schemata, about ourselves, about categories of events and so on. These knowledge structures enable us to process, with speed, what is happening and help us render the environment predictable. It is accepted that, in general, schema develop from early childhood and subsequently predispose a person to interpret themselves, the world and the future in a particular way.

Williams et al. (1997) give a succinct description of a schema as 'a *stored body of knowledge* which interacts with the encoding, comprehension and/or retrieval of new information within its domain, by guiding attention, expectancies, interpretation and memory search … [a] consistent internal structure, used as a template to organise new information' (p. 211). You might ask: 'What does this mean in practice?' Consider the following brief passage:

Mary walked down the aisle, the congregation was silent and her parents looked on proudly. She readjusted her mortarboard slightly.

You probably quickly concluded that this was Mary's graduation ceremony even though there is no mention of graduation. Your previous knowledge of ceremonies furnished you with the information that you needed to 'read between the lines' and to anticipate what was happening. This body of knowledge resides in a schema. Schemata are highly functional and flexible (there is a reasonable chance that you were holding out for a wedding until you read 'mortarboard' and switched to an alternative possibility). This generally serves us well, but problems arise when the content of a schema is biased or is inflexible. When this happens, a person can 'read between the lines' inaccurately. For example:

> Rosie's boss had barely finished saying: 'You look well today!' when she felt overwhelming distress and had to get out of the room. The thought running through her mind was: 'He thinks I look fat!' and the feelings that she experienced were fear and self-loathing.

Rosie's self-schema was so biased towards the negative that when her boss commented on her appearance, she 'read between the lines', and, instead of perceiving a compliment, she believed that she had been criticised.

Beck et al. (1979) recognised the position of schemata in the cognitive model of depression. He acknowledged that accessible thoughts (automatic thoughts) are coloured by 'deeper' mental structures (schemata). For example, a self-schema represented by the label 'hopeless' could well underpin NATs such as 'There's no point in trying' or 'Things will never go well for me'; an interpersonal schema, represented by 'mistrust', might explain NATS such as 'He's only saying that to manipulate me', or 'Others will leave me in the end'.

Although schemata have long been recognised as 'enduring structures of knowledge' (Neisser, 1976), they are flexible to varying degrees, enabling us to change our attitudes and expectations as we have new experiences. For example, with managerial experience, a person's view of self might shift from 'I can't handle people' to 'I can manage others'; following a traumatic experience, a person's view of the world might shift from 'basically safe' to 'threatening and dangerous'. CBT exploits this by working in the 'here and now', offering clients new possibilities, encouraging new experiences which might have an impact at the schema level.

Schema-focused work

Some clients, however, present with schemata that seem resistant to change even in the face of new evidence. This is seen to be pivotal in the maintenance of chronic psychological problems, including those associated with personality disorders. Typically, clients with change-resistant schemata cannot embrace a positive experience that challenges a negative belief. Instead, they *repeatedly* dismiss it with comments such as, 'Yes but he's only saying that out of pity', or 'Yes but that was down to luck'. Some clients, such as Rosie, never get as far as appreciating the positive experience; they rapidly distort it to a negative event that sits comfortably with their inner, negative perspective.

This is the client group for whom schema-focused, or 'second generation', cognitive therapy (Perris, 2000) was evolved. The resilience of unhelpful schema(ta) demanded the development of strategies that could more directly target them and an approach that could facilitate this. Thus schema-focused work is an elaboration of traditional CBT with a shift of emphasis – it is not a distinct, new approach.

The approach puts greater emphasis on understanding the childhood and adolescent origins of psychological problems and on the client–therapist relationship, placing the formulation in a greater historical context. Beck et al. (1979) suggested that 'the use of childhood material is not crucial in treating the acute phase of depression or anxiety, but it is important in the chronic personality disorders'.

Practitioners have emphasised using the client–therapist interaction to more readily uncover sensitive or elusive core themes, to engage clients with interpersonal difficulties or profound hopelessness and to use the relationship as a mediator of change (Perris, 2000, Beck et al., 2004). In cognitive therapy, transference is not assumed to be operating but is a possibility to be explored. Young et al. (2003) particularly emphasise the therapeutic value of 'partial re-parenting' and 'empathic confrontation' in schema therapy, both of which assume that the therapeutic relationship represents a medium for change.

Schema work is about developing new, helpful belief systems which will be to the client's advantage and will compete with old perspectives – simply demolishing old beliefs can leave a client in something of a void. Many of these strategies are elaborations of 'classic' CBT techniques and include the following.

Positive data logs (Padesky 1994) are systematically compiled lists of positive experiences that serve to build new, more constructive belief systems and that challenge old, less helpful perspectives. For example, Rosie collected information which was consistent with a new possibility: 'I am an attractive person'. First, she compiled a list of qualities which she found attractive in others:

> A ready smile
> Genuine warmth
> Kindness
> Tolerance
> Fairness.

Rosie was interested that her list did not contain descriptions of physical appearance, and she reflected that others might share similar views. She used this list as a checklist and noted each time she became aware that she fulfilled one of her criteria, or when someone paid her a compliment indicating that she was attractive. At first, it was difficult to recognise the positives, but, with practice, Rosie became more adept at doing so.

This technique reflects the data-collecting exercises that we use in traditional CBT, but it is likely to span a longer period.

Continuum work or 'scaling' (Pretzer 1990) is a strategy for helping clients combat an unhelpful dichotomous thinking style. In classic CBT, we often help clients recognise their 'all-or-nothing' thinking and prompt them to take stock of the range of possibilities linking the extremes. Continuum work builds on this and involves drawing out the spectrum that lies between the extremes, discussing and weighing up the validity of an 'all-or-nothing' perspective. In Rosies's case, she held a dichotomy of 'ugly *or* attractive' and, unless she was given a very unambiguous message that she was attractive, she perceived comments as confirming that she was ugly. In therapy, she began to realise a continuum of attractiveness existed and that it included more than physical appearance.

Historical logs (Young 1984) are retrospective thought records. Key incidents from the past are re-evaluated in a systematic way, reviewing the historical reasons why a belief might have seemed compelling and why its validity might now be doubted. Rosie dated her belief that she was ugly to several incidents from her past, including an incident at age eight when a group of children surrounded her and chanted that she was 'repulsive'. She reflected on why it was that she believed them at the time:

> *I was overweight and my parents never did anything but criticise me.*

Now, however, she could use her 'wise mind' to challenge the conclusion she drew as an eight-year-old:

> *I was a regular-looking, slightly chubby girl who was scape-goated by a group of kids who knew no better.*

She then drew a new conclusion:

> *I was vulnerable to believing criticism because of my home life, but I can now see that those kids were being superficial and cruel, which reflects badly on them rather than on me.*

Responsibility pies (Greenberger & Padesky, 1995): It is not uncommon for clients to assume that they are predominantly, if not totally, responsible for bad things that have happened and to feel painfully ashamed. The 'responsibility pie' technique encourages a client to consider who or what else might have contributed to a difficult situation. In Rosie's case, she blamed herself for being overweight, which fuelled self-loathing, shame and depressed mood. Her therapist prompted her to think who or what else might have contributed to her being overweight. At first she struggled, but slowly generated a list:

1. The food industry, who package and advertise food to make it so appealing.
2. My depression, which leads me to comfort eat.
3. My parents, who were unsupportive so that I turned to comfort eating.
4. My mother, who was always dieting but fed me the food she craved, which made me a fat child.
5. The children, who teased me for being 'fat', which triggered my obsession with weight.
6. My dance school, which indoctrinated us with the idea that only thin is acceptable and contributed to my obsession with weight.
7. My obsession with weight: I am preoccupied with food.
8. My aunt, though I love her dearly, who tried to cheer me up with chocolate treats, which is probably why I find chocolate particularly tempting.

When she had exhausted all possibilities, she added her name to the bottom of the list. For some clients, this alone is sufficient to modify an extreme view of responsibility, as they now realise that there were many contributors to the problem. However, Greenberger and Padesky suggest taking it further and asking clients to estimate *how much* each person/ thing contributed and then to convert this to a pie chart. While this is too demanding for some clients, it can be helpful to others. In Rosie's case, her ratings were as follows:

1. The food industry   5%
2. My depression   10%
3. My parents   40%
4. My mother   10%
5. The children   10%
6. My dance school   5%
7. My weight obsession   15%
8. My aunt   1%
9. Myself   4%

When she reached the bottom of the list, Rosie discovered that she only had 4% left to apportion to herself, and, as a consequence, felt less shameful and angry with herself. Her 'pies' are shown in Figure 17.1.

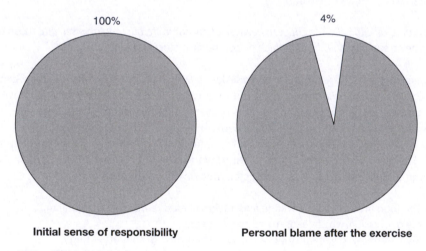

Initial sense of responsibility   Personal blame after the exercise

Figure 17.1   Rosie's 'pies'

It is important that you encourage your client not to conclude, 'I am not responsible, therefore there is nothing I can do about it.' Although a person no longer feels responsible for something happening to them, they can take responsibility for moving on. You might not be responsible for your central heating breaking down, but you can take responsibility for getting it fixed.

Schema-change strategies have also involved the development of 'experiential techniques', reflecting the role plays and visualisations used in classic CBT but also drawing on

Gestalt techniques and complex imagery exercises. For example, Rosie benefited from what Padesky calls psychodrama (Padesky 1994), a role play of an interaction with her dead father which enabled her to confront him about his emotional and physical abuse. She was also helped by engaging in image restructuring (Layden et al., 1993), where she reviewed the image of being ridiculed by schoolchildren, reconsidered her responses and con clusion and then rescripted an ending with positive connotations. For Rosie, this new image was of her walking away feeling tall and attractive (rather than cowed and ugly), confident in her knowledge that they were wrong and that she was morally superior. She particularly focused on the physical sensations of feeling tall and attractive, as this challenged her 'felt sense' of ugliness. Such body-image transformation can be particularly helpful in those with a long-standing 'sense' of being unattractive or uncomfortable (Kennerley, 1996). Another experiential technique is schema dialogue (Young et al., 2003), where a client conducts a dialogue between the old, unhelpful belief system and the more adaptive one. In a session, the therapist played the part of Rosie's assumption that she was ugly, and Rosie rehearsed responding with compassionate, positive statements that supported the belief that she was attractive. Initially, the therapist modelled arguments to undermine the validity of the negative perspective, but Rosie was soon able to take on this role and, in debate, became adept at generating convincing arguments that she was attractive. To help the client in the early stages of challenging, Young advises the use of schema flashcards which summarise the process for the client.

The techniques used to address fundamental beliefs are predominantly developments of 'classic' CBT strategies and are summarised in Table 17.1.

Table 17.1 Classic and schema-focused CBT strategies

'Classic' CBT	Schema-focused CBT
Collecting data as part of a behavioural experiment	Positive data logs
Identifying dichotomous thinking and recognising gradations	Continuum or scaling technique
Thought records	Historical log
Questioning blame	Responsibility pies
Role play	Psychodrama
Simple imagery transformation	Transformation of meaning of early memories; complex imagery transformation
Physical techniques	Body-image transformation
Challenging unhelpful thoughts	Schema dialogue
Progress review	Core belief logs
Aides-memoire	Schema flashcards

The experiential techniques have been shown to be particularly effective in achieving schema-level changes (Arntz & Weertman, 1999). However, they can be very evocative of strong emotion and should be used with caution, i.e. only when clearly justified and when you are confident that your client can tolerate the consequent effect.

The more ambitious aims of schema-focused work often make it necessary to offer clients longer therapy – sometimes several years (Young et al., 2003). Thus, you need to ask not only, 'Have I the skills to engage in a schema-focused therapy?' but also, 'Can both the client and I commit to a long-term intervention?'

It is striking that schema-focused therapy has achieved popularity in the world of cognitive therapy, and across a range of disorders (Riso et al., in press), without a substantial empirical foundation. There are single case reports (e.g. Morrison, 2000), examination of specific schema-change methods (e.g Arntz & Weertman, 1999) and open clinical trials (Brown et al., 2004), but these are few in number, and, as yet, no RCT data have been published. For this reason alone, schema-focused approaches should be used with caution; traditional CBT should be the first choice for a client who has been assessed and considered suitable for cognitive therapy.

Compassion-based therapy

What is it?

A commonly reported emotion among those seeking psychotherapy is shame (Gilbert & Andrews, 1998). For example, it has been associated with depressive disorder (Gilbert, 1992), and eating disorders and childhood abuse (Andrews, 1997). There is evidence that those who are highly self-critical do less well with traditional CBT (Rector et al., 2000), and the explanation might lie in the nature of long-standing negative schemata. Compassion-based therapy aims to help those with internal shame, self-criticism and self-condemnation develop compassion towards themselves and thus reduce or eliminate their feelings of shame.

Shameful clients often adopt the techniques of cognitive therapy but fail to feel an emotional shift, because shame and self-criticism pervade their responses. One reason might be that they use a harsh tone when challenging unhelpful cognitions. This can perhaps be likened to a parent 'comforting' a child by saying 'Don't be afraid' in a stern tone, as though fear is ridiculous and contrasting this with a parent who uses the same words but with a tone of empathy and genuine caring.

Gilbert's (2005) approach combines familiar cognitive behavioural interventions with *compassionate mind training* directed at addressing self-criticism and shame. This combines the technical aspects of cognitive reappraisal with developing an attitude of caring and concern.

Social mentality theory

Compassionate mind training is based on Gilbert's social mentality theory, which proposes that self-relevant information is often processed through systems ('social mentalities') which were originally evolved for social relating. Thus, each of us has an internal relationship with the self, and our thinking and feelings can reflect this 'self-to-self' relating. For example, a person can be self-attacking and feel attacked, or a person can feel needy for care and be self-soothing. Compassion-based therapy focuses on this internal relationship, training clients to develop inner compassion and warmth so that they might self-soothe and counter self-attack effectively.

Compassion-based therapy in practice

Compassion-based therapy shares many similarities with classical CBT. A sound therapeutic relationship is crucial to therapy. The therapist uses guided discovery and thought-monitoring to identify key cognitive-emotional processes which relate to feelings of shame and to self-criticism. A formulation is shared and, through this, patterns are identified, as well as blocks to therapy such as beliefs like: 'Self-criticism is good for me: it is character building.' The shared understanding of how the problem developed and why it persists allow what Gilbert calls 'de-shaming and de-guilting' (p. 287), which is similar to Linehan's concept of *validation* (1993). He advocates using imagery to capture the experience of being cared for, thus promoting feelings of acceptance, safeness and self-soothing. This compassionate state of mind is then used to promote a *compassionate reframe* of unhelpful automatic thoughts.

Compassion-based therapy uses experiential interventions, many similar to those employed in the schema-focused treatments. Techniques include promoting imagery of the compassionate self and restructuring past, traumatic experiences; achieving a detachment from the emotional impact of NATs by learning to name the critical process; and developing inner dialogues with the hostile self – sometimes using the Gestalt two-chairs technique. Compassionate meditations are also advocated, with similarities in form and purpose to the mindfulness exercises of DBT and MBCT (see below).

Compassionate mind training is a 'young' psychotherapy, but its popularity is growing, and the approach has been adapted for the treatment of depression (Gilbert, 2005), PTSD (Lee, 2005) and anxiety disorders (Bates, 2005; Hackmann, 2005). At present, the evidence base for CMT is not extensive, but it is growing (see Gilbert and Irons, 2005, for a review).

Mindfulness-based cognitive therapy (MBCT)

What is it?

This novel treatment approach was developed as a relapse-prevention intervention for depression (Segal et al., 2002). It combines elements of classic cognitive therapy with 'mindfulness' training, a therapeutic meditation approach developed by Kabat-Zinn (1994), who described mindfulness as 'paying attention in a particular way: on purpose, in the present moment and non-judgementally' (Kabat-Zinn, 1994, p. 4).

Over a decade ago, Teasdale et al. (1995) proposed an alternative to the assumption that CBT was effective because of changes in belief in the *content* of negative cognitions. They suggested that CBT might work because, by prompting clients to pause, identify cognitions and evaluate the accuracy or usefulness of their content, it helps them 'stand back' from problem cognitions. This allows 'distancing' or 'decentring'. Teasdale et al. (2002) highlighted the importance of decentring and increased meta-cognitive awareness as an effective intervention in reducing relapse in depression.

This raises the possibility that relief from psychological distress might be achieved by helping clients switch to a state of mind in which unhelpful thoughts and feelings are viewed from a decentred perspective. As the meditative stance of mindfulness training enhances decentring, mindfulness was incorporated into CBT, and MBCT was developed.

Interacting cognitive subsystems (ICS)

MBCT is based on a model of information-processing known as interacting cognitive subsystems (ICS) which regards the mind as a collection of interacting components (Teasdale & Barnard, 1993). Each of these components receives information from the senses or from other components of the mind. Each component then processes this information and passes the transformed information to other components. Thus, there is an *interacting network* within which recurring patterns appear in response to certain stimuli. In particular, those with previous experiences of depressive disorder get caught up in escalating self-perpetuating cycles of cognitive–affective ruminations more readily than those without a history of major depression. This pattern of rumination increases the likelihood of relapse into depression (Teasdale, 1988).

Teasdale calls the recurring patterns of interaction between mental components 'modes of mind' and likens them to the gears of a car:

> *Just as each gear has a particular use (starting, accelerating, cruising, etc.), so each mode of mind has a characteristic function. In a car, change of gear can be prompted either automatically (with an automatic transmission, by a device that detects when the engine speed reaches certain critical values) or intentionally (by the individual consciously choosing to rehearse a particular intention or to deploy attention in a particular way) (Teasdale, 2004: 275).*

He goes on to say that, just as with a car, the mind cannot be simultaneously in two gears or modes. Thus, operating in one mode of mind precludes a person from being in another state of mind at the same time. MBCT aims to help clients recognise a 'mental gear' which is unhelpful, to disengage from it and to shift to a more functional cognitive mode. Mindfulness is seen as an alternative and helpful cognitive mode, as it is the antithesis of rumination. Depressive rumination is characterised by repeatedly and automatically thinking about negative material, and mindfulness appears to decrease the likelihood of relapse into depression by putting the client into a state of mind which is incompatible with rumination, namely:

- Intentional: focusing on present experience rather than processing thoughts about the past or the future.
- Regards thoughts as mental events, rather than valid reflections of reality.
- Non-judgemental: viewing events as events, rather than 'good' or 'bad'.
- Fully present: that is, experiencing the moment, which reduces cognitive and experiential avoidance.

MBCT in practice

MBCT is a manualised group skills training programme for clients in remission from recurrent major depression (Segal et al., 2002). It integrates mindfulness with compatible elements of CBT. However, there is little emphasis on *changing* unhelpful thoughts but rather on cultivating greater mindfulness with respect to them. The key to this is achieving a stance of non-judgement and radical acceptance. MBCT aims to help clients become more aware of, and to relate differently to, their cognitive, emotional and physical experiences. Clients are taught to disengage from habitual and dysfunctional cognitive routines as a way to reduce future relapse and recurrence of depression.

Groups meet weekly for eight two-hour sessions, with homework assignments between meetings. These take the form of awareness exercises and tasks designed to integrate the application of awareness skills into daily life. Following the initial eight meetings, follow-up sessions are scheduled at increasing intervals.

Two clinical trials have evaluated the effects of MBCT for recurrent depression, and more are being carried out. So far, the results of trials indicate that MBCT is a cost-efficient preventative programme that can reduce the risk of relapse and recurrence in those with three or more previous episodes of depression. It is also being used to help sufferers of other problems such as chronic fatigue and cancer, and we can look forward to a continued refinement of the model and further clinical trials.

The radical behavioural interventions

What are they?

Some practitioners and researchers have developed cognitive behavioural interventions which have a clear cognitive component but emphasise the importance of the behavioural aspect of treatment. These include Linehan's dialectic behaviour therapy (1993), acceptance and commitment therapy (Hayes et al., 1999), and Jacobsons' behavioural activation (Martell et al., 2001). Below is a brief summary of each of these increasingly popular approaches.

Dialectical behaviour therapy (DBT)

Linehan et al. (1993) devised this intervention specifically for para-suicidal women diagnosed as having borderline personality disorder (BPD), a diagnosis associated with poor treatment outcome. DBT comprises a broad array of cognitive and behavioural strategies, tailored to address problems associated with BPD, including suicidal behaviours. The core skills which are taught are:

- emotion regulation;
- interpersonal effectiveness;
- distress tolerance;
- mindfulness; and
- self-management.

Treatment requires both individual and group sessions to run concurrently.

The defining characteristic of DBT is an emphasis on 'dialectics' or the reconciliation of opposites – for example, achieving self-acceptance whilst recognising the need to change, or balancing the alternating high and low aspirations which are common in those with BPD. Together with this focus on dialectical processes, there is more emphasis on process than on structure and content.

DBT differs from CBT in several other respects. Rather than aiming to challenge, it promotes acceptance and validation of the client's behaviour and reality. The therapeutic relationship is deemed central to DBT, and there is an emphasis on identifying and address-ing therapy-interfering behaviours.

DBT has now been evaluated in several trials comparing it with treatment as usual (for example, see Bohus et al., 2004). Overall, it is associated with better retention rates and is effective in reducing self-harmful behaviours. Although DBT appears to diminish a partic-ularly dangerous behaviour, so far its effectiveness seems quite specific, and it does not nec-essarily target the wide range of problems suffered by many clients with BPD.

Acceptance and commitment therapy (ACT)

ACT assumes that psychological problems are due to a lack of behavioural flexibility and effectiveness, and the goal of therapy is to help clients choose effective behaviours even in the face of interfering thoughts and emotions. Therapy is based on Hayes's relational frame theory (Hayes et al., 2001), which views psychological problems as a reflection of psycho-logical inflexibility and experiential avoidance. The model has two main components: *acceptance and mindfulness processes* and *commitment and behaviour change processes* – hence, 'acceptance and commitment therapy'. In ACT, these processes are balanced to pro-duce: greater 'psychological flexibility' (which Hayes views as the ability to experience the present moment fully as a conscious, historical being); and, depending on the situation, changing or persisting in behaviour in the service of chosen values.

Therapists are advised to adopt a compassionate attitude towards the client, echoing Gilbert's therapeutic guidelines. Hayes also emphasises the importance of being in the pre-sent moment, advocating the therapeutic use of mindfulness, echoing MBCT and DBT.

To support ACT, there are several randomised controlled studies indicating its efficacy with, for example, psychotic symptoms (Bach & Hayes, 2002) and specific anxiety (Zettle, 2003).

Behavioural activation (BA)

Behavioural activation emerged as a stand-alone treatment for depression following a com-ponent analysis study of CBT (Jacobson et al., 1996). BA was found to equal in efficacy a more complete version of CT, which also incorporated coping skills to counter depressive thinking.

BA helps depressed people re-engage in their lives through focused activation strategies. This counters patterns of avoidance, withdrawal and inactivity that may exacerbate depres-sive episodes by generating additional secondary problems. BA is also designed to help clients reintroduce positive reinforcement in their lives, which can have an antidepressant effect. This approach is also mentioned in Chapter 12, which more fully details the role of activity scheduling in the management of depression. See Martell et al. (2001) for a full account of BA.

Conclusion

Cognitive therapy has been used with an increasing variety of clinical populations and with client groups of increasing complexity and/or chronicity. This has demanded devel-opments in cognitive therapies and augmentations of CBT.

It is interesting (and reassuring) that there are themes common to several of the newer approaches, including the relevance of schemata and the utility of mindfulness and validation.

There can be no doubt that these developments have been exciting and have been met with enthusiasm. However, in general, the empirical status of the interventions is still poor and some are highly specific – for recurrent depression in the case of MBCT and for para-suicidal women with BPD in the case of DBT – and, until there is further evidence, we cannot assume that the approaches will generalise to other populations.

Problems

The therapist is not competent to offer the therapy

Clinicians not only need to be familiar with the basic principles of CBT and the augmentations of it but need to be able to work with clients who might have challenging interpersonal difficulties and who might present with a range of problems – some dangerous to themselves and others. Thus, additional training combined with good supervision is essential.

The therapist is stressed by the complexity and the demands of the therapy

These therapies tend to be reserved for complex clients who can be taxing on the therapist's skills and resources. As before, supervision is essential, and additional peer support can offset some of the stress. Nevertheless, therapists need to be realistic and only take on cases when they are reasonably confident that they can provide long-term or intensive care when necessary. It is also important to have a caseload with a 'balance' of clients that matches the therapist's skills and resources.

The case seems never-ending

Clients with complex needs can need 'longer-term' therapy that, in the literature, can mean anything from 20 sessions to several years. In order to guard against unnecessarily prolonging therapy and to guard against fostering dependence, you are advised to use supervision and to review progress regularly with a view to ending if there is little indication that cognitive therapy is helpful.

Vicarious trauma

Some of the more complex case-work invariably involves working with clients who will describe traumatic events, and vicarious traumatisation can occur in therapists exposed to this (McCann & Pearlman, 1990). Good supervision and support can help you identify the early signs of vicarious trauma, such as experiencing traumatic intrusions or taking actions to avoid triggering them – by drinking, for example.

18 Evaluating CBT Practice

What is evaluation and why should we do it?

By evaluating practice, we mean gathering data with the aim of determining how well therapy is working or whether one form of therapy is better than another. We believe that CBT practitioners should attempt to evaluate the effectiveness of their therapy for several reasons:

1. It places us in the great tradition of 'scientist-practitioners' (Committee on Training in Clinical Psychology, 1947; Raimy, 1950), aiming to expand knowledge through 'real world' research by practitioners. See also Salkovskis (1995; 2002) and Margison et al. (2000). The idea behind these approaches is that although traditional, university-based, controlled research is essential to progress, some questions are best answered through research based in clinical practice and carried out by ordinary clinicians.
2. It allows us to give both clients and purchasers more accurate information about what kind of outcomes clients can expect. Such evaluation is, therefore, an important part of accountability to our commissioners and of informed consent for our clients. It also allows both our clients and ourselves to see whether we are doing as well as expected and, therefore, whether there are areas that we need to improve.
3. It gives us a baseline of data against which we can compare changes we introduce in running our services. For instance, if we introduce a change, hoping to reduce the proportion of people who drop out of therapy, then it is helpful to know what the original proportion was; if we do some training, hoping to improve outcomes with depression, then we need to know what our outcomes were before the training. This kind of routine data can be an enormously useful support for clinical audits.

Thus, some system for routinely evaluating therapy is important, and while one short chapter can only cover a fraction of the issues of research design that arise in this area, we hope we can give you some useful pointers.

Types of evaluation

There are two main foci for evaluation:

- individual clinical case outcome (including evaluating a single group); and
- whole clinical service outcome (whether provided by one clinician or 100).

We shall look at each of these in turn.

Evaluating individual clinical cases

The major purposes of evaluating individual outcomes are (a) to allow you and your client to see what, if any, changes have occurred in therapy; and (b) in some cases to look more closely at the effects of a clinical intervention, perhaps using what has been called *single-case experimental designs*.

The first of these is fairly straightforward: we take some relevant measures, perhaps at the beginning and end of therapy, and see whether and by how much they change. Used at this level, such evaluation is straightforward good clinical practice. It gives both therapist and client a clear view of how much difference therapy has made to target problems.

Specific single-case research designs are probably less familiar to many readers, and we shall briefly introduce some of the ideas behind these approaches, although we cannot do more than scratch the surface. The interested reader is directed to classic texts such as Barlow et al. (2006) and Kazdin (1982).

The aim of these designs is to allow us to be more confident about evaluating the impact of treatment or some component of treatment. The most common approaches to single-case design rely on regularly repeated measures. The basic logic is that we establish some measure of the problem in which we are interested and then repeat that measure sufficiently often to establish a trend – the so-called *baseline* – against which we can compare subsequent changes when we introduce an intervention. The baseline gives us some protection against the likelihood that changes we observe are actually due to chance or some other factor, rather than our intervention. If we just take one measurement before therapy and one after, with just one individual, then it is impossible to rule out the chance that something external to therapy – for example, that our client won the lottery, or fell in love, or got a wonderful new job – caused any changes we see. If we have larger numbers of measurements, it becomes much less plausible that an external change just happened to occur at the time when we changed our intervention.

Figure 18.1 illustrates this logic. Imagine that the vertical axis here represents some relevant measure: score on a depression questionnaire, or number of obsessional thoughts in a day, or ratings of fear in a particular situation. In the left-hand part of this figure, with a single measurement before and after treatment, there is nothing to assure us that the reduction in score is not due to some external cause unrelated to therapy. We have only two measurements – anything could have happened in the intervening time and had an impact on whatever the measure is. In the right-hand chart, however, the frequent repeated measures give us greater reason to believe that the treatment that has caused the change because it is less likely that a sequence of repeated measurements should happen to respond to such an event *just at the specific time* that the treatment is introduced.

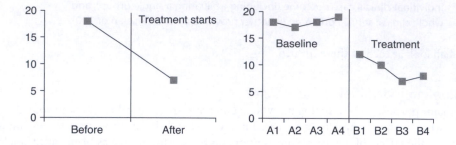

Figure 18.1 **'Before and After' versus 'Repeated measurements'**

The basic logic of many single-case designs follows this principle. We look at the *pattern* of measurements to see whether changes coincide with changes of treatment: if they do, that gives us some reason to believe that the treatment was responsible for the change (but we can still not be *sure* that some coincidental event has not caused the change).

The simple design on the right-hand side of Figure 18.1, consisting of a baseline before treatment and a continuation over the course of treatment, is often known as an A–B design: the baseline is Condition A and treatment is Condition B. If the treatment is one that we would expect not to have a lasting effect but only to work whilst it is being implemented (e.g. perhaps a sleep-hygiene programme), then there is scope for extending the A–B design to variations such as A–B–A, in which we first introduce the treatment and then withdraw it; see Figure 18.2 for an illustration of this.

The basic logic is strengthened here by the measure's not just responding to the introduction of the treatment but also responding again to its withdrawal. The likelihood that such opposite responses should coincide with treatment changes just by chance is even smaller, and, thus, our conviction that the treatment caused a change is stronger. Of course, if the treatment is one that we would expect to have a persisting effect – e.g. CBT for

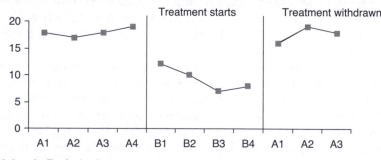

Figure 18.2 **A–B–A design**

depression leading to improved mood – then this A–B–A model is not usable: we do not expect the client's mood to drop as soon as the treatment is withdrawn.

We shall briefly describe two further common designs. The first, the *alternating treatments design*, is a way of determining in a single case which of two treatments is more effective (but requires that the treatment's effect will be measurable rapidly). During each segment (e.g. a treatment session, or some other unit of time), one of the two treatments is chosen randomly, and the measure is repeated for each segment. If the measure shows a clear separation of the two conditions, as in Figure 18.3, then we have some evidence that one treatment is more effective than the other. For example, suppose we wanted to test the hypothesis that talking about a particular topic makes our client anxious. Then we could agree with the client to decide randomly in some sessions to talk about the topic; and in other sessions not to; and to take ratings of anxiety. In Figure 18.3, if A marks the 'avoiding' sessions and B marks the 'talking' sessions, then the pattern suggests that avoiding leads to lower scores on our measure than talking does.

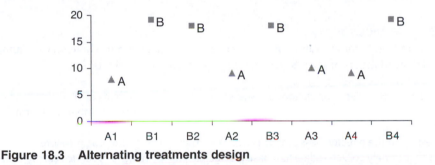

Figure 18.3   Alternating treatments design

This design can also be adapted as a useful design for patients' BEs (Chapter 9), for example to help an obsessional patient decide whether repeated checking of the front door actually causes more or less anxiety than doing one quick check and walking away.

Finally, there is the *multiple baseline design*, where we look at several different measurements at the same time, hence the name. There are several variations: multiple baseline across *behaviours*, across *settings* or across *subjects*. Consider this simple example of multiple baselines across behaviours. A client has two different obsessional rituals, both of which we monitor regularly during the baseline period (see Figure 18.4, where the triangles represent the frequency of one ritual and the squares the other ritual). Then we introduce the treatment for one behaviour only (one ritual in this case). After a delay, we introduce the treatment for another behaviour (the second ritual in this case). If we get a pattern like Figure 18.4, where each behaviour shows a change *just at the time treatment was introduced for that behaviour*, then this gives us some reason to believe it was the treatment that caused the change (see Salkovskis & Westbrook, 1989, for an example of this design).

The same principles apply to multiple baseline designs across subject or settings: of course, the number of different baselines does not have to be two, as in our example above, but can be any number. In the example in Figure 18.4, each set of data represents one *behaviour* (a ritual in our example); in the case of multiple baseline across *subjects*, each set of data represents a person, to whom we introduce the treatment at different times after baseline; in the case of multiple baseline across *settings*, each data set represents one situation (for example, a programme for disruptive behaviour that is introduced first in the school setting and then later at home). Note that this design can only work when we would expect some independence between the behaviours, subjects or settings: if the treatment is likely to generalise from one of these to the others, then the synchronised change we are looking for will not happen.

Finally, note that we have described here the common approach of analysing the results of such single case designs by *visual inspection* – i.e. by looking at the pattern of results and seeing what they seem to show. Over the past 20 years, there have also been developments in the statistical analysis of single-case designs, but such statistics are not yet straightforward enough for most ordinary clinicians to use.

Evaluating services

The other common form of evaluation is the collection of data about whole services and, therefore, larger numbers of clients. The main purposes of such evaluations are:

- to describe the client population (e.g. age, sex, chronicity of problems etc.);
- to describe the nature of the service (e.g. drop-out rates, average number of treatment sessions, etc.);
- to establish the effectiveness of the service's treatments, using outcome measures;
- to use routinely collected data as a baseline against which changes of service can be evaluated (e.g. does this change result in better outcomes, or greater client satisfaction?).

It is impossible to specify what kind of data should be collected, as that depends on your own service's interests and goals, but most services collect various forms of data, including:

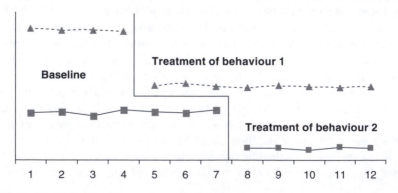

Figure 18.4   Multiple baseline across behaviours

- client outcome data (e.g. mental-health questionnaire measures, administered before and after treatment – see below);
- client demographic data (e.g. age, sex, duration of problems, employment status, etc.);
- service parameters, such as dates of referral, etc. (from which waiting times can be calculated);
- service outcomes such as dropping out of treatment or not attending appointments.

Some frequently used questionnaires

What outcome measures to use is again a matter for each service to decide according to its needs, but the following are suitable for routine clinical use in that they (a) do not take too long for a client to complete; (b) are widely used, so that comparisons can be made with other services and/or research trials; and (c) assess aspects of mental health which are common in most populations.

- The Beck Depression Inventory (BDI: Beck et al., 1961) is probably the best- known measure of depression. The latest revision is the BDI II (Beck et al., 1996), although the original version is still sometimes used in research in order to retain comparability with earlier work.
- The Beck Anxiety Inventory (BAI: Beck et al., 1988) is a similar measure of anxiety.
- The Clinical Outcomes in Routine Evaluation – Outcome Measure (CORE–OM: Evans et al., 2002; see also the web site at www.coreims.co.uk) is an increasingly popular general measure of mental health used in UK primary-care settings.
- The Hospital Anxiety and Depression Scale (HADS: Zigmond & Snaith, 1983), which, despite the name, is suitable for community settings. The name arose because it was originally designed for use in general hospital settings and, therefore, aimed to avoid confounding mental-health problems with physical-health problems. This characteristic makes it particularly useful for settings where one might expect a significant proportion of clients to have physical-health problems as well as mental-health problems.

A literature search will quickly turn up other measures suitable for almost any specific mental-health problem. See also the list of downloadable measures on the BABCP website under 'Members' resources' (BABCP, 2006).

Other measures

Standardised questionnaires are often supplemented by other measures such as individual problem ratings; belief ratings for particular cognitions; problem frequency counts or duration timings; and so on (see Chapter 5).

Clinical significance statistics

Service-evaluation data can be analysed using any of the standard statistical approaches. However, an approach known as 'clinical significance' analysis is particularly suited for clinical services, and especially an approach developed by Jacobson (Jacobson & Revenstorf, 1988; Jacobson et al., 1999). The aim of clinical significance analysis is to deal with the problem in conventional statistical testing that almost any change in average scores, even a tiny one, will emerge as significant if the number of participants in the study is large enough. Conventional testing tells us that such a change is 'significant' in the sense that it is unlikely to have emerged by chance but does *not* tell us that it is significant in the sense of being important. Thus, given large enough numbers, a change in patients' mean BDI score of a couple of points from start to end of treatment might be statistically significant – and rightly so, in the sense of being 'not due to chance'. But clinicians would not regard such a change of score as *clinically* significant, in the sense that their clients would not be happy if this was the kind of benefit they could expect.

Jacobson's approach to testing for clinical significance looks at each participant in a study individually and asks two questions:

1. Did this person's score on a particular measure change sufficiently for it to be unlikely to be due to chance? A 'reliable change' index, dependent on the reliability of the measure and its natural variation in the population, is calculated. If a patient's change score is greater than the calculated criterion, then that patient may be described as reliably improved (or deteriorated) on the measure.
2. If the patient *has* reliably changed, has the change also taken them across a cut-off point into the normal range for this measure? If so, we may consider the person not just improved but also 'recovered'. Jacobson et al., set out different possible ways of setting this 'normal cut-off' criterion, e.g. by calculating the point beyond which a patient is statistically more likely to belong to a normal population than a dysfunctional population.

Table 18.1 shows the possible outcomes resulting from this analysis for each client. Depending on the above two calculations, every client is classified as: reliably deteriorated, no reliable change, reliably improved (but not recovered) or recovered.

Table 18.1   Classification of change scores for clinical significance

		1. Change score larger than reliable change criterion?		
		Yes, for the worse	No	Yes, for the better
2. Score crossed cut-off into normal range?	No	Reliably deteriorated	No reliable change	Reliably improved (but not recovered)
	Yes			Recovered

The results of the analysis are reported as the proportion of clients falling into each of these categories.

The advantages of this approach are:

(a) that it gives us more meaningful statistics to report: most clinicians would agree that a client who meets both of the Jacobson criteria has truly made clinically significant progress;

(b) that the resulting figures are more comprehensible to clients and/or service commission-ers: it is much easier for most people to understand 'On average 56% of clients recover' than 'On average, clients' scores on the BDI move from 17.3 to 11.2' – Westbrook & Kirk (2005) give an example of this kind of analysis for routine clinical data.

Incidentally, it is worth noting that although these 'bench-marking' strategies (see also Wade et al., 1998; Merrill et al., 2003) typically find that CBT is an effective treatment in clinical prac-tice as well as in research trials, clinical significance analysis is sobering for anyone who believes that CBT (or any other kind of psychological therapy) is a panacea that can help all clients: most such analyses find that only around a third to a half of clients achieve recovery.

Difficulties in evaluation

Keep it simple

There is always a temptation to gather more data: it is easy to think 'Whilst we're at it, let's find out about this . . . and this . . . and this . . .' The result can be an unwieldy mass of data that overburdens the client, is too time-consuming to collect reliably and is even more time-consuming to analyse. In general, it is better to have a small number of data items which can be collected and analysed reasonably economically.

Repeating measures

Sometimes clients become overfamiliar with regularly used measures and begin to com-plete them on 'automatic pilot'. Always spend a minute or two discussing questionnaire results with your client so that you can assess how valid the responses are.

Keep it going

Most routine data collection starts enthusiastically, but this cannot be sustained. We sug-gest two factors are important in keeping data collection going. First, having a 'champion' at a reasonably senior level – someone who will support data collection and analysis and make sure that people are prompted if they forget about collecting data. Second, it is cru-cial that clinicians collecting data see that something is done with it and that results are fed back to them periodically. Data which are never analysed are useless anyway; and the chances are low that people will continue to collect it when no results appear.

Research design

Clinical service evaluation usually cannot reach the highest standards of research design, such as RCTs. All research designs involve some compromise between (a) the tightly controlled research that eliminates as much uncertainty as possible but, in doing so, may end up not resembling real clinical practice; and (b) the more 'real-world' research which is very close to clinical practice but, as a result, leaves room for ambiguity about causal factors. Service evalua-tion therefore often works on the principle that some evidence is better than nothing and accepts some lack of rigour for the sake of being able to describe everyday outcomes. Robson's (2002) book on 'real-world research' is a useful resource to look further at these issues.

Using Supervision in CBT

Introduction

As anyone who tries it soon discovers, the practice of good therapy is not something you can learn quickly or easily. You cannot just read a book, or attend a workshop, and then go off and do good CBT: effective clinical training demands a much longer process of learning in which you bring together what you have learned about theory and therapeutic strategies with the complex reality of the clients you see. Clinical supervision is one of the main ways in which this continued learning can occur. It can take different forms (see below), but the basic idea is that by having someone else to discuss or directly observe your therapy, you can examine how well it is going, identify problems, find solutions and develop your skills. The need for supervision applies to CBT practitioners at any level, but most crucially for novices.

These views of the positive value of supervision would probably gain support from most CBT practitioners. However, embarrassingly for an approach as empirical as CBT, there is not much evidence about whether supervision actually makes a difference, either to the supervisee's skills or to the outcomes for clients. What follows is, therefore, based on the clinical experience and beliefs of ourselves and others rather than on a strong evidence-base. Much of what we have to say can and should be challenged as new evidence emerges.

Goals of supervision

Although we are unaware of any single generally agreed definition of clinical supervision in CBT, there is agreement that clinical supervision can help achieve any or all of the following goals:

- developing therapist skills: honing and improving existing skills, and learning new skills;
- protecting clients: providing a form of quality control for therapy, both at the practical level of ensuring appropriate strategies are being used and at the emotional level of enabling an external, more objective view of therapeutic relationships;

- providing support for therapists in dealing with the difficulties therapy may cause for them;
- monitoring and evaluating therapist skills and practice.

The balance between these different components will vary according to factors such as the characteristics and experience of therapist and supervisor, the context of the supervision and so on.

In thinking about the last of the goals, i.e. evaluation, it is worth considering a distinction between *summative* and *formative* evaluation.

- Summative evaluation refers to evaluation whose primary aim is to arrive at a summary judgement: is the subject of evaluation 'good enough' in some sense (e.g. is the trainee good enough to pass the course)?
- Formative evaluation refers to evaluation whose primary aim is to enable the subject to improve, i.e. where the main point is not 'Is *X* good enough?' but rather 'How can we make *X* better?' Almost all clinical supervision contains elements of formative evaluation, but summative evaluation is usually only important in the context of a training course or similar process.

A useful tool to evaluate cognitive-therapy skills for both summative and formative purposes is the cognitive therapy scale (CTS: Young & Beck, 1980; Dobson et al., 1985; Blackburn et al., 2001).

Modes of supervision

We can distinguish two important dimensions of supervision: first, whether the supervision is for an individual therapist or a group; second, whether the supervision is from one person considered to be more expert to another considered less expert or is between people of roughly equal expertise. Combining these categories gives us four modes of supervision, which we have given arbitrary names, illustrated in Table 19.1.

It is sometimes thought – wrongly in our view – that all supervision must have an identified leader. We feel that peer supervision can be very useful, even if none of the participants is highly expert. We would draw an analogy with CBT therapy: just as the therapist may be able to help the client in an area about which she knows little, through a process of guided discovery, so peers may be able to use the same processes to open up new ways of thinking for the therapist in supervision. Although there is a danger of 'the blind leading the blind' if *none* of the participants has any CBT experience, such supervision can be better than nothing at all in situations where access to expert supervision is limited.

There are pros and cons to each of these modes.

1. Apprenticeship

This is probably what most people think of as typical supervision: a skilled and experienced practitioner meeting a relative novice, one to one, to develop the novice therapist's skills. It is undoubtedly a good model, with excellent scope for detailed examination and

Table 19.1   Modes of supervision

	Individual	Group
Identified leader	1. 'Apprenticeship'	2. 'Led group'
No identified leader	3. 'Consultation' (mutual or one-way)	4. 'Peer group'

rehearsal of therapy skills, finely tuned to the supervisee's needs. The main disadvantages are that it is relatively extravagant (and thus expensive) in its use of the leader's time; and because there is only one supervisor, the range of views and expertise available to the supervisee is limited.

2. Led group

The main selling point of the led group is that it has the advantages of the apprenticeship model in terms of offering expertise, whilst being more economical and therefore more practical in many settings. Another advantage is that supervisees can learn from hearing about other practitioner's cases as well as their own. Possible disadvantages include the fact that each person in the group gets less individual time and that it can sometimes become more like a seminar – although this too can sometimes be helpful.

3. Consultation

For very experienced practitioners, this may well be the only available mode of supervision, since there may be no one with more expertise available. Consultation can either be one-way – one of the pair consults the other for supervision – or can be mutual, where each supervises the other.

4. Peer group

The advantages of the peer group include its being relatively cheap and easy to set up; that it allows vicarious learning; and that by being more egalitarian it may encourage less-experienced participants to be creative and to share their ideas. Disadvantages include the risk that 'the blind can lead the blind', with no one really knowing what they are talking about; that, as with any form of group supervision, each supervisee gets less time; and that there is no leader to take responsibility for group dynamics.

Alternative channels for supervision

In addition to the above modes, it is worth considering that some of them can be practised using other means of communication such as telephone and e-mail. These alternative channels probably work best with individual supervision: managing group interactions without any face-to-face contact is not easy! Such methods may lose some of the subtleties of face-to-face communication, especially when it comes to emotional issues, and there are possible technical difficulties in playing audio- or video-tapes. Nevertheless, they can offer a useful alternative if no supervisor is available to meet your needs.

Supervision or therapy?

It is recognised in all forms of therapy that there may be times when the therapist's own problems or beliefs may impinge on therapy. Is such material suitable for exploration in supervision, or should it be considered as personal therapy that should take place in another setting? Is there a limit to the personal material dealt with in supervision sessions? If so, where will you go with material which it is agreed should not be part of supervision? There are no right answers to these questions, but most CBT practitioners would say that such material should only be part of supervision to the extent that it has a direct impact on your work with your clients (e.g. Padesky, 1996). If one of your own beliefs (for example, 'I must never do anything that clients will find distressing' or 'I am solely responsible for my clients' progress') is blocking you from implementing a therapeutic strategy that appears relevant in other respects, then it may be appropriate to look at that in supervision. If it appears that the belief is part of a wider problem, it probably cannot be dealt with in the limited time available in supervision. If it is not something that directly affects your work with patients, then it should probably be taken elsewhere.

Use of tapes

The use of audio- or video-tapes of client sessions (just 'tapes' from here on) has always been a distinctive feature of CBT supervision. Instead of the supervisor having to rely on the supervisee's account of therapy, the supervisee records sessions and plays back (parts of) the tapes during supervision so that the supervisor can observe what happens more directly. Although almost everyone initially feels anxious about presenting their therapy openly to others in this way, it gets easier and is extremely useful once the initial inhibitions have been overcome. We therefore strongly advise using tapes. Advantages include:

- *Self-reflection*. Although not always comfortable, it is good practice to listen to your therapy tapes and critically appraise your performance. In addition, you can better prepare your supervision question and identify the most relevant parts of the tape to share with your supervisor.
- *Avoiding omissions and distortions* (positive or negative) in the therapist's view and account of clients. It could be the case that what is important in the sessions is something you have not noticed or are reluctant to report – and tapes give you and the supervisor a chance to spot that.
- It therefore allows a *depth and precision of supervision* which is almost impossible if supervision is based just on the therapist's account. Instead of an inevitably partial account from the therapist, the supervisor can hear or see more of the full complexity of the interaction. Think how long it would take you to give a detailed verbal *description* of a therapeutic interaction, compared to what can be gleaned from listening to a couple of minutes of tape! It is difficult for most people to convey a full sense of what a client is like through

verbal description. Via tapes, the supervisor can get a much better impression of your client, as well as what is happening in the therapy, and may therefore be better able to offer useful suggestions for how to manage the client's behaviour.

If you are using tapes then you need to consider the practicalities of how to do so effectively and ethically:

- Clients must give full informed consent before any sessions are recorded. You therefore need to establish processes to obtain and record the client's consent. Your hospital or other organisation may have a policy that you need to follow. If not, you should think about developing a policy of your own which includes informing clients what will be done with the tapes, who will hear them and what arrangements will be made for destroying or securely wiping the tapes after supervision.
- If you have decided to use tapes, then it is usually much easier if you get into the habit of recording *all* your client sessions rather than thinking about it only when something has gone wrong or a specific need has arisen. It is usually much easier to get clients' consent to a routine procedure at the start of therapy rather than negotiating recording with the client when some particular difficulty has come up.

Choosing a supervisor

In some situations, particularly when training, you may have no choice about who your supervisor is because he or she is allocated to you, but if you have a choice then you may want to consider the following:

- Is the supervisor someone you think you can trust and be comfortable with? You do need to form a good working relationship which is as important, and sometimes as difficult, as a therapeutic relationship.
- Does the supervisor have the skills that you need to learn from? For example, you might want someone who is expert in treating certain problems, or someone who can work more with the therapeutic process. It may be difficult to judge initially how well someone will meet your needs, hence the importance of agreeing an initial trial period (see below).
- Is the supervisor motivated to supervise you and willing to commit to the agreed period of supervision?
- Is the supervisor receiving supervision? It is increasingly common for supervisors to seek supervision of their practice.

Negotiating supervision arrangements

Whether you are choosing a supervisor or have one allocated to you, we suggest it is always important to have a preliminary meeting in order to clarify hopes and expectations. You may want to consider:

- Practical arrangements: when supervision will take place, where, how long will sessions be, how often, etc.?
- Confidentiality issues.
- Is the supervision to be 'general' or are there specific objectives (e.g. to get better at formulating, or dealing with clients with OCD, or managing clients who are self-harming)? If you have specific objectives, does the supervisor feel she has the necessary skills to help?
- Do you or the supervisor have priorities regarding the possible aims of supervision outlined above? For example, are you on a training course where summative evaluation is an important part of supervision?
- Although it is often impossible to predict in advance what will happen during a course of supervision, it is worth considering your views and the supervisor's about the boundaries between supervision and personal therapy.
- It is usually wise to have a trial period and then review so that if it is not working well the arrangements can be changed.

See the Appendix to this chapter for an example template for a supervision agreement, provided by the British Association for Behavioural & Cognitive Psychotherapy (BABCP, 2005).

For any kind of group supervision, similar questions will arise, and there will also be others unique to the group setting. For example, how will the available time be divided between the group members? Options include equal time for all group members in every session; or one person presenting at each session (with possibly long intervals between supervision sessions for any one individual); or a combination of these, in which one person takes a larger chunk of time in a session but others also take smaller amounts of time. There may be more need for explicit feedback from the supervisee(s) to the group and/or the leader about their experience of supervision. If, as sometimes happens, most or all of the group members disagree with a supervisee's approach, the supervisee can be left feeling very exposed and isolated. Careful attention to group process may be needed to avoid excessively painful and off-putting experiences for supervisees.

Preparing for a supervision session

You will get the most out of supervision if you prepare carefully for it. This does not need to take hours, but it needs more than two minutes' thought before supervision starts, grabbing the client's notes and running off to meet the supervisor! In particular, we would recommend that you identify a reasonably clear *supervision question* for each client you will discuss. This does not necessarily mean a simple question but, rather, what is it that you want to focus on. The potential range of questions is limitless, but might include:

- How can I develop a formulation for this client?
- What might I do to manage this client's tendency to get dependent on me?
- What behavioural experiments could I usefully do with this client?
- Can we look at what makes me get angry with this client?
- Where can I learn more about treating OCD?

Preparation is also important in using tapes for supervision. It is almost impossible for supervisors to listen to complete tapes of all your clients, as that would take many hours. It is therefore best to make this a two-stage process. First, listen to your tapes yourself. This alone will provide you with useful insights about how you might improve. As you listen, make a note of any points where problems seem to emerge: those are the issues you might want to take to supervision. Select segments of a few minutes that illustrate the points you want to discuss, then, before the supervision session, have your tape ready to run from those points. With this kind of preparation, tapes can be used effectively and economically.

In preparing for supervision, Padesky's (1996) questions for supervisors can be helpful for supervisees as well. These questions include the following sequence of factors that might contribute to difficulties in therapy:

1. *Is there a CBT formulation and consequent treatment plan for this client?*
   If not, developing one may be a supervision question.
2. *Is the formulation and consequent treatment plan being followed?*
   If not, the supervision question might be thinking about what is stopping you from following the formulation and treatment plan – either something in your own beliefs or some characteristic or behaviour of the client.
3. *Do you have the knowledge and skills to implement the required treatment?*
   If not, you might want to use supervision to gain knowledge, practise skills or get advice on where you can go to achieve those goals.
4. *Is the client's response to therapy as expected?*
   If not, you might want to use supervision to consider what client beliefs, life circumstances, developmental history, etc., might be blocking progress.
5. *If all the above have satisfactory answers, what else might be interfering?*
   Supervision might need to consider therapist factors, problems in the therapeutic relationship, whether the formulation needs modifying, whether a different treatment approach is needed and so on.

During a supervision session

The form of a supervision session can usefully follow the model of a CBT session, as outlined in Chapter 11. Thus, supervision might go through the same sequence:

- Agenda-setting: what are today's main topics and how will we divide the available time between them? Both parties should be able to raise topics for the agenda, and the supervisee should take increasing responsibility for the agenda as she becomes more experienced. Reviewing homework should always be on the agenda.
- Main topics: the bulk of the session will be taken up with going through the agreed main agenda items.
- Homework assignment: supervisees will often leave supervision with some agreed list of tasks to be carried out, ranging from reading a particular article to trying out a particular strategy with a client.
- Review: what feedback does the supervisee have about the session, what has she learned, what was difficult and so on. You might ask yourself whether your supervision question has been answered; whether the supervisor made it easy for you to use supervision; whether the balance of informality and rigidity, being didactic and being non-directive, or support and constructive criticism was right.

Other aspects of your contribution to successful supervision include: keeping on track; being as open as possible, rather than feeling you have to show only competence; and not being defensive about admitting difficulties. You will not learn much from supervision if you say everything is OK and your supervisor says that sounds fine! Everyone does imperfect therapy, and your best chance of getting more skilled is through openness about what goes wrong.

Finally, remember that supervision can involve a range of techniques beyond straightforward verbal discussion of cases. It is useful to use role play, in two ways. Either you play the client and the supervisor models how you might respond to that client; or the supervisor plays the client whilst you rehearse a particular strategy as therapist (tapes come in useful here – it is much easier for supervisors to play your clients if they have heard or seen them on tape). There may also be times when straightforward didactic teaching or recommended reading is a useful part of supervision.

Problems with supervision

Not being able to find a supervisor

Although we must stress the importance of securing regular, competent supervision, you might sometimes find yourself between supervisors or unable to contact your supervisor. We would then suggest that you first consider self-supervision. Set aside time to review your supervision question (perhaps using the Padesky guidelines above) and critically reflect on your practice and resources – in short, discover whether or not you can resolve the difficulty yourself. If you cannot, you could consider trying to obtain a one-off consultation from a colleague or external 'expert'. Do not simply resign yourself to not having supervision.

Problems with the supervisor

Common problems include a lack of commitment from the supervisor (e.g. regularly being late or interrupting supervision sessions to take phone calls, etc.); or feeling poorly supported by the supervisor. It is possible that such problems arise because a supervisor and supervisee are not well matched and an alternative arrangement is needed. However, it is worth considering if the working relationship can be improved. Is the supervisor aware of your needs? If not, why not? Are your expectations of your supervisor realistic, or do you need to supplement your supervision with further support or personal therapy?

Feeling unable to bring along tapes of sessions for evaluation

Try to discover what is handicapping you. Perhaps you need to think through the reasons for using tapes; or perhaps you need to do a BE to see whether the pros or cons are as you imagine them to be.

Is the problem performance anxiety or fears of being 'found out' as incompetent? That kind of worry is extremely common, even in experienced therapists, and it is important to try to work with it. Use guided discovery to help you unpack the reason(s) for your reluctance, and consider taking the problem along to supervision.

Agreeing strategies which are not carried out

Again, you need to understand the thoughts and beliefs that account for this. For example, is it overcompliance with your supervisor, agreeing to take actions that you do not really agree with? If so, what makes it difficult for you to tell your supervisor that you disagree?

Or is it that you genuinely think the plans are good, but then in your therapy sessions you get sidetracked? Again, try to understand what leads to that. Therapy tapes may be very helpful in looking at where therapy sessions go off track. And, as always, you can take these questions to supervision.

Negative beliefs about supervision

We have occasionally come across therapists who have negative views about supervision. For instance, the primary purpose of supervision may be seen as 'overseeing' or making sure that it is done 'right', and it may therefore be perceived as an aversive experience in which you are likely to be subjected to managerial control or trenchant criticism. On review, it might well become apparent that the primary purpose of supervision is usually to help you get better at what you do and to be able to help your clients more effectively. Supervision could therefore be seen as an opportunity to learn, not as a threat. As in our clinical work, it is crucial to identify the negative beliefs that interfere with progress. Thus, you need to be aware of your own unhelpful beliefs and use your CBT skills to evaluate them.

Appendix 1: Example supervision agreement from the British Association for Behavioural & Cognitive Psychotherapy (BABCP 2005)

Supervision Agreement between ——————— &——————

Confidentiality

- All professional and clinical issues discussed are confidential and are not to be discussed outside the supervision session. The exceptions to this are where professional malpractice may be evident, or if requested to release information by a court of law, coroners office or professional body.
- All cases or professionals discussed during supervision must be made anonymous.
- Where tape recording of sessions takes place, this must be agreed with and have the informed consent of the service user, carer or professional. Arrangements must also be made to destroy/wipe any recordings. The supervisee is responsible for ensuring this process is followed.

Comments

Content of supervision

- Content of supervision will focus on the acquisition of knowledge, conceptualisation and clinical skills within a cognitive behavioural model(s).

- Associated issues will also be discussed when it is relevant to do so, e.g. medication, hospitalisation, case management.
- Identification (and collaborative change of these if appropriate) of supervisee thoughts, attitudes, beliefs and values and the impact of these on therapeutic and professional behaviour.
- Discussion and working through relationship and process aspects of supervision.

There will be an equal split between the time spent on each of the above in the time available.

Comments

Practicalities

- One session each ——————— for ——— hours/minutes
- The venue the session(s) will take place at is ———————
- The person responsible for booking the accommodation is ———————
- Fees for supervision are ——————
- Cancellation arrangements —————

Supervision methods and content

- Discussion of therapeutic relationship and engagement issues.
- Case conceptualisation/formulation.
- Rehearsal of therapeutic techniques, e.g. simulation, role play.
- Discussion about therapeutic strategies.
- Case presentations.
- Homework.
- Review of tapes (at least one per month).
- Direct observation of practice – at least once a month per supervisee.
- Identification of supervisee thoughts, attitudes and beliefs with exploration of the impact of these on therapeutic and professional behaviour.
- Review of risk and therapist/service-user safety.
- Review of clinical guidelines/manuals.

- Review of psycho-educational material.
- Experiential exercises.
- Other strategies as agreed.

Comments

Aims of supervision

The primary focus of supervision is the welfare of the client through the supervisee's learning process, in terms of knowledge attainment, attitude refinement and skills development.

Goals for supervision

1.
2.
3.
4.

Comments

Anti-discriminatory practice

Practice will follow the policy of ————————— (employer/professional body)

Comments

Steps in the event of a breakdown in the arrangements for clinical CBT supervision

In the event of inappropriate behaviour by the supervisor/supervisee, this should be discussed together initially.
If this is unsuccessful or if the behaviour is of a serious and immediate nature, then —————————————— should be informed IMMEDIATELY.

In the unlikely event that the relationship between the supervisees and supervisor deteriorates, each person is responsible for attempting to work together to resolve the problem.

Comments

Changes to this agreement and timescale

Changes to this agreement can be negotiated at any time.

This agreement covers the period ——————————

Signed ————————— Supervisor ——————————

Date —————————

Signed ————————— Supervisee ——————————

Date —————————

With thanks to Michael Townend

Please feel free to circulate and edit the document as you wish.

References

Abramson, L.Y., Alloy, L.B., Hogan, M.E., Whitehouse, W.G., Donovan, P., Rose, D.T., Panzarella, C. & Raniere, D. (2002). Cognitive vulnerability to depression: theory and evidence. In R.L. Leahy & E.T. Dowd (Eds), *Clinical advances in cognitive psychotherapy: theory and application*. New York: Springer.

American Psychiatric Association (APA) (2000). *Diagnostic and statistical manual of metal disorders,* 4th edition (text revision). Washington, DC: American Psychiatric Association.

Andrews, B. (1997). Bodily shame in relation to abuse in childhood and bulimia. *British Journal of Clinical Psychology*, 36, 41–50.

Antonuccio, D.O., Thomas, M. & Danton, W.G. (1997). A cost-effective analysis of cognitive behaviour therapy and Fluoxetine (Prozac) in the treatment of depression. *Behaviour Therapy*, 28, 187–210.

Arntz, A., Rauner, M. & van den Hout, M.A. (1995). 'If I feel anxious there must be a danger': ex-consequentia reasoning in inferring danger in anxiety disorders. *Behaviour Research & Therapy*, 33, 917–25.

Arntz, A. & Weertman, A. (1999). Treatment of childhood memories: theory and practice. *Behaviour Research & Therapy*, 37, 715–40.

British Association for Behavioural and Cognitive Psychotherapy (BABCP) (2005). BABCP supervision template. Retrieved 28 March 2006 from BABCP web site: http://www.babcp. org.uk/downloads/supervision_agreement_ 2004.pdf.

BABCP (2006). Members' resources. Retrieved 9 July 2006 from the BABCP web site: http://www. babcp.org.uk/members/resources.htm.

Bach, P. & Hayes S.C. (2002). The use of acceptance and commitment therapy to prevent the re-hospitalization of psychotic patient: a randomised controlled trial. *Journal of Consulting & Clinical Psychology*, 70, 1129–39.

Baddeley, A. (1996). *Your memory: a user's guide.* London: Prion.

Barlow, D.H., Andrasik, F. & Hersen, M. (2006) '*Single case experimental designs*, 3rd edn. Boston: Allyn & Bacon.

Barlow, D.H., Hayes, C.H. & Nelson, R.O. (1984). *The scientist practitioner: research and accountability in clinical and educational settings*. Oxford: Pergamon Press.

Bartlett, F. (1932). *Remembering*. Cambridge: Cambridge University Press.

Basco, M. & Rush, A. (1996). *Cognitive behavioural therapy for bipolar disorder.* New York: Guildford Press.

Bates, A. (2005). The expression of compassion in group therapy. In P. Gilbert (Ed.), *Compassion: conceptualisations, research and use in psychotherapy.* Hove: Brunner-Routledge.

Beck, A.T. (1963). Thinking and depression, 1: Idiosyncratic content and cognitive distortions. *Archives of General Psychiatry*, 9, 324–33.

Beck, A.T. (1964). Thinking and depression, 2: Theory and therapy. *Archives of General Psychiatry*, 10, 561–71.

Beck, A.T. (1967). *Depression: clinical, experimental and theoretical aspects.* New York: Harper & Row.

Beck, A.T. (1988). *Love is never enough.* New York: Harper & Row.

Beck, A.T. (1999). *Prisoners of hate.* New York: HarperCollins.

Beck, A.T., Brown, G. & Steer, R.A. (1996). *Beck Depression Inventory II manual.* San Antonio, TX: The Psychological Corporation.

Beck, A.T., Emery, G. & Greenberg, R.L. (1985). *Anxiety disorders and phobias: a cognitive perspective.* New York: Basic Books.

Beck, A.T., Epstein, N., Brown, G. & Steer, R.A. (1988). An inventory for measuring clinical anxiety: psychometric properties. *Journal of Consulting & Clinical Psychology*, 56, 893–7.

Beck, A.T., Freeman, A. et al. (1990). *Cognitive therapy of personality disorders.* New York: Guilford Press.

Beck, A.T., Freeman, A. et al. (2004). *Cognitive therapy of personality disorders,* 2nd edn. New York: Guilford Press.

Beck, A.T., Rush, A.J., Shaw, B.F. & Emery, G. (1979). *Cognitive therapy of depression.* New York: Guilford Press.

Beck, A.T., Ward, C.H., Mendelson, M., Mock, J. & Erbaugh, J. (1961). An inventory for measuring depression. *Archives of General Psychiatry*, 4, 561–71.

Beck, A.T., Wright, F.D., Newman, C.F. & Liese, B.S. (1993). *Cognitive therapy of substance abuse.* New York: Guilford Press.

Beck, R. & Fernandez, E. (1998). Cognitive-behavioral therapy in the treatment of anger: a meta-analysis. *Cognitive Therapy & Research*, 22, 63–74.

Bennett-Levy, J. (2003). Mechanisms of change in cognitive therapy: the case of automatic thought records and behavioural experiments. *Behavioural and Cognitive Psychotherapy*, 31, 261–77.

Bennett-Levy, J., Butler, G., Fennell, M., Hackmann, A., Mueller, M. & Westbrook, D. (Eds) (2004). *The Oxford guide to behavioural experiments in cognitive therapy.* Oxford: Oxford University Press.

Bieling, P.J. & Kuyken, W. (2003). Is cognitive case formulation science or science fiction? *Clinical Psychology: Science & Practice*, 10, 52–69.

Blackburn, I.M., James, I.A., Milne, D.L., Baker, C., Standart, S., Garland, A. & Reichelt, K. (2001). The revised cognitive therapy scale (CTS-R): psychometric properties. *Behavioural & Cognitive Psychotherapy*, 29, 431–46.

Bohus, K., Haaf, B., Simms, T., Limburger, M.F., Schmahl, C., Unckel, C., Lieb, K. & Linehan, M.M. (2004). Effectiveness of inpatient dialectical behavioural therapy for borderline personality disorder: a controlled trial. *Behaviour Research & Therapy*, 42, 487–99.

Bootzin, R.R. (1972). Stimulus control treatment for insomnia. *Proceedings of the American Psychological Association*, 7, 395–6.

Bordin, E.S. (1979). The generalisation of the psychoanalytic concept of the working alliance. *Psychotherapy*, 16, 252–60.

Borkovec, T.D. (1994). The nature, functions and origins of worry. In G.C.L. Davey and F. Tallis (Eds), *Worrying: perspectives on theory, assessment and treatment.* Chichester: Wiley.

Borkovec, T.D. & Newman, M.G. (1999). Worry and generalized anxiety disorder. In P. Salkovskis (Ed.), *Comprehensive clinical psychology, Vol. 6.* Oxford: Elsevier.

Borkovec, T.D., Newman, M.G., Lytle, R. & Pincus, A.L. (2002). A component analysis of cognitive behavioural therapy for generalized anxiety disorder and the role of interpersonal problems. *Journal of Consulting & Clinical Psychology,* 70, 288–98.

Borkovec, T.D. & Sides, J.K. (1979). Critical procedural variables related to the physiological effects of progressive relaxation: a review. *Behaviour Research & Therapy,* 17, 119–25.

Bower, P., Richards, D.A. & Lovell, K. (2001). The clinical and cost effectiveness of self-help treatments for anxiety and depressive disorders in primary care: a systematic review. *British Journal of General Practice,* 51, 838–45.

British Psychological Society (1995). *Recovered memories: the report of the working party of the BPS.* Leicester: BPS Publications.

Brown, G.K., Newman, C.F., Charlesworth, S.E., Crits-Christoph, P. & Beck, A.T. (2004). An open clinical trial of cognitive therapy for borderline personality disorder. *Journal of Personality Disorders,* 18, 257–71.

Brown, G.W. and Harris, T.O. (1978). *The social origins of depression: a study of psychiatric disorder in women.* London: Tavistock.

Brown, G.W., Harris, T.O. & Bifulco, A. (1986). Long-term effects of early loss of parent. In M. Rutter, Izard, L. & Read, P. (Eds), *Depression and childhood: developmental perspectives.* New York: Guilford.

Bruch, M. & Bond, F.W. (1998). *Beyond diagnosis: case formulation approaches in CBT.* Chichester: Wiley.

Burns, D. (1980). *Feeling good: the new mood therapy.* New York: William Morrow.

Burns, D. (1999). *The feeling good handbook.* New York: Plume.

Burns, D. & Nolen-Hoeksema, S. (1991). Coping styles, homework compliance, and the effectiveness of cognitive-behavioural therapy. *Journal of Consulting & Clinical Psychology,* 59, 305–11.

Butler, G. (1998). Clinical formulation. In A.S. Bellack & M. Hersen (Eds), *Comprehensive clinical psychology.* New York: Pergamon.

Butler, G. & Hackmann, A. (2004). Social anxiety. In J. Bennett-Levy, G. Butler, M. Fennell, A. Hackmann, M. Mueller & D. Westbrook (Eds), *Oxford guide to behavioural experiments in cognitive therapy.* Oxford: Oxford University Press.

Butler, G. & Hope, T. (1995). *Manage your mind.* Oxford: Oxford University Press.

Butler, G. and Rouf, K. (2004). Generalized anxiety disorder. In J. Bennett-Levy, G. Butler, M. Fennell, A. Hackmann, M. Mueller & D. Westbrook (Eds), *Oxford guide to behavioural experiments in cognitive therapy.* Oxford: Oxford University Press.

Butler, G. and Surawy, C. (2004). Avoidance of affect. In J. Bennett-Levy, G. Butler, M. Fennell, A. Hackmann, M. Mueller & D. Westbrook (Eds), *Oxford guide to behavioural experiments in cognitive therapy.* Oxford: Oxford University Press.

Chadwick, P., Birchwood, M. & Trower, P. (1996). *Cognitive therapy for delusions, voices and paranoia.* Chichester: Wiley.

Clark, D.M. (1986). A cognitive approach to panic. *Behaviour Research & Therapy,* 24, 461–70.

Clark, D.M. (1989). Anxiety states: panic and generalised anxiety. In K. Hawton, P. Salkovskis, J. Kirk, & D. Clark, (Eds), *Cognitive-behaviour therapy for psychiatric problems: a practitioner's guide.* Oxford: Oxford University Press.

Clark, D.M. (1999). Anxiety disorders: why they persist and how to treat them. *Behaviour Research & Therapy*, 37, S5–S27.

Clark, D.M. (2002). A cognitive perspective on social phobia. In W.R. Crozier & L.E. Alden (Eds), *International handbook of social anxiety*. Chichester: Wiley.

Clark, D.M. & Beck, A.T. (1988). Cognitive approaches. In C. Last and M. Hersen (Eds), *Handbook of anxiety disorders*. New York: Pergamon.

Clark, D.A., Beck, A.T. & Alford, B. (1999). *Scientific foundations of cognitive theory and therapy of depression*. New York: John Wiley.

Clark, D.M. & Wells, A. (1995). A cognitive model of social phobia. In R. Heimberg, M. Liebowitz, D.A. Hope & F.R. Schneier (Eds), *Social phobia: diagnosis, assessment and treatment*. New York: Guilford Press.

Close, H. & Schuller, S. (2004). Psychotic symptoms. In J. Bennett-Levy, G. Butler, M. Fennell, A. Hackmann, M. Mueller & D. Westbrook (Eds), *Oxford guide to behavioural experiments in cognitive therapy*. Oxford: Oxford University Press.

Committee on Training in Clinical Psychology (1947). Recommended graduate training program in clinical psychology. *American Psychologist*, 2, 539–58.

Craft, L.L. and Landers, D.M. (1998). The effect of exercise on clinical depression and depression resulting from mental illness: a meta-analysis. *Journal of Sport and Exercise Psychology*, 20, 339–57.

Dattilio, F.M. & Padesky, C.A. (1990). *Cognitive therapy with couples*. Sarasota, FL: Professional Resource Exchange.

Davey, G.C.L. & Tallis, F. (Eds) (1994). *Worrying: perspectives on theory, assessment and treatment*. Chichester: Wiley.

Devon Book Prescription Scheme (2004). Book list retrieved 18 February 2006, from http://www.research.plymouth.ac.uk/pei/projects/selfhelpbookspresc/booklist.htm.

Dobson, K., Shaw, B. & Vallis, T. (1985). Reliability of a measure of the quality of cognitive therapy. *British Journal of Clinical Psychology*, 24, 295–300.

Duckro, P., Beal, D. & George, C. (1979). Research on the effects of disconfirmed client role expectations in psychotherapy: a critical review. *Psychological Bulletin*, 86, 260–75.

Dugas, M.J., Gagnon F., Ladouceur, R. & Freeston, M. (1998). Generalized anxiety disorder: a preliminary test of a conceptual model. *Behaviour Research & Therapy*, 36, 215–26.

Durham, R.C. and Turvey, A.A. (1987). Cognitive therapy vs behaviour therapy in the treatment of chronic general anxiety. *Behaviour Research & Therapy*, 25, 229–34.

Ehlers, A. & Clark, D.M. (2000). A cognitive model of post-traumatic stress disorder. *Behaviour Research & Therapy*, 38, 319–45.

Ehlers, A., Clark, D.M., Hackmann, A., McManus, F., Fennell, M., Herbert, C. & Mayou, R. (2003). A randomised controlled trial of cognitive therapy, a self-help booklet, and repeated assessments as early interventions for posttraumatic stress disorder. *Archives of General Psychiatry*, 60, 1024–32.

Eisler, I., le Grange, D. & Asen, E. (2003). Family interventions. In J. Treasure, U. Schmidt & E. van Furth (Eds), *Handbook of eating disorders*, 2nd edn. Chichester: Wiley.

Emmelkamp, P.M.G., Aardema, A. (1999). Metacognitive, specific obsessive-compulsive beliefs and obsessive compulsive behaviour. *Clinical Psychology and Psychotherapy*, 6, 139–46.

Enright, S.J. (1991). Group treatment for obsessive-compulsive disorder: an evaluation. *Behavioural Psychotherapy*, 19, 183–92.

Espie, C.A. (1991). *The psychological treatment of insomnia*. Chichester. John Wiley.

Espie, C.A. (2001). Insomnia: conceptual issues in the development, persistence, and treatment of sleep disorders in adults. *Annual Review of Psychology*, 53, 215–43.

Evans, C., Connell, J., Barkham, M., Margison, F., McGrath, G., Mellor-Clark, J. & Audin, K. (2002). Towards a standardised brief outcome measure: psychometric properties and utility of the CORE-OM. *British Journal of Psychiatry*, 180, 51–60.

Eysenck, H.J. (1952). The effects of psychotherapy: an evaluation. *Journal of Consulting & Clinical Psychology*, 16, 319–24.

Fairburn, C.G., Cooper, Z. & Shafran, R. (2003). Cognitive behaviour therapy for eating disorders: a 'transdiagnostic' theory and treatment. *Behaviour Research & Therapy*, 41, 509–28.

Fairburn, C.G., Kirk, J., O'Connor, M., Anastadies, P. & Cooper, P.J. (1987). Prognostic factors in bulimia nervosa. *British Journal of Clinical Psychology*, 26, 223–4.

Fairburn, C.G., Shafran, R. & Cooper, Z. (1999). A cognitive-behavioural theory of anorexia nervosa. *Behaviour Research & Therapy*, 37, 1–13.

Fennell, M. (1989). Depression. In K. Hawton, P. Salkovskis, J. Kirk & D. Clark (Eds), *Cognitive-behaviour therapy for psychiatric problems: a practitioner's guide*. Oxford: Oxford University Press.

Fennell, M. (1999). *Overcoming low self esteem: a self-help guide using cognitive-behavioural techniques*. London: Constable Robinson.

Fennell, M., Bennett-Levy, J. & Westbrook, D. (2004). Depression. In J. Bennett-Levy, G. Butler, M. Fennell, A. Hackmann, M. Mueller & D. Westbrook (Eds), *The Oxford guide to behavioural experiments in cognitive therapy*. Oxford: Oxford University Press.

Flavell, J.H. (1979). Metacognition and cognitive monitoring: a new area of cognitive developmental inquiry. *American Psychologist*, 34, 906–11.

Foa, E.B. & Riggs, D.S. (1993). Post-traumatic stress disorder in rape victims. In American Psychiatric Association, *Annual review of psychiatry*. Washington, DC: APA.

Fowler, D., Garety, P. & Kuipers, E. (1995). *Cognitive behaviour therapy for psychosis: theory and practice*. Chichester: Wiley.

Fox, K.R. (2000). The effects of exercise on self-perceptions and self-esteem. In S.J.H. Biddle, K.R. Fox, and S.H. Boutcher (Eds), *Physical activity and psychological well-being*. London: Routledge.

Freeman, A. (1983). *Cognitive therapy with couples and groups*. New York: Springer.

Freeman, A., Schrodt, R., Gilson, M. and Ludgate, J.W. (1993). Group cognitive therapy with inpatients. In J.H. Wright, M.E. Thase, A.T. Beck and J.W. Ludgate (Eds), *Cognitive therapy with inpatients*. New York: Guilford Press.

Freud, S. (1909). Analysis of a phobia in a five-year-old boy. *Standard Edition*, Vol. X, 5–149.

Frude, N. (2005). Prescription for a good read. *Counselling & Psychotherapy Journal*, 16, 28–31.

Gabbard, G.O. (1991). Psychodynamics of sexual boundary violations. *Psychiatric Annals*, 21, 651–5.

Garety, P., Kuipers, E., Fowler, D., Freeman, D. & Bebbington, P. (2001). A cognitive model of the positive symptoms of psychosis. *Psychological Medicine*, 31, 189–95.

Garfield, S.L. (1986). Research in client variables in psychotherapy research. In S.L. Garfield & A. Bergin (Eds), *Handbook of psychotherapy and behaviour change*, 3rd edn. New York: Wiley.

Ghaderi, A. (2006). Does individualization matter? A randomized trial of standardized (focused) versus individualized (broad) cognitive behavior therapy for bulimia nervosa. *Behaviour Research & Therapy*, 44, 273–88.

Gilbert, P. (1992). *Depression: the evolution of powerlessness*. New York: Guilford Press.

Gilbert, P. (2000). *Overcoming depression: a self-help guide using cognitive-behavioural techniques* rev. edn,. London: Constable Robinson.

Gilbert, P. (2005). *Compassion: conceptualisations, research and use in psychotherapy.* Hove: Brunner-Routledge.

Gilbert, P. & Andrews, B. (1998). *Shame: interpersonal behaviour, psychopathology and culture.* New York: Oxford University Press.

Gilbert, P. & Irons, C. (2005). Focused therapies and compassionate mind training for shame and self-attacking. In P. Gilbert (Ed.), *Compassion: conceptualisations, research and use in psychotherapy.* Hove: Brunner-Routledge.

Gottlieb, M.C. (1993) Avoiding exploitative dual relationships: a decision-making model. *Psychotherapy*, 30, 41–48.

Greenberger, D. and Padesky, C. (1995). *Mind over mood.* New York: Guilford Press.

Greist, J.H. & Klein, M. (1985). Running as treatment for depression. *Comprehensive Psychiatry*, 20, 41–54.

Grey, N., Young, K. and Holmes, E. (2002). Hot spots in emotional memory and the treatment of posttraumatic stress disorder. *Behavioural & Cognitive Psychotherapy*, 30, 37–56.

Hackmann, A. (1998). Cognitive therapy with panic and agoraphobia: working with complex cases. In N. Tarrier, A. Wells & G. Haddock (Eds), *Treating complex cases: the cognitive behavioural approach.* Chichester: Wiley.

Hackmann, A. (2005). Compassionate imagery in the treatment of early memories in Axis I anxiety disorders. In P. Gilbert (Ed.), *Compassion: conceptualisations, research and use in psychotherapy.* Hove: Brunner-Routledge.

Harvey, A.G. (2002). A cognitive model of insomnia. *Behaviour Research & Therapy*, 40, 869–93.

Hayes, S.C. (2004). Acceptance and commitment therapy, relational frame theory, and the third wave of behavioral and cognitive therapies. *Behavior Therapy*, 35, 639–65.

Hayes, S.C., Barnes-Holmes, D. & Roche, B. (2001). *Relational frame theory: a post-Skinnerian account of human language and cognition.* New York: Plenum Press.

Hayes, S.C., Strosahl, K. & Wilson, K.G. (1999). *Acceptance and commitment therapy: an experiential approach to behaviour change.* New York: Guilford Press.

Heimberg, R.G. (2002). Cognitive behaviour therapy for social anxiety disorder: current status and future directions. *Biological Psychiatry*, 51, 101–8.

Hollon, S.D. & Shaw, B.F. (1979). Group cognitive therapy for depressed patients. In A.T. Beck, A.J. Rush, B.F. Shaw & G. Emery (Eds), *Cognitive therapy for depression.* New York: Guilford Press.

Honey, P. & Munford, A. (1992). *The manual of learning styles.* Maidenhead: Peter Honey.

Hope, D.A. & Heimberg, R.G. (1993). Social phobia and social anxiety. In D.H. Barlow et al. (Eds), *Clinical handbook of psychological disorders: a step-by-step manual*, 2nd edn. New York: Guilford Press.

Horvarth, A.O. (1995). The therapeutic relationship: from transference to alliance. *In Session: Psychotherapy in Practice*, 1, 7–17.

Jacobson, E. (1970). *Modern treatments of tense patients.* Springfield, IL: Thomas.

Jacobson, N.S., Dobson, K.S., Truax, P.A., Addis, M.E., Koerner, K., Gollan, J.K., Gortner, E. & Prince, S.E. (1996). A component analysis of cognitive-behavioural treatment for depression. *Journal of Consulting & Clinical Psychology*, 64, 295–304.

Jacobson, N.S. & Margolin, G. (1979). *Marital therapy: strategies based on social learning and behaviour exchange principles.* New York: Brunner/Mazel.

Jacobson, N.S., Martell, C.R. & Dimidjian, S. (2001). Behavioural activation treatment for depression: returning to contextual roots. *Clinical Psychology: Science & Practice,* 8, 255–70.

Jacobson, N.S. & Revenstorf, D. (1988). Statistics for assessing the clinical significance of psychotherapy techniques: issues, problems, and new developments. *Behavioral Assessment*, 10, 133–45.

Jacobson, N.S., Roberts, L.J., Berns, S.B. & McGlinchey, J.B. (1999). Methods for defining and determining the clinical significance of treatment effects: description, application and alternatives. *Journal of Consulting & Clinical Psychology,* 67, 300–7.

Kabat-Zinn, J. (1994). *Wherever you go, there you are: mindfulness meditation in everyday life.* New York: Hyperion.

Kazdin, A.E. (1982). *Single-case research designs: methods for clinical and applied settings.* New York: Oxford University Press.

Kennerley, H. (1995). Presentation at BABCP annual conference, Lancaster.

Kennerley, H. (1996). Cognitive therapy of dissociative symptoms associated with trauma. *British Journal of Clinical Psychology*, 35, 325–40.

Kennerley, H., Whitehead, L., Butler, G. & Norris, R. (1998). *Recovering from childhood abuse: therapy workbook.* Oxford: Oxford Cognitive Therapy Centre.

Kirk, J. & Rouf, K. (2004). Specific phobias. In J. Bennett-Levy, G. Butler, M. Fennell, A. Hackmann, M. Mueller & D. Westbrook (Eds), *Oxford guide to behavioural experiments in cognitive therapy.* Oxford: Oxford University Press.

Kischka, U., Kammer, T., Maier, S., Thimm, M. & Spitzer, M. (1996). Dopaminergic modulation of semantic network activation. *Neuropsychologia*, 34, 1107–13.

Kolb, D. (1984). *Experiential learning: experience as the source of learning and development.* Englewood Cliffs, NJ: Prentice-Hall.

Krakow, B., Hollifield, M., Johnston, L., et al. (2001). Imagery rehearsal therapy for chronic nightmares in sexual assault survivors with posttraumatic stress disorder. *Journal of the American Medical Association*, 286, 537–45.

Kuyken, W. (2006). Evidence-based case formulation: is the emperor clothed? In N. Tarrier, (Ed.), *Case formulation in cognitive behaviour therapy: the treatment of complex and challenging cases.* Hove: Brunner-Routledge.

Ladouceur, R., Dugas, M.J., Freeston M.H., Leger, E., Gagnon, F. & Thibodeau, N. (2000). Efficacy of cognitive behavioural therapy for generalized anxiety disorder: evaluation in a controlled clinical trial. *Journal of Consulting & Clinical Psychology*, 68, 957–64.

Lam, D., Jones, S., Bright, J. & Hayward, P. (1999). *Cognitive therapy for bipolar disorder: a therapist's guide to concepts, methods and practice.* Chichester: Wiley.

Lambert, M.J. and Bergin, A.E. (1994). The effectiveness of psychotherapy. In A. Bergin and S. Garfield (Eds), *Handbook of psychotherapy and behaviour change,* 4th edn. New York: Wiley.

Lang, P.J. (1968). Fear reduction and fear behavior: Problems in treating a construct. In J.M. Shlien, (Ed.), *Research in psychotherapy, Vol. I.* Washington, DC: APA

Layden. M., Newman, C., Freeman, A. & Morse, S.B. (1993). *Cognitive therapy of borderline personality disorder.* Boston, MA: Allyn & Bacon.

Lee, D.A. (2005). The perfect nurturer: a model to develop a compassionate mind within the context of cognitive therapy. In P. Gilbert (Ed.), *Compassion: conceptualisations, research and use in psychotherapy.* Hove: Brunner-Routledge.

Lewin, K. (1946). Action research and minority problems. *Journal of Social Issues*, 2, 34–46.

Lewis, G., Anderson, L., Aray, R., Elgie, R., Harrison, G., Proudfoot, J., Schmidt, U., Sharp, D., Weightman, A. and Williams, C. (2003). *Self-help interventions for mental health problems. Report to the Department of Health R&D Programme.* London: Department of Health.

Liese, B.S. & Franz, R.A. (1996). Treating substance use disorders with cognitive therapy: lessons learned and implications for the future. In P.M. Salkovskis (Ed.), *Frontiers of cognitive therapy*. New York: Guilford Press.

Linehan, M.M. (1993). *Cognitive-behavioural treatment for borderline personality disorder: the dialectics of effective treatment*. New York: Guilford Press.

Lovell, K. and Richards, D.A. (2000). Multiple access points and levels of entry (MAPLE): ensuring choice, accessibility and equity for CBT services. *Behavioural and Cognitive Psychotherapy*, 28, 379–91.

Lovell, K., Richards, D.A. & Bower, P. (2003). Improving access to primary mental health care: uncontrolled evaluation of a pilot self-help clinic. *British Journal of General Practice*, 53, 133–5.

Mansell, W. & Clark, D.M. (1999). How do I appear to others? Social anxiety and biased processing of the observable self. *Behaviour Research & Therapy*, 37, 419–34.

Margison, F., Barkham, M., Evans, C., McGrath, G., Mellor-Clark, J., Audin, K. and Connell, J. (2000). Measurement and psychotherapy: evidence-based practice and practice-based evidence. *British Journal of Psychiatry*, 177, 123–30.

Marlatt, G.A. & Gordon, J.R. (1985). *Relapse prevention: maintenance strategies in the treatment of addictive disorders*. New York: Guilford Press.

Marlatt, G.A., Larimer, M.E., Baer, J.S. & Quigley, L.A. (1993). Harm reduction for alcohol problems: moving beyond the controlled drinking controversy. *Behaviour Therapy*, 24, 461–504.

Martell, C.R., Addis, M.E. & Jacobson, N.S. (2001). *Depression in context: strategies for guided action*. New York: Norton.

Martinsen, E.W., Medhus, A. & Sandvik, L. (1985). Effects of aerobic exercise on depression: a controlled study. *British Medical Journal*, 291, 109.

McCann, I.L. & Pearlman, L.A. (1990). Vicarious traumatization: a framework for understanding the psychological effects of working with victims. *Journal of Traumatic Stress*, 3, 131–49.

McNally, R.J. (2003). *Remembering trauma*. Cambridge, MA: Harvard University Press.

Meichenbaum, D.H. (1975). A self-instructional approach to stress management: a proposal for stress inoculation training. In C.D. Spielberger & I. Sarason (Eds), *Stress and anxiety, Vol. 2*. New York: Wiley.

Merrill, K.A., Tolbert, V.E. & Wade, W.A. (2003). Effectiveness of cognitive therapy for depression in a community mental health center: a benchmarking study. *Journal of Consulting & Clinical Psychology*, 71, 404–9.

Michelson, L. (1986). Treatment consonance and response profiles in agoraphobia: the role of individual differences in cognitive, behavioural, and physiological treatments. *Behaviour Research & Therapy*, 24, 263–75.

Miller, W. & Rollnick, S. (1991). *Motivational interviewing: preparing people to change addictive behaviour*. New York: Guilford Press.

Moore, R. & Garland, A. (2003). *Cognitive therapy for chronic and persistent depression*. Chichester: Wiley.

Morrison, A.P., Renton, J.C., Dunn, H., et al. (2003). *Cognitive therapy for psychosis: a formulation-based approach*. London: Psychology Press.

Morrison, N. (2000). Schema-focused cognitive therapy for complex long-standing problems: a single case study. *Behavioural & Cognitive Psychotherapy*, 38, 269–83.

Morrison, N. (2001). Group cognitive therapy: treatment of choice or sub-optimal option? *Behavioural & Cognitive Psychotherapy*, 29, 311–32.

Mullen, P.E., Martin, J.L., Anderson, J.C., Romans, S.E. & Herbison, G.P. (1993). Child sexual abuse and mental health in adult life. *British Journal of Psychiatry*, 163, 721–32.

Mynors-Wallis, L., Davies, I. & Gray, A., et al. (1997). A randomised controlled trial and cost analysis of problem-solving treatment for emotional disorders given by community nurses in primary care. *British Journal of Psychiatry*, 170, 113–19.

Mynors-Wallis, L., Gath, D. H. & Baker, F. (2000). Randomised controlled trial of problem solving treatment, antidepressant medication, and combined treatment for major depression in primary care. *British Medical Journal*, 320, 26–30.

National Institute of Mental Health (NIMH) (2001). *Facts about anxiety disorders*. Retrieved 21 May 2006 from NIMH web site: http://www.nimh.nih.gov/publicat/adfacts.cfm.

Neisser, U. (1976). *Cognition and reality: principles and implications of cognitive psychology.* San Francisco, CA: W.H. Freeman.

Newman, C.F. (1994). Understanding client resistance: methods for enhancing motivation to change. *Cognitive and Behavioural Practice*, 1, 47–69.

Nezu, A.M., Nezu, C.M. & Perri, M.G. (1989). *Problem-solving therapy for depression: theory research and clinical guidelines.* New York: Wiley.

National Institute for Clinical Excellence (NICE) (2002). *Schizophrenia: core interventions in the treatment and management of schizophrenia in primary and secondary care.* Retrieved 9 May 2005 from NICE web site: http://www.nice.org.uk/page.aspx?o=42461.

NICE (2004a). *Depression: management of depression in primary and secondary care.* Retrieved 9 May 2005 from NICE website: http://www.nice.org.uk/page.aspx?o=235367.

NICE (2004b). *Eating disorders: core interventions in the treatment and management of anorexia nervosa, bulimia nervosa and related eating disorders.* Retrieved 9 May 2005 from NICE website: http://www.nice.org.uk/page.aspx?o=101246.

NICE (2004c). *Anxiety: management of anxiety (panic disorder, with or without agoraphobia, and generalised anxiety disorder) in adults in primary, secondary and community care.* Retrieved 9 May 2005 from NICE web site: http://www.nice.org.uk/page.aspx?o=235400.

NICE (2005). *Post-traumatic stress disorder (PTSD):The management of PTSD in adults and children in primary and secondary care.* Retrieved 9 May 2005 from NICE web site: http://www.nice.org.uk/page.aspx?o=248146.

Niemeyer, R.A. & Feixas, G. (1990). The role of homework and skill acquisition in outcome of group cognitive therapy for depression. *Behaviour Therapy*, 21, 281–92.

Norris, R. (1995). Pair therapy with adult survivors of sexual abuse. Thesis submitted for MSc in Clinical Psychology.

Norris, R. & Küchemann, C. (Undated). *How to relax*. Oxford: Oxford Cognitive Therapy Centre.

Novaco, R.W. (1979). The cognitive regulation of anger and stress. In P.C. Kendall & S.D. Hollon (Eds), *Cognitive-behavioral interventions: theory, research, and procedures.* New York: Academic Press.

Novaco, R.W. (2000). Anger. In A.E. Kazdin (Ed.), *Encyclopedia of psychology.* Washington, DC: American Psychological Association & Oxford University Press.

Obsessive-Compulsive Cognitions Working Group (1997). Cognitive assessment of obsessive-compulsive disorder. *Behaviour Research & Therapy*, 35, 667–81.

Orlinsky, D., Grawe, K. & Parks, B. (1994). Process and outcome in psychotherapy. In A. Bergin and S. Garfield (Eds), *Handbook of psychotherapy and behaviour change,* 4th edn. New York: Wiley.

Öst, L.G. (1987). Applied relaxation: description of a coping technique and review of controlled studies. *Behaviour Research & Therapy*, 25, 397–410.

Öst, L.G. & Sterner, U. (1987). Applied tension: a specific behavioural method for treatment of blood phobia. *Behaviour Research & Therapy*, 25, 25–30.

Öst, L.G., Sterner, U. & Lindhal, J.-L. (1984). Physiological responses in blood phobics. *Behaviour Research & Therapy*, 22,109–27.

Ottavani, R. & Beck, A.T. (1987). Cognitive aspects of panic disorder. *Journal of Anxiety Disorders*, 1, 15–28.

Padesky, C. (1993). *Socratic questioning: changing minds or guiding discovery?* Keynote address delivered at European Association for Behavioural & Cognitive Therapies conference, London.

Padesky, C. (1994). Schema change processes in cognitive therapy. *Clinical Psychology & Psychotherapy*, 1, 267–78.

Padesky, C. (1996). Developing cognitive therapist competency: teaching and supervision models. In P. Salkovskis, (Ed.), *Frontiers in cognitive therapy*. New York: Guilford Press.

Padesky, C. (1996a). *Guided discovery using Socratic dialogue*. Oakland, CA: New Harbinger.

Padesky, C. (1997). A more effective treatment focus for social phobia? *International Cognitive Therapy Newsletter*, 11, 1–3.

Padesky, C. (2005). *Constructing a new self: cognitive therapy for personality disorders*. Workshop presented in London, England, 23–4 May 2005.

Padesky, C. & Greenberger, D. (1995). *Clinician's guide to mind over mood*. New York: Guilford Press.

Palmer, B. (2003). Concepts of eating disorders. In J. Treasure, U. Schmidt & E. van Furth (Eds), *Handbook of eating disorders,* 2nd edn. Chichester: Wiley.

Perris, C. (2000). Personality-related disorders of interpersonal behaviour: a developmental–constructivist cognitive psychotherapy approach to treatment based on attachment theory. *Clinical Psychology & Psychotherapy*, 7, 97–117.

Persons, J.B. (1989). *Cognitive therapy in practice: a case formulation approach*. New York: Norton.

Persons, J.B., Burns, D.D. & Perloff, J.M. (1988). Predictions of drop-out and outcome in cognitive therapy for depression in a private practice setting. *Cognitive Therapy & Research*, 12, 557–75.

Peruzzi, N. & Bongar, B. (1999). Assessing risk for completed suicide in patients with major depression: psychologists' views of critical factors. *Professional Psychology: Research and Practice*, 30, 576–80.

Petrak, J. and Hedge, B. (2002). *The trauma of sexual assault: treatment, prevention and practice*. Chichester: Wiley.

Pilling, S., Bebbington, P., Kuipers, E., Garety, P., Geddes, J., Orbach, G. & Morgan C. (2002). Psychological treatments in schizophrenia: I. Meta-analysis of family intervention and cognitive behaviour therapy. *Psychological Medicine*, 32, 763–82.

Pope, K.S. & Bouhoutsos, J. (1986). *Sexual intimacy between therapists and patients*. New York: Praeger.

Pope, K.S., Tabachnick, B.G. & Keith-Spiegel, P. (1987). Ethics of practice: the beliefs and behaviours of psychologists as therapists. *American Psychologist*, 42, 993–1006.

Pretzer, J. (1990). Borderline personality disorder. In A.T. Beck, A. Freeman et al., *Cognitive therapy of personality disorders*. New York: Guilford Press.

Prochaska, J. and DiClemente, C. (1984). *The trans-theoretical approach: crossing the traditional boundaries*. Homewood, IL: Dow Jones Irwen.

Prochaska, J.O. and DiClemente, C.C. (1986). Towards a comprehensive model of change. In W. Miller and H. Heather (Eds), *Treating addictive behaviours: processes of change*. New York: Plenum Press.

Rachman, S.J. & de Silva, P. (1978). Abnormal and normal obsessions. *Behaviour Research & Therapy*, 16, 233–48.

Rachman, S.J. and Hodgson, R. (1974). Synchrony and de-synchrony in fear and avoidance. *Behaviour Research & Therapy*, 12, 311–18.

Raimy, V. (Ed.) (1950). *Training in clinical psychology*. New York: Prentice-Hall.

Raue, P.J. & Goldfried, M.R. (1994). The therapeutic alliance in cognitive-behaviour therapy. In A.O. Horvath and L.S. Greenberg (Eds), *The working alliance*. New York: Wiley.

Rector, N.A., Bagby, R.M., Segal, Z.V., Joffe, R.T. & Levitt, A. (2000). Self-criticism and dependency in depressed patients treated with cognitive therapy or pharmacotherapy. *Cognitive Therapy & Research*, 24, 571–84.

Ree, M. & Harvey, A.G. (2004). Insomnia. In J. Bennett-Levy, G. Butler, M. Fennell, A. Hackmann, M. Mueller & D. Westbrook (Eds), *The Oxford guide to behavioural experiments in cognitive therapy*. Oxford: Oxford University Press.

Resick, P.A. & Schnicke, M.K. (1993). *Cognitive processing therapy for rape victims*. Newbury Park, CA: Sage.

Richards, A., Barkham, M., Cahill, J., Richards, D., Williams, C. & Heywood, P. (2003). PHASE: a randomised controlled trial of supervised self-help cognitive behavioural therapy in primary care. *British Journal of General Practice*, **53**, 764–70.

Richardson, R. & Richards, D.A. (2006). Self-help: towards the next generation. *Behavioural & Cognitive Psychotherapy*, 34, 13–23.

Riso, L.P., duToit, P.T. & Young, J.E. (in press). *Cognitive schemas and core beliefs in psychiatric disorders: a scientist-practitioner guide*. New York: American Psychiatric Association.

Robson, C. (2002). *Real world research*. Oxford: Blackwell.

Roth, A. & Fonagy, P. (2005). *What works for whom?* 2nd edn. New York: Guilford Press.

Rothschild, B. (2000). *The body remembers: the psychophysiology of trauma and trauma treatment*. New York: Norton.

Rush, A.J., Beck, A.T., Kovacs, M. & Hollon, S.D. (1977). Comparative efficacy of cognitive therapy and pharmacotherapy in the treatment of depressive outpatients. *Cognitive Therapy & Research*, 1, 17–37.

Rush, A.J. & Watkins, J.T. (1981). Group versus individual therapy: a pilot study. *Cognitive Therapy and Research*, 5, 95–103.

Safran, J.D. & Muran, J.C. (1995). Resolving therapeutic alliance ruptures: diversity and integration. *In Session: Psychotherapy in Practice*, 1, 81–92.

Safran, J.D. & Segal, Z.V. (1990). *Interpersonal process in cognitive therapy*. New York: Basic Books.

Safran, J.D., Segal, Z.V., Vallis, T.M., Shaw, B.F. & Samstag, L.W. (1993). Assessing patient suitability for short-term cognitive therapy with an interpersonal focus. *Cognitive Therapy & Research*, 17, 23–38.

Salkovskis, P.M. (1985). Obsessive-compulsive problems: a cognitive-behavioural analysis. *Behaviour Research & Therapy*, 23, 571–83.

Salkovskis, P.M (1988). Phenomenology, assessment and the cognitive model of panic. In S.J. Rachman & J. Maser (Eds), *Panic: psychological perspectives*. Hillsdale, NJ: Erlbaum.

Salkovskis, P.M. (1991). The importance of behaviour in the maintenance of anxiety and panic: a cognitive account. *Behavioural Psychotherapy*, 19, 6–19.

Salkovskis, P.M. (1995). Demonstrating specific effects in cognitive and behavioural therapy. In M. Aveline & D. Shapiro (Eds.), *Research foundations for psychotherapy practice*. Chichester: Wiley.

Salkovskis, P.M. (1999). Understanding and treating obsessive-compulsive disorders. *Behaviour Research & Therapy*, 37, S29–S52.

Salkovskis, P.M. (2002). Empirically grounded clinical interventions: cognitive-behavioural therapy progresses through a multi-dimensional approach to clinical science. *Behavioural & Cognitive Psychotherapy*, 30, 3–9.

Salkovskis, P.M. & Bass, C. (1997). Hypochondriasis. In D.M. Clark and C.G. Fairburn (Eds), *Science and practice of cognitive-behaviour therapy*. Oxford: Oxford University Press.

Salkovskis, P.M., Jones, D.R.O. & Clark, D.M. (1986). Respiratory control in the treatment of panic attacks: replication and extension with concurrent measurement of behaviour and pCO2. *British Journal of Psychiatry*, 148, 526–32.

Salkovskis, P.M. & Warwick, H.M. (1986). Morbid preoccupations, health anxiety and re-assurance: a cognitive-behavioural approach to hypochondriasis. *Behaviour Research & Therapy*, 24, 597–602.

Salkovskis, P.M. & Westbrook, D. (1989). Behaviour therapy and obsessional ruminations: can failure be turned into success? *Behaviour Research & Therapy*, 27, 149–60.

Scholing, A. & Emmelkamp, P.M.G. (1993). Exposure with and without cognitive therapy for generalised social phobia: effects of individual and group treatment. *Behaviour Research & Therapy*, 31, 667–81.

Schulte, D., Kuenzel, R., Pepping, G. & Schulte, B.T. (1992). Tailor-made versus standard-ized therapy of phobic patients. *Advances in Behaviour Research & Therapy*, 14, 67–92.

Scott, J. (2001). *Overcoming mood swings: a self-help guide using cognitive behavioural techniques*. London: Robinson.

Scott, M.J. & Stradling, S.G. (1994). Post-traumatic stress without the trauma. *British Journal of Clinical Psychology*, 33, 71–4.

Segal, Z.V., Williams J.M. & Teasdale, J.D. (2002). *Mindfulness-based cognitive therapy for depression: a new approach to prevent relapse*. New York: Guilford Press.

Simon, R.I. (1991). Psychological injury caused by boundary violation precursors to therap-ist–patient sex. *Psychiatric Annals*, 21, 616–19.

Smith, D. & Fitzpatrick, M. (1995). Patient–therapist boundary issues: an integrative review of theory and research. *Professional Psychology: Research and Practice*, 26, 499–506.

Sobell, M.B. & Sobell, L.C. (1993). *Problem drinkers: guided self-change treatment*. New York: Guilford Press.

Stuart, G.L., Treat, T.A. & Wade, W.A. (2000). Effectiveness of an empirically based treat-ment of panic disorder delivered in a service clinic setting: 1-year follow-up. *Journal of Consulting & Clinical Psychology*, 68, 506–12.

Stuart, R. (1980). *Helping couples change: a social learning approach to marital therapy*. New York: Guilford Press.

Tarrier, N., Wells, A. & Haddock, G. (1998). *Treating complex cases: the cognitive behav-ioural approach*. Chichester: Wiley.

Tavris, C. (1989). *Anger: the misunderstood emotion*. New York: Simon & Schuster.

Taylor, A.H. (2000). Physical activity, anxiety, and stress. In S.J.H. Biddle, K.R. Fox & S.H. Boutcher (Eds), *Physical activity and psychological well-being*. London: Routledge.

Teasdale, J.D. (1988). Cognitive vulnerability to persistent depression. *Cognition & Emotion*, 2, 247–74.

Teasdale, J.D. (1996). Clinically relevant theory: integrating clinical insight with cognitive science. In P. Salkovskis (Ed.), *Frontiers of cognitive therapy*. New York: Guilford Press.

Teasdale, J.D. (2004). Mindfulness-based cognitive therapy. In J. Yiend (Ed.), *Cognition, emotion and psychopathology: theoretical, empirical and clinical directions*. Cambridge: Cambridge University Press.

Teasdale, J.D. & Barnard, P.J. (1993). *Affect, cognition and change: re-modelling depressive thought.* Hove: Erlbaum.

Teasdale, J.D., Moore, R.G., Hayhurst, H., Pope, M., Williams, S. & Segal, Z.V. (2002). Metacognitive awareness and prevention of relapse in depression: empirical evidence. *Journal of Consulting & Clinical Psychology*, 70, 275–89.

Teasdale, J.D., Segal, Z.V. & Williams, J.M.G. (1995). How does cognitive therapy prevent depressive relapse and why should attentional control (mindfulness) training help? *Behaviour Research & Therapy*, 33, 25–39.

Telch, M.J., Luxcas, J.A., Schmidt, N.B., Hanna, H.H., Jaimez, T.L. & Lucas, R.A. (1993). Group cognitive-behavioural treatment of panic disorder. *Behaviour Research & Therapy*, 31, 279–87.

Terr, L.C. (1991). Childhood traumas: an outline and overview. *American Journal of Psychiatry*, 148, 10–20.

Thase, M.E., Greenhouse, J.B., Frank, E., Reynolds, C.F., Pilkonis, P.A., Hurley, K., et al. (1997). Treatment of major depression with psychotherapy or psychotherapy–pharmacotherapy combinations. *Archives of General Psychiatry*, 54, 1009–15.

Treasure, J.L., Katzman, M., Schmidt, U., Troop, N., Todd, G. & de Silva, P. (1999). Engagement and outcome in the treatment of bulimia nervosa: first phase of a sequential design comparing motivation enhancement therapy and cognitive behaviour therapy. *Behaviour Research & Therapy*, 37, 405–18.

Treasure, J.L., Schmidt, U., and van Furth, E. (2003). *Handbook of Eating Disorders*, 2nd edn. Chichester: Wiley.

Vanderlinden, J. & Vandereycken, W. (1997). *Trauma, dissociation and impulse dyscontrol in eating disorders.* Bristol, PA: Brunner/ Mazel.

Vitousek, K.B. (1996). The current status of cognitive behavioural models of anorexia nervosa and bulimia nervosa. In P.M. Salkovskis (Ed.), *Frontiers of cognitive therapy.* New York: Guilford Press.

Wade, W.A., Treat, T.A. & Stuart, G.L. (1998). Transporting an empirically supported treatment for panic disorder to a service clinic setting: a benchmarking strategy. *Journal of Consulting & Clinical Psychology*, 66, 231–9.

Waller, G. & Kennerley, H. (2003). Cognitive behavioural treatments. In J. Treasure, U. Schmidt & E. van Furth (Eds), *Handbook of eating disorders,* 2nd edn. Chichester: Wiley.

Warwick, H.M.C. & Salkovskis, P.M. (1989). Hypochondriasis. In J. Scott, J.M.G. Williams & A.T. Beck (Eds), *Cognitive therapy in clinical practice.* London: Croom Helm.

Waters, A., Hill, A. & Waller, G. (2001). Bulimics' responses to food cravings: is binge-eating a product of hunger or emotional state? *Behaviour Research & Therapy*, 39, 877–86.

Watson, J.C. and Greenberg, L.S. (1995). Alliance ruptures and repairs in experiential therapy. *In Session: Psychotherapy in Practice*, 1, 19–31.

Wells, A. (1997). *Cognitive therapy of anxiety disorders: a practice manual and conceptual guide.* Chichester: Wiley.

Wells, A. (2000). *Emotional disorders and metacognition.* Chichester: Wiley.

Wells, A. & Mathews, G. (1994). *Attention and emotion: a clinical perspective.* Hove: Lawrence Erlbaum.

Wenzlaff, R.M. & Bates, D.E. (2000). The relative efficacy of concentration and suppression strategies of mental control. *Personality and Social Psychology Bulletin*, 26, 1200–12.

Wenzlaff, R.M., Wegner D.M. & Klein, F.B. (1991). The role of thought suppression in the bonding of thought and mood. *Journal of Personality and Social Psychology*, 60, 500–8.

Westbrook, D.J. & Kirk, J. (2005). The clinical effectiveness of cognitive behaviour therapy: outcome for a large sample of adults treated in routine practice. *Behaviour Research & Therapy*, 43, 1243–61.

Westen, D. (1996). *Psychology: mind, brain and culture*. New York: Wiley.

White, J. (1998). 'Stress control' large group therapy for generalized anxiety disorder: two year follow-up. *Behavioural & Cognitive Psychotherapy*, 26, 237–46.

White, J. (2000). *Treating anxiety and stress: a group psycho-educational approach using brief CBT*. Chichester: Wiley.

White, J., Keenan, M. & Brooks, N. (1992). 'Stress control': a controlled comparative investigation of large group therapy for generalized anxiety disorder. *Behavioural Psychotherapy*, 20, 97–114.

Williams, C. (2001). Use of written cognitive-behavioural therapy self-help materials to treat depression. *Advances in Psychiatric Treatment*, 7, 233–40.

Williams, J.M.G. (1992). *The psychological treatment of depression: a guide to the theory and practice of cognitive behaviour therapy*. London: Routledge.

Williams, J.M.G. (1997). Depression. In D.M. Clark and C.G. Fairburn (Eds), *Science and practice of cognitive behaviour therapy*. Oxford: Oxford University Press.

Williams, J.M.G., Watts, F.N., McCleod, C. & Mathews, A. (1997). *Cognitive psychology and emotional disorders,* 2nd edn. New York: Wiley.

Wolpe, J. (1958). *Psychotherapy by reciprocal inhibition*. Stanford, CA: Stanford University Press.

Wright, J.H. & Davis, D. (1994). The therapeutic relationship in cognitive-behaviour therapy: patient perceptions and therapist responses. *Cognitive and Behavioural Practice*, 1, 25–45.

Young, J.E. (1984). *Cognitive therapy with difficult patients*. Workshop presented at the meeting of the Association for Advancement of Behaviour Therapy, Philadelphia, PA.

Young, J.E. (1990). *Cognitive therapy for personality disorders: a schema focused approach*. Sarasota, FL: Professional Resource Exchange.

Young, J. & Beck, A.T. (1980). Cognitive therapy scale: rating manual. Unpublished MS, University of Pennsylvania, PA.

Young, J.E., Klosko, J. & Weishaar, M.E. (2003). *Schema therapy: a practitioner's guide*. New York: Guilford Press.

Zettle, R.D. (2003). Acceptance and commitment therapy (ACT) versus systematic desensitization in treatment of mathematics anxiety. *The Psychological Record*, 53, 197–215.

Zigmond, A.S. & Snaith, R.P. (1983). The Hospital Anxiety And Depression Scale. *Acta Psychiatrica Scandinavica*, 67, 361–70.

Zipfel, S., Lowe, B. & Herzog, W. (2003) Medical complications. In J. Treasure, U. Schmidt & E. van Furth (Eds), *Handbook of eating disorders,* 2nd edn. Chichester: Wiley.

Index